Britain Against the
Xhosa and Zulu Peoples

Britain Against the Xhosa and Zulu Peoples

Lord Chelmsford's South African Campaigns

Stephen Manning

Pen & Sword
MILITARY

First published in Great Britain in 2022 by
Pen & Sword Military
An imprint of
Pen & Sword Books Ltd
Yorkshire – Philadelphia

ISBN 978 1 39901 056 6

A CIP catalogue record for this book is
available from the British Library.

Typeset by Mac Style
Printed and bound in the UK by CPI Group (UK) Ltd,
Croydon, CR0 4YY.

Pen & Sword Books Limited incorporates the imprints of Atlas,
Archaeology, Aviation, Discovery, Family History, Fiction, History,
Maritime, Military, Military Classics, Politics, Select, Transport,
True Crime, Air World, Frontline Publishing, Leo Cooper, Remember
When, Seaforth Publishing, The Praetorian Press, Wharncliffe
Local History, Wharncliffe Transport, Wharncliffe True Crime
and White Owl.

For a complete list of Pen & Sword titles please contact

PEN & SWORD BOOKS LIMITED
47 Church Street, Barnsley, South Yorkshire, S70 2AS, England
E-mail: enquiries@pen-and-sword.co.uk
Website: www.pen-and-sword.co.uk

Or

PEN AND SWORD BOOKS
1950 Lawrence Rd, Havertown, PA 19083, USA
E-mail: Uspen-and-sword@casematepublishers.com
Website: www.penandswordbooks.com

To Jack Gibson

A dear friend who has been so supportive of my endeavours during the writing of this book and has travelled the Zulu battlefields with me.

Contents

Acknowledgements

I would like to thank the librarians at the University of Exeter and Exeter City Library for obtaining research materials for me during the challenging period of the global pandemic of the last few years. I am also grateful to Jan Dwan for her proof-reading skills and Anthony Grattan-Cooper for his ongoing advice and support. At Pen & Sword, I thank my editor, Alison Flowers, for her patience and commissioning editor, Rupert Harding, for his continuing support and trust.

Maps

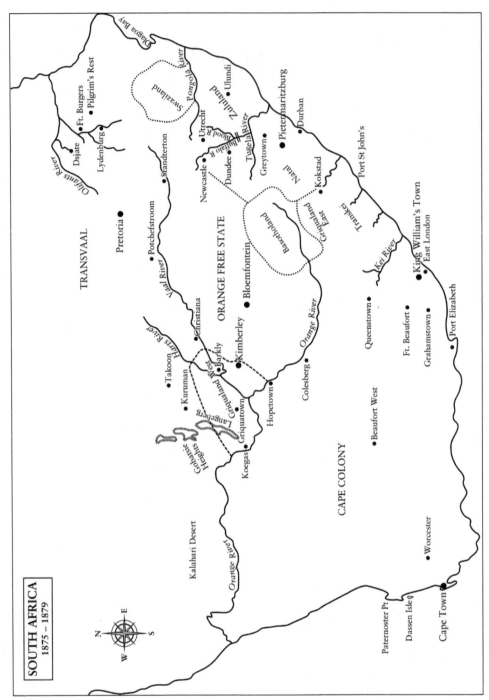

Southern Africa, 1875–9.

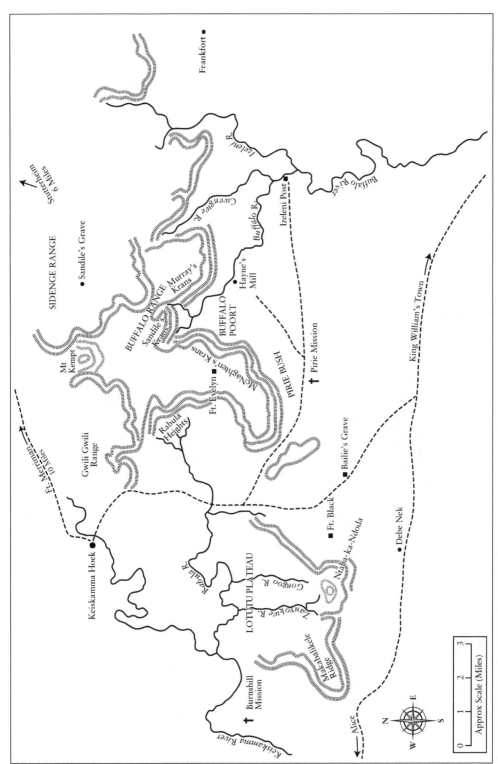

Scene of operations in the Eastern Amatholes.

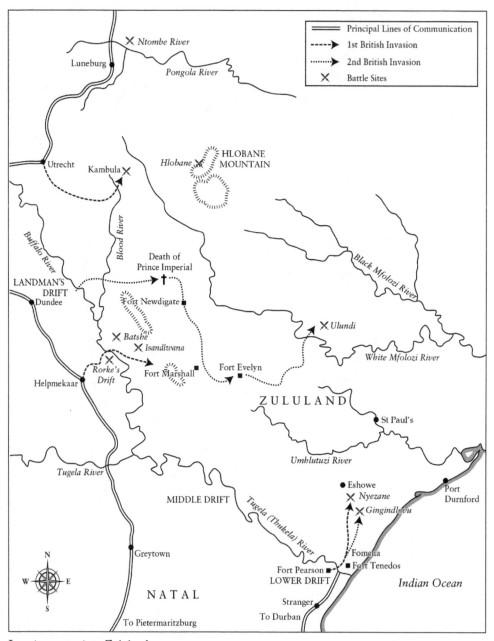

Invasion routes into Zululand.

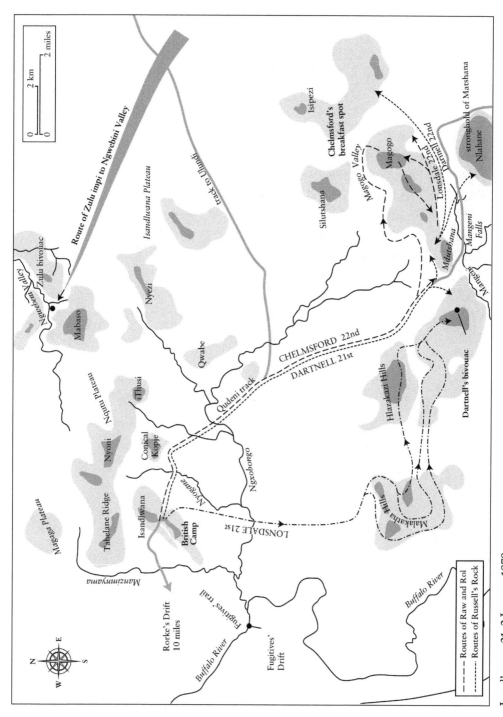

Isandlwana, 21–2 January 1879.

Abbreviations

ADC	Aide-de-Camp
DAG	Deputy Adjutant General
FAMP	Frontier Armed and Mounted Police
FLH	Frontier Light Horse
NMP	Natal Mounted Police
NNC	Natal Native Contingent
NNH	Natal Native Horse
TNA	The National Archives, Kew
WO	War Office (records held at TNA)

Introduction

This is a book about bravery, injustice, conquest and incompetence.

A brief introduction is necessary to explain the format of the book to the reader. The Anglo-Zulu War of 1879 has been written about extensively. Indeed, the word exhaustively might be used, and the subject has encouraged many historians to write their own interpretations of the events surrounding the war. This volume was never intended to be just another book about the conflict, and therefore its brief is wider. The history of British contact with both the Xhosa and Zulu peoples is examined. The events of the nine wars Britain undertook against the Xhosa, which culminated in 1878 with Frederic Thesiger's final victory and the capitulation of the Xhosa, are detailed.

Thesiger, now 2nd Baron Lord Chelmsford following the death of his father in autumn 1878, moved on to to Natal where with the connivance of the High Commissioner, Sir Bartle Frere, began to assemble a force for an invasion of Zululand. No signficant biography of Lord Chelmsford has been published for many decades and this book does not claim to be that. However, it endeavours to offer a better understanding of the man and his thinking and provide fresh insight into why he made many of the fateful and fatal decisions that he did. Whilst this is not an attempt to redeem the man, the book seeks to place him in the context of his time and also illustrate that, contrary to the views held by many, he was capable of change.

Many writers on the Anglo-Zulu War have tended to 'not see the wood for the trees' and have consequently become somewhat lost in unnecessary or even fanciful conjecture. The focus of this volume is the command of Lord Chelmsford and as such avoids lengthy descriptions of events that he did not take part in. For example, some readers may be disappointed that the text does not dwell on the clash of arms at Rorke's Drift and covers this in terms of Chelmsford's direct involvement with the aftermath of the battle. By adopting this approach an original analysis of this well-known war is offered, which it is hoped the reader enjoys as much as I have enjoyed writing it.

Dr Stephen Manning
Exeter, March 2022

Chapter 1

The Road to Ulundi

The Battle of Ulundi, fought on 4 July 1879, was the final and decisive battle of the Anglo-Zulu War. Ulundi was also the last engagement in which Lieutenant General Lord Chelmsford, Frederic Thesiger, was to command British forces in action. Chelmsford claimed a notable victory against the Zulu army and with this last act was able to resign his command and return to England with some of his battered reputation restored. Within Britain today the Anglo-Zulu War is the most well known of the many conflicts in which British troops fought during Queen Victoria's reign and this can be attributed to a number of factors. Arguably, the most significant is that British soldiers, under the overall command of Chelmsford, suffered the worst defeat at the hands of an indigenous foe during the Victorian era when the Zulu army overwhelmed the British camp at Isandlwana Hill on 22 January 1879.

The defeat at Isandlwana has defined how historians have viewed Chelmsford's abilities and the consensus is that the commander was found wanting. Yet, only the year before, Chelmsford had successfully concluded the Ninth Frontier War against the Xhosa people of the Eastern Cape of South Africa and honours and praise had been showered upon him. Throughout the nineteenth century Britain engaged in a series of conflicts with the Xhosa and many a British commander's reputation was sullied as they struggled to overcome both the various tribes and the terrain of the Eastern Cape. It is to Chelmsford's credit that the Ninth Frontier War was brought to a prompt and successful end. Furthermore, Chelmsford demonstrated that he was able to learn from the mistakes of Isandlwana and his victories at Gingindlovu (2 April 1879) and at Ulundi were models of control in utilizing British troops in a defensive formation, and furthermore they showed that he had learnt to respect his brave and skilful Zulu enemy. Although numerous books have been written about the Anglo-Zulu War, few, with the notable exception of Gerald French's 1939 work, have offered a defence of Chelmsford. Whilst it is undoubtedly true that he made some fundamental errors, which will be highlighted, and that his strategy for both his First and Second invasions of Zululand was flawed, it will be argued that a blanket condemnation of Chelmsford is unfair and fails to examine or properly understand the circumstances of his command.

Chelmsford was very much a product of his background and his appointment to the position of Commander-in-Chief of British Army in Southern Africa in 1878 can be viewed as a part of a battle that raged for much of Victoria's reign between the ultra-conservative Duke of Cambridge, Commander-in-Chief of the British Army between 1856 and 1895, and the more progressive and forward-thinking officer corps that had Sir Garnet Wolseley as its leading proponent. Cambridge would consistently resist change and innovation during his tenure, sometimes stubbornly so, and all the Secretaries of State for War during this period had to carefully manage the dynamic between political authority and royal powers and influence. It was Edward Cardwell, with his ambitious plans for army reform, who had to learn more than others how to handle the duke's paranoia regarding the loss of his and the queen's prerogative powers over the army, and in this Cardwell was largely successful. Although never wishing to erode the status and authority of Cambridge, Cardwell was adamant that the duke had to recognize the paramount role of the government and Parliament in determining the future structures at the War Office and the funding of the army. Critically though, Cardwell acknowledged that the duke would retain control over the selection and promotion of senior officers, even after the purchase system was abolished in 1871. This was to include the prerogative to appoint senior commanders to campaigns, although this could sometimes be overruled as happened in 1873, when Cardwell gave command of the Asante Expedition to Wolseley, much to the Cambridge's disgust.

Thesiger was very much the establishment choice for the Southern African command when the situation and circumstances, both political and military, undoubtedly called for a more innovative thinker to be appointed. It was Cambridge who pressed for Thesiger's appointment, for the duke, throughout his tenure, favoured the promotion and advancement of those individuals with the 'right' background or family connections. This was often at the expense of those that through their individual efforts and skills merited greater opportunities. The fact that Thesiger knew, and had a friendship with, the High Commissioner in Southern Africa, Sir Henry Bartle Frere, from his time serving in India might well have influenced his appointment to the Southern Africa Command. In 1875 Frere had advised and attended the Prince of Wales on his tour of India. After this he had maintained friendly contact with the royal family and seems to have enjoyed the confidence of Victoria and Cambridge and it is possible that when looking to appoint a new commander to Southern Africa that Frere and the duke might have concluded that Thesiger would suit both men's designs. It was also the duke that became one of the staunchest public defenders of Chelmsford after the disaster of Isandlwana, although privately Cambridge was well aware of the general's failings during the Zulu Campaign.

The Thesigers were descendants of a yeoman Saxon gentleman who emigrated to England from the Dresden area in the middle of the eighteenth century and found a position as secretary to the Marquess of Rockingham. Frederic's grandfather, Charles, who died in 1831 was the first Thesiger to really begin to enhance the family's social standing. He obtained a position on the island of St Vincent, in the West Indies Lesser Antilles chain, where he was Comptroller and Collector of Customs. Charles was able to use savings to buy a large sugar producing estate, which was reliant on slave labour. His only surviving son, Frederick (1794–1878), studied law which was considered a good training for administering the estate as well as offering social prestige. The Thesiger family fortunes suffered a major setback on 30 April 1812 when the La Soufrière volcano on the island erupted and destroyed the estate. The family were impoverished and forced to return to England where Frederick threw himself into his law career. He was an incredibly successful lawyer and Member of the Bar. He married a general's daughter, Anna Maria Tinling, in 1822. His distinguished legal service allowed Frederick to enter politics and he sat in the House of Commons on the Tory benches. He was raised to the peerage on 1 March 1858, and as Lord Chelmsford he moved to the House of Lords. He held the office of Lord Chancellor in the years 1866–7 in the Lord Derby government.

Frederic Augustus Thesiger was born on 31 May 1827, the eldest of seven children. The young Frederic was schooled at Eton. Whilst his father had gained his social advancement as a lawyer, Frederic, in need of earning a living because his family's wealth was relatively modest, decided to enter the army. For the eldest son of a lord, albeit a landless one, an army career was a logical choice for it offered a position held in high regard and confirmed social prestige. Furthermore, other members of the family would turn to the services. Two uncles had careers in the navy and army respectively and his younger brother, Charles, eventually reached the rank of lieutenant general. Frederic set his own sights high by aiming to obtain a commission in the Grenadier Guards and his father endeavoured to use his friendship with the then Lord Chancellor, Lord Saint Leonards, to ease his entry into the regiment. However, despite the Lord Chancellor's intervention Frederic was to be initially frustrated for a suitable vacancy did not exist. On 22 July 1843, the Duke of Wellington wrote to Lord Saint Leonards:

My dear Lord Chancellor, I have received your note of the 18th with its enclosure from Mr Thesiger [Frederick]. His son's name was placed on my list of candidates for Grenr. Guards some time ago and I will not lose sight of his Father's wishes; but there have been very few vacancies lately and there are still more names I am sorry to say before his. Believe me, ever yours most sincerely, Wellington.[1]

Frustrated in his attempts to obtain a position in the Guards for his son, Frederick resolved to purchase a commission into the Rifle Brigade and Frederic was gazetted on 31 December 1844 as a second lieutenant. Although not all regiments required a purchase for entry, and the system did not apply to the Royal Artillery or Royal Engineers, the more fashionable regiments, such as the cavalry and the Guards, demanded purchase into the regiment. In addition, further advancement, rather than based on merit, was often down to purchasing a higher rank, although a notable act of gallantry might also enable promotion. Having paid the initial sum of about £450 (roughly £58,000 today) for his son's commission into the Rifle Brigade, it is not known whether Frederick would have been thrilled to learn of a vacancy becoming available in the Grenadier Guards the following year. There seems to have been no hesitation for the required sum was again paid and on 28 November 1845 Frederic exchanged by purchase and became an ensign and lieutenant in the Grenadier Guards.

The purchase system, which was to survive until the Cardwell Army Reforms of the early 1870s, had started in 1683, during the reign of Charles II. Initially it had been viewed as a cash bond for ensuring good behaviour. In the event of cowardice, gross misbehaviour or desertion, the purchase price of the commission, or bond, would be forfeited and the monies given to the army's cashiers. Over the centuries the purchase system evolved into one by which a commission as an officer could initially be secured.

Later as vacancies became available for more senior ranks these could also be purchased from the individual officer who was either being promoted himself or retiring, thus avoiding the need to wait to be promoted by merit or seniority.

The existence of such a practice had to be justified by a set of rationale and this altered over the centuries. Like the original idea of the bond, the purchase system served as a check on the abuse of authority or incompetence. Officers who disgraced the regiment by their behaviour could be cashiered by the Crown and thus stripped of their commission without a reimbursement of the purchase price. It was felt too that the system reduced the risk of officers profiteering by pilfering army supplies and that they would be less likely to engage in looting on campaigns, if they felt that this would put them at risk of loss of their purchase price.

Crucially, as the cost of purchase was high it very frequently meant that the officer class would be drawn from those who had a vested interest in ensuring that the political and social systems remained in limbo; conservatism was at its heart for it was felt that it reduced the possibility of the military becoming involved in politics or at the most extreme in revolutionary behaviour or even coup attempts. Further to this, the purchase system contributed to the social exclusivity of the officer class. Lastly, it provided retiring officers with a direct source of capital for upon leaving the service they were able to sell their commission to another officer who wished to assume their rank. This had the added benefit of reducing the liability of the Crown to provide either any or a reduced pension for the retiring officer.

It is clear that the purchase system defined and then self-perpetuated the social composition of the officer corps in the British army throughout the nineteenth century; indeed, it continued to do so long after it was abolished in 1871. The initial cost of purchasing a commission and then subsequent 'promotions' was prohibitive to many. Indeed, Garnet Wolseley, who had limited personal means, only managed to gain a commission in the 12th Foot (Suffolks), aged 18, after he and his mother had personally petitioned the Duke of Wellington on three separate occasions. Even then it was only given on the basis that it recognized Wolseley's deceased father's meritorious army service. Wolseley's subsequent rapid rise through the officer ranks was based on merit and personal bravery which seemed to to be evident in the number of times he was wounded in his early career. It is open to conjecture how many similarly talented and brave men were lost to the British army because they did not possess sufficient funds for the initial purchase of the commission.

In 1838, just a year after Victoria succeeded to the throne, there were 6,173 officers on the active list and of these 21 per cent could be described as aristocratic, with the majority of these directly related to a peer or a baronet. This trend would continue after the abolition of the purchase system and throughout the rest of the century. In the 1870s there were over two-and-a-half times as many aristocrats in the ranks of major general or above than would be expected as a proportion of aristocrats in the whole corps. Indeed, the aristocracy and landed gentry provided more than half of the officer recruits and a much higher percentage of the higher ranks well into the twentieth century.[2]

The majority of the rest of the officer corps, and again this is directly related to the existence and legacy of the purchase system, was from the upper sections of the middle class, to which Frederic belonged when he first gained his commission. The critics of the purchase system, who became more vocal from the Crimean War onwards (1853–6), contested that as long as an officer could be appointed with no reference to his abilities and he could then be promoted without consideration of his knowledge of military matters, what then was the importance of professional expertise. In fact, many examples existed of very limited military competence throughout the officer corps. For some a commission was viewed as a social statement or allowed for membership of a larger social group. For others, the existence of purchase meant that if there was a danger of his regiment being sent on foreign service, an officer could simply, by careful inter-regimental exchange, avoid such service and continue to enjoy society. Many Victorian officers had limited professional commitment or personal involvement in their chosen 'career'. Indeed, some viewed their professional 'career' as complementary to their membership of the landed classes.

As Victoria's reign progressed so did the debate about the ills of the purchase system. Numerous commissions, sub-committees of Parliament and debates in the House of Commons all noted the failings of purchase and Edward Cardwell became determined that the changes to purchase were to be part of his wider reforms of the army, which was to include a link battalion system and short service periods for the rank and file. He felt that although purchase should remain for the initial commission, selection based on merit needed to be put in place for the ranks of captain or major and above. Yet, when he took his planned reforms to the House in late 1869, Cardwell met with a surprising degree of opposition. From the Radical benches, who wanted to see an end to purchase altogether, the Members felt that his reforms did not go far enough, whilst the Conservatives were angered that his plans made no provision for compensating those officers who had invested large sums in the purchase system and had not taken into account their views as to whether they wanted the purchase system to continue. The Cabinet refused to consider compensation and Cardwell was forced to withdraw his plans for abolition from his wider reforms. Instead, a Royal Commission, chaired by Sir George Grey, was appointed to examine a way forward to end the purchase system. This duly reported in June 1870 and over-whelmingly supported the officers' rights in justifying a continuation of purchase, and if it was to be abolished then compensation must be paid.

During the summer of 1870 Cardwell dwelt on the matter and consulted with colleagues, particularly Lord Northbrook. He finally concluded that complete abolition of purchase and the payment of compensation to the officers concerned was the only way forward. Yet, very difficult months lay ahead as the government attempted to ease the abolition bill through Parliament. The greatest opposition came from a group of largely retired army officers, known as 'the Colonels', and these Members were very vocal in defence of the status quo. Although the Bill passed its first reading in the Commons, it only scraped through its second with the qualified and somewhat reluctant support of Disraeli. Realizing that the passage of the third reading might be threatened, Gladstone insisted on firm Liberal party discipline, and this ensured that those Liberal Members who were apathetic on the matter finally turned out to vote and on 13 July 1871 the Abolition of Purchase Bill, including substantial financial compensation to the officers concerned, was passed through the Commons. Cardwell recognized that the passage of the Bill through the House of Lords would be very problematic and called on Cambridge to speak in this Chamber in support of it. The duke's incoherent mumblings were mostly inaudible and certainly noncommittal and failed to influence the debate. The Bill provoked violent partisanship and was defeated on its second reading.

Cardwell and the Cabinet had considered a reversal in the Lords as likely and had already resolved to push through abolition via a Royal Warrant. Within days of the Lords defeat the queen had signed the said Warrant and on 1 November 1871 the purchase, sale and exchange of commissions was duly cancelled. The matter of compensation to officers was agreed over the following two years. Although now abolished, the ending of the purchase system did not fundamentally alter the internal social structure within the Victorian officer corps. The possession of a large private income was still necessary especially in the more fashionable regiments, and previous attendance at the right private boarding school was something that mattered. This basis for recruitment was to the critics of the army at the heart of its perceived low level of professionalism and was certainly considered a factor by the various commissions that investigated the army's poor initial performance in the Anglo-Boer War at the end of the nineteenth century. There were few internal mechanisms by which officers' standards and wider knowledge and experience could be improved. Much training of junior officers was undertaken in situ in their own regiments in which their education could be at best minimal or even non-existent. Of course, this varied across regiments with a lack of uniformity in training or thinking. There was little questioning of how things were done and a large acceptance that practices happened because they had always been done that way.

Although the Staff College had been founded in Camberley in 1858, it received scant encouragement from the General Staff, and with Cambridge's firm belief that purchase rather than merit should enhance promotion, many officers saw little advantage in taking the two-year course. There was minimal incentive to move beyond regimental training and indeed students at the college were seen by many of their contemporary officers as 'slackers' who by taking the course evaded their regimental duties, and who then obtained staff appointments. It would not be until the appointment of Sir Edward Hamley, commandant for seven years from 1870, that fresh life was breathed into the Staff College. As author of *The Operations of War*, Hamley's enthusiasm and wide knowledge rapidly saw an improvement in not only what was taught but a widening of the range of subjects covered. This included many technique subjects, such as map-making, logistics and intelligence-gathering. The reputation of the college was further enhanced as Wolseley, who, following the success of the Red River Expedition of 1870 and the Asante War of 1873–4, was a rising star, at least amongst the political classes, favoured the appointment of Staff College graduates. It is perhaps not surprising that two of the most successful officers on the Asante Expedition, Redvers Buller and Evelyn Wood, were both recent graduates of Camberley and is it even less of a surprise that these two officers received plaudits for their actions in Southern Africa under Thesiger's command. There is no evidence to suggest that Thesiger, surrounded as he was by the conservative hierarchy of the army, ever considered attending the Staff College.

Thesiger's brief spell with the Rifles was spent largely on foreign service for between February and November 1845, when he transferred to the Grenadier Guards, he served in Halifax, Nova Scotia. Although foreign service was to be a feature of his career, Frederic spent much of his early years of regimental duty at home. He was promoted to lieutenant and captain in December 1850, again via purchase, which would have cost in the region of a further £525 (£71,000 today), this being the difference in price between his old and new commissions. Although not specified, payments of up to double the regulated price were often agreed upon, and there is no reason to suggest that in the fashionable and elite Grenadier Guards this would not have been the case at this time. Yet another anomaly within the system meant that a commission purchased into the Guards was at a higher rank than in other regiments, right up to the rank of lieutenant colonel. In February 1852 Thesiger was appointed Aide-de-Camp (ADC) to the Lord Lieutenant of Ireland, Lord Eglington, working from Dublin Castle. Just eleven months later he became ADC to General Sir Edward Blakeney, commander of British troops in Ireland.

In 1853 war in the Crimea broke out and this presented Frederic with yet another opportunity. He was again given an ADC role, this time to Lieutenant General Frederick Markham, commander of the Second Division. There seems little doubt that Thesiger's family and social connections helped him secure these important and influential positions at a time when such things mattered greatly. However, it is also clear that he was a good administrator and organizer who flourished in these early roles. Alongside this Frederic, now a tall, thin, imposing figure, with a hooked nose and thick bushy eyebrows, who spoke in sharp, jerky sentences, displayed a courteous and gentlemanly character, and lived a modest and moderate life. His friends knew him as 'Fred', even after he assumed the title of Lord Chelmsford and he was a teetotaller who enjoyed physical activity and sports. Although naturally shy, if not introspective, his background, including his schooling, had provided him with the ability to adopt a genial, confident social manner. His creative side was seen in a love of amateur dramatics and his competent clarinet-playing. Frederic epitomized the 'gentleman ideal', which the engrained conservatism of the Victorian British army so valued.

In November 1855 Frederic was made brevet major, which reflected that his service had been distinguished. The brevet conferred a rank in the army higher than that in his regiment. In the same month he was made deputy assistant quartermaster general on the Headquarters Staff in the Crimea and here he was kept very busy trying to resolve the many supply issues that bedevilled British forces. Whilst serving in the Crimea Thesiger was Mentioned in Despatches and at the end of his service, he received the Crimean medal, with Sebastopol clasp, as well as the Turkish and Sardinian medals and the Order of the Medjidie (5th Class).

Whilst in the Crimea, it appears that he managed to find time to write letters home and two pieces of correspondence he sent to his brother-in-law Sir John Inglis, who was at the time commanding a brigade in India, have survived and tell of Frederic's experiences in the Crimea, which included the French and British attacks upon the Russian Redans outside of Sebastopol. Inglis was to later gain fame for the gallant eighty-seven-day defence of the Lucknow Residency during the Indian Rebellion. In a letter dated 5 August 1855, Frederic told Inglis of some of the hardships the troops faced due to problems with supplying the army as well as having to endure the appalling weather. In contrast he wrote of the good and ample food General Markham and his staff enjoyed. He also informed Inglis that as long as Lord Hardinge remained as Commander-in-Chief of the British Army both men could hope for further advancement as, 'my father will almost be able to get anything he applies for', which clearly illustrates the importance of social and family connections at this time. Frederic concluded the letter by stating that, 'I am now bearded like a pard [a leopard's coat] and have all the appearance of a bronzed veteran.'[3]

In the second letter, dated 20 September 1855, Frederic wrote to Inglis describing the successful French attempts to take the 'Malakoff' position outside of Sebastopol and the unsuccessful efforts of the British troops to hold onto the 'Redan' after they had taken it from the Russians. There is an underlying frustration, if not anger, in Frederic's writing when he discussed the inability of the British to reinforce the 'Redan' and stated that after the British were forced to retreat that, 'The Authorities ... seem content with the beating'.[4] Although Frederic clearly was close to the fighting in the Crimea, he never fought in any general engagements and this was to be something of a feature of his career.

Frederic's service in the Crimea had been successful and equally importantly he had worked with and around the senior command where his abilities, affability and social conformity and been noticed by those who could influence his career. Yet, his immediate advancement was again initially via the purchase system. He returned with the Grenadier Guards to England and when an opportunity arose in August 1857 for promotion to captain and lieutenant colonel, he seized it, despite the purchase price of £1,150 (roughly £131,000 today). Thesiger, via his father's purse and the patronage of family contacts, had risen to high rank in a very short period of time, yet for all his apparent success, and clear ability, an important problem remained, that of money. The purchasing of commissions had been a hard burden to bear for his father, despite his glowing career at the bar. Furthermore, life as an officer in such a prestigious regiment as the Grenadier Guards involved a significant financial outlay just to maintain a position. The Grenadiers were renowned for their extravagant uniforms and high mess bills and there was undoubtedly a social pressure or etiquette to match the spending of fellow officers. In addition, living in London imposed a further financial burden. Indeed, any officer in Thesiger's regiment could spend up to £900 (over £100,000 today) a year above his pay.[5] For Frederic, with his moderate and modest way of living, such extra outlays must have been particularly hard to stomach.

Thesiger realized that he was living beyond his means and that he could not continue to rely upon his father's financial support. Indeed, it is a wonder that Frederic remained in the Grenadier Guards as long as he did, although his decision to initially purchase into this regiment undoubtedly accelerated his career, via social connections. An officer of Thesiger's then rank was paid an annual salary of £365 (around £47,000 today) and this was generally insufficient to meet the cost of uniforms, mess bills, etc.[6] In April 1858, Frederic took the opportunity to exchange as a lieutenant colonel into the 95th (Derbyshire) Regiment of Foot, which following the 1881 reorganization of the army became the 2nd Battalion of the Sherwood Foresters. The 95th was due to serve in Southern Africa but, with the uprising in India, had been diverted to the sub-continent and their new lieutenant colonel joined his new Indian command in November 1858. The regiment was part of Sir Robert Napier's Central Indian Field Force which was tasked with eradicating the last elements of dissent from British rule and participated in fourteen engagements. Frederic, however, arrived after these actions and once more did not see any direct fighting, although he was Mentioned in Despatches and received the Indian Mutiny medal.

Frederic now, at last, had command of a regiment and he had the added benefit of an Indian command, which offered generous allowances and pay as well as providing a better standard of living and high status in Indian society. Furthermore, with the Indian rebellion just recently over, Thesiger must have felt that there had to be a high chance of more conflict, whether in India or perhaps Burma or even Afghanistan and military success was a sure way to accelerate further promotion. Thesiger was now to spend the greatest part of his army career in India, serving there until 1874, but rather than gaining practical experience of commanding troops in the field much of his tenure there was spent in administrative and staff duties. It seems that his early reputation for thoroughness, attention to detail and organizational ability had followed him to India. In addition, it is probable that his experiences at the tail end of the rebellion, and the stories that he must have heard from his brother-in-law, Sir John Inglis, and others could have clouded his view on the native threat once he was finally given a field command in Southern Africa.

Thesiger travelled extensively around India with his new command but on 13 July 1861 he was appointed Deputy Adjutant General, British Troops, based at the Bombay Presidency. Here he could again demonstrate his organizational skills whilst allowing time to enjoy the social life of the British Raj. On 30 April 1863, Thesiger was promoted once more, this time to brevet colonel. It was in Bombay that he met for the first time the Governor of Bombay, Sir Henry Bartle Frere. These two men, whose paths would cross again in Southern Africa and whose destinies and legacies would be so tightly entwined, befriended each other. It is not known how strong the friendship was between the two men, but there is little doubt that in 1878 and 1879 the fact they already had a relationship certainly influenced how they worked together in Southern Africa. It was also in Bombay that Frederic met and fell in love with Adria Fanny Heath, eldest daughter of Major General Heath of the Bombay army. Adria was twenty years Frederic's junior which was not an uncommon age gap at this time. The couple married on 1 January 1867 and the union was a very happy one which blessed them with four sons, though tragically a further two children died in infancy.

In little over a year Frederic was separated from his new bride when he was selected by Sir Robert Napier as DAG on the staff of the Abyssinian

Expeditionary Force. In a letter to his wife written as he left with Napier, Thesiger opened his heart and revealed his inner insecurities that were to haunt him later during his Southern Africa command. He wrote:

> I am afraid if anyone saw me writing these lines, they would not believe that I was an Adjutant General proceeding to join an army in the field – I feel more like a schoolboy leaving home the second time, when the novelty of the new life has vanished and nothing remains but the miseries of the moment. It is of course, when alone, that I feel as I have written; I do not let the outside world penetrate into my secret thoughts.[7]

The British expedition to Abyssinia was initially viewed as a rescue mission following the imprisonment of several missionaries and two representatives of the British government by the mentally unstable Emperor Tewodros of Ethiopia in his citadel of Magdala. These acts of kidnapping by the emperor were an attempt to force London to comply with his requests for military assistance. The hostages had been taken several years before and public opinion in Britain had grown in support of some sort of military action to not only free them, but to teach the emperor a sharp lesson. Patient negotiations by the British came to nothing and with public pressure demanding action, the government of the Earl of Derby decided, in August 1867, to despatch an expedition, although it would be the subsequent government of Benjamin Disraeli which would gain the plaudits for the success of the campaign. Given the remote location, it was decided to use troops from the Bombay army, both British and Indian, rather than send regiments from Britain. Sir Robert Napier was given command, a veteran of the Sikh Wars, the Indian Rebellion and of the taking of the Taku Forts outside Peking in 1860.

Napier's command consisted of 4,000 European troops, 9,000 Indian troops and a further 7,000 camp followers, with 25,000 head of cattle. Whilst the Indian troops were armed with either smooth-bore Enfields or obsolete muzzle-loading muskets, the British regiments, which included the 4th (King's Own Royal) Regiment of Foot and the 33rd (Duke of Wellington's Regiment), were issued with the latest British rifle, the Snider–Enfield, which was the first breech-loading rifle to enter British service. To march the 400 miles from the East African coast to Tewodros' fortress of Magdala, where the hostages were being held, was an enormous logistical challenge and one that Napier and Thesiger relished and rose to. Forty-four elephants were required to carry the heavy components of the four Armstrong artillery pieces and two mortars across high mountainous terrain. In addition, the force was supplied with nearly 1,000 bullocks, 1,800 camels and almost 5,000 mules and ponies. All water and food supplies had to be carried along with the new metal cartridges for the Snider rifles, which were packed in 70lb boxes for the mules to carry. This was a significant and major campaign and Thesiger thrived in his staff role.

By 10 April 1868, after nearly three months of arduous marching, Napier's force had reached its goal of the Aroge plain, below the Magdala citadel. The British force comprised an advanced 'flying column' of around 5,000 troops with the remaining men strung out along the line of advance. To face his adversaries Tewodros had 7,000 warriors behind the walls of his fortress. These men were generally armed with long curved swords, stabbing spears and had some protection in the form of round, leather shields, 3ft or more in diameter. Around 2,000 were armed with ancient muskets, flintlocks and matchlocks, whilst some thousand men carried a double-barrelled percussion weapon, which had been imported from Europe. All these weapons required that Tewodros' men engage with the enemy at close quarters, something Napier was very keen to avoid. Little did he know it at the time, but Thesiger was to later see parallels with the Zulu forces he faced in 1879.

However, as Napier's advance forced reached the Aroge plain, 1,000ft below the fortress of Magdala, the commander quickly perceived that he had inadvertently given Tewodros an opportunity to launch a potentially catastrophic attack. By taking an easier route than the main body, the mule train and baggage column had arrived in advance of their supporting cavalry and infantry, with only the 23rd Punjab Pioneers in position to protect this vulnerable force. Napier riding ahead realized the danger immediately and despatched his ADC, Captain Scott, at full gallop back down the difficult mountain pass to spur on the men of the 4th who were wearily toiling some distance behind. From his lofty position Tewodros saw his opportunity to attack the prize of the expedition's baggage whilst it was so exposed. At 4pm on the afternoon of 10 April 1868, the first artillery volleys began to fall disconcertingly near to the troops of the 23rd Punjab regiment and Napier and his staff officers; Thesiger was at last close to a general action.

After some worrying moments, 300 men of the 1st Battalion of the 4th King's Own Regiment arrived exhausted, just as Tewodros unleashed his main attack and around 6,500 warriors descended the slope from Magdala in a rush of screams onto the Aroge plain. Tewodros delegated command of the assault to one of his most-trusted chieftains, Fitaurari Gabri, who rather conspicuously wore a scarlet robe. Along with the foot soldiers, Gabri also had some 500 chiefs, or principal men, mounted upon either mules or sure-footed Galla ponies, which seemed to fly over the precipitous drop to the plains below. With a thunderstorm as a dramatic backdrop, Gabri led the mile-wide crescent of screaming warriors from the front. As the mass approached the baggage train, hopeful of easy pickings, they were confronted by the men of the 4th in skirmishing order. The small, thin line of infantry waited patiently, and resolutely, for the order to fire. As the warriors approached to within 250yd of the British skirmish line, Colonel Cameron of the 4th calmly gave the order for volley fire.

Simultaneously, 300 rifles were raised to shoulders. Hammers clicked back to full cock and suddenly, and violently, the first volley erupted. As the smoke cleared a wide gap could be seen in the centre of the Abyssinian line. Gabri fell in this first volley, along with hundreds of his men. The remaining warriors discharged their obsolete muskets in an ineffective salvo and prepared to reload. The British, now firing independently, gave these men no time to do so, as the British fire was continuous. As one man fired, another had rapidly reloaded his Snider. With the men of the 4th able to fire between six to eight rounds a minute the line was producing between thirty to forty well-aimed shots every second. The effect of this rate of fire upon the mass of warriors was totally devastating and its intensity seemed to have even taken the men of the 4th by surprise. With a steady breeze blowing the black gunpowder smoke away, the British riflemen had an uninterrupted view of their unfortunate targets.

Tewodros' warriors fell in their hundreds until the line, smashed beyond endurance, wavered and fled. The 4th now began a steady advance, firing slowly as targets presented themselves. Some of the Abyssinians, still defiant, stopped to fire their ineffectual muskets only to meet death as dozens of Sniders fired back riddling their bodies. Despite some flanking movements by Tewodros' troops upon the baggage train which had to be beaten back by men of the Sikh pioneers in fierce hand-to-hand fighting, the battle was effectively won. It had lasted 3 hours and, in that time, some 2,000 of Tewodros' men had fallen, with around 700 confirmed as dead. British casualties amounted to just twenty wounded of whom two subsequently died. Thesiger, watching from the rear as the 4th advanced, must surely have been impressed by how the Snider had decimated the Abyssinians and the lesson seemed clear – superior firepower could decide a battle, even when the enemy vastly outnumbered the British. He would take this view with him to Southern Africa, where he would place huge value on the Martini-Henry rifle and its ability to stop the Zulu army in its advance. In that situation his view was to be shown to be flawed and ultimately costly.

Although defeated in open battle, Tewodros and 500 of his most loyal supporters remained defiantly behind the walls of the Magdala citadel. Napier knew the emperor's fortress would have to be assaulted and in the early morning of 13 April 1868, led by men of the 33rd Regiment, the British stormed the fortress gates. Despite Napier's fears, the assault proved easier than expected and its success owed much to the firepower of the Snider, which kept the defenders' heads down as the British clambered over the walls. Tewodros, with his last remaining followers, retreated to the inner wall. Finally, as the men of the 33rd approached nearer, Tewodros drew a pistol, ironically presented to him as a gift from Queen Victoria, placed its barrel in his mouth and ended his own personal suffering. With his death all further resistance ceased.

Napier and his staff rightfully received huge praise not only for the successful release of the hostages and the military defeat of a belligerent foe, but more especially for how the massive logistical demands of the expedition were undertaken and handled so smoothly. Napier fully recognized Frederic's tremendous efforts and was full of praise for his conspicuous service throughout the campaign. Thesiger was Mentioned in Despatches by Napier in which he wrote in glowing terms of his 'great ability and untiring energy'.[8] In addition to receiving the Abyssinian medal Thesiger was awarded a CB, Order of the Bath. He was also rewarded with the honour of being appointed as ADC to Queen Victoria and he returned briefly to England between August 1868 and March 1869 to fulfil this role. Little is known of how he fared during this time and certainly Victoria made no mention of Frederic in her journal, although it seems clear from how the queen followed events in Southern Africa in 1879, and then welcomed him on his return from that campaign, that she thought fondly of Thesiger.

Napier clearly respected Thesiger both as a person and for his abilities. There must also have been a deep friendship between the two men for Thesiger's first son was christened Frederic John Napier. On his return to

India the commander-in-chief pressed for Thesiger's appointment to the position of adjutant general in India. Frederic assumed the role on 17 March 1869 and again his natural organizational skills shone. Bindon Blood first met Thesiger at this time and described him as 'being universally liked and respected and considered one of the best Adjutant-Generals there had ever been'.[9] Thesiger held the position for five years and did gain some experience of handling troops in the field. In 1874 Napier selected him to lead the camp exercises and Thesiger received written thanks from both the government of India and the commander-in-chief for the manner in which the exercises were conducted. Soon after he returned to England and on 1 October 1874 Thesiger assumed command of the troops at the Shorncliffe camp, near Cheriton in Kent, with the title of Colonel on the Staff. On departing India, he received letters of thanks from Napier and the government for the ability and service he demonstrated whilst adjutant general in India.

Back in England, Thesiger took command of a brigade in the manoeuvres at Aldershot. He remained at Shorncliffe until December 1876, and in January of the following year he was promoted to brigadier general in command of the 1st Infantry Brigade at Aldershot. Also, in 1877, Thesiger was offered the significant home command of deputy adjutant general based at Horse Guards. Thesiger declined this prestigious position, citing his desire to return to India where he felt that his years of service had given him a good understanding of the sub-continent and what it took to be an effective senior officer there. However, it is also probable that Thesiger was well aware of the financial commitments that would be placed upon himself if he had accepted the Horse Guards appointment, and this may well have influenced him. Yet, Thesiger's decision to not take the promotion did not hamper further advancement for on 15 March 1877 he was promoted to the rank of major general, which was backdated to November 1868. It was fairly common at this time to ante-date promotions and Thesiger certainly benefited from this, and this promotion needs to be viewed in terms of the ending of the purchase system by Cardwell in 1871.

The Thesiger family had invested, via the purchase system, heavily in Frederic career and advancement. As part of the agreement to pacify and reimburse those officers who had spent so much on commissions the government, via the terms of the Royal Warrant of 30 October 1871, made a commitment to repay the cost of the commissions purchased as long as the officers then accepted retirement. Between November 1871 and November

1873, 888 officers accepted this offer at a cost to the Treasury of more than £7,000,000 (roughly £830,000,000 today). Thesiger, by, deciding to pursue his army career and accept promotion, forfeited any claim to compensation and lost the substantial amount of capital he and his family had invested. This was certainly an issue of huge contention for Frederic, but the choice had been made. The backdating of his promotion to major general would have lessened some of Thesiger's disquiet at the loss of his 'purchase' investment. Now as a relatively young major general he was in line for an active field command should one become available.

Frederic did not have long to wait for his opportunity for on 1 February 1878 he was selected as General Officer Commanding (GOC) in Southern Africa, to replace General Sir Arthur Cunynghame. The Duke of Cambridge had actively pushed for Thesiger's appointment and clearly Cambridge viewed Frederic as a safe and sound choice. Thesiger must have felt a mixture of emotions at the appointment. Certainly, it was what he had been working towards for many years, but he must have been nervous and perhaps unsure, yet at the same time no doubt excited by the prospect of, at last, a field command. However, was Thesiger ready for such an appointment? He was certainly as well qualified as many of his contemporaries, yet he was perhaps, more than most, a product of the army system and that system clearly had many ingrained faults that were likely to surface at critical moments.

None of his contemporaries, nor subsequent writers, have ever criticized Thesiger's bravery or effort. Those under his command found him essentially a decent and fair man and he earned the loyalty of most who served under him. He was conscientious and no doubt a very good staff officer. Unlike many of his contemporaries in senior ranks, he seemed incapable of insincerity or intrigue. Again, unlike others, he was a modest man, although some considered him too self-effacing, too ready to listen to subordinates or the last opinion offered, and too ready to change his mind in deference to others. He was viewed as a gentleman by all, especially the rank and file, and he was almost paternalistic towards his men. In civilian clothes he might have been mistaken for a university professor or even a clergyman. As a teetotaller he encouraged abstinence amongst the troops. In contrast, he allowed flogging for troops who misbehaved whilst serving on a campaign. Indeed, flogging of British troops did occur during the Anglo-Zulu War and this was to be the last campaign in which this punishment was permitted within the British army.

Yet, despite Thesiger's attributes and skills none of these would necessarily make for a successful field commander. His years of diligent staff work certainly influenced Thesiger when he came to his own field command. He was to appoint a very small inner circle of Staff officers, selected mostly from the Aldershot command, and he failed to delegate tasks even to this group, meaning that he became overwhelmed, on occasion, by both detail and long hours at a time when he should have been focusing on the bigger picture of the campaign itself. In addition, his introspective personality, if not shyness, made him appear aloof and diffident to many and this hardly encouraged discussion and debate amongst his inner circle of officers.

Despite the Cardwell reforms, the British army remained a highly conservative institution. Thesiger himself opposed the linked battalion system and short-service enlistments which Cardwell had introduced and preferred the Indian system of battalions serving for long periods on the sub-continent. In these views he was very much supported by Cambridge. Indeed, the duke, whilst recognizing that ultimate control of the army rested with the Secretary of State for War, and thus Parliament, retained huge influence and power and did not hesitate to voice his own opposition to reforms. He even led many officers, of all ranks, to believe that the Cardwell reforms would likely be rejected before too long. The abolition of the purchase system had not altered the social composition of the officer corps, especially in the higher ranks and this, in itself, enhanced the conservative nature of the army. Field exercises, whether in Britain or India, followed much the same formula with little opportunity for recognition of initiative. Intelligence-gathering and even obtaining adequate maps were not given the importance they deserved both within regiments and on field exercises.

Although the Staff College, and its graduates, tried to rectify the inherent reluctance to change and adapt, such progressive thinking was seen by many as radical and even disloyal to the long-standing teachings of the regiments. Thesiger was very much a product of this conservatism; for example, at the beginning of the Zulu Campaign he had not appointed a staff officer to the role of intelligence officer. He simply did not consider the role of importance. In contrast, Wolseley recognized how vital it was to have a large group of able and competent staff officers around him on campaign and he actively promoted the advancement of those officers who had graduated from the Staff College. The question was could Thesiger, who had risen to a field command through promotion in an inherently unquestioning organization, and had assimilated much of that conservative thinking, rise to the enormous challenges imposed upon him by commanding a substantial force, with all the logistical demands that would be placed upon it when invading onto enemy soil, and then be able to fight successfully against a formidable foe? It seemed that Thesiger, through his background, his conservatism and his own introspective character, could be placed in a situation that might overwhelm him, although Cambridge clearly had no such concerns when appointing Thesiger to the Southern African command.

One area in which Thesiger displayed a reluctance to involve himself was politics. Unlike Wolseley, Thesiger was a strong believer that military operations and politics were distinct spheres and should not be vested in any one commander. This was in part due to his own nature, but he was also probably conditioned by his service in India, where the two areas remained distinct. Once he arrived in Southern Africa, he was to serve alongside the High Commissioner, Sir Bartle Frere, his old Indian hand and friend from his own service in Bombay. Thesiger showed a natural deference, or even subservience, towards Frere and just when the political situation required an element of military input and control against the feral politics of the time, Thesiger was most certainly not the commander to show it. To offer some defence, Thesiger had witnessed his predecessor, Cunynghame, fail because of his political stance and meddling and this must have made him somewhat reluctant to involve himself in politics and oppose Frere's strategy, and of course his friendship with Frere would almost certainly have influenced how Frederic would have reacted towards the High Commissioner. However, acting to oppose or even influence a politician was just not Thesiger's style, nor something that his conservative background would have allowed him to consider, and indeed he bent over backwards to assist Frere's firm-line position against the Zulu king, Cetshwayo. He would do everything in his power to ready his command for the invasion of Zululand. Yet, in February 1878, Thesiger was fully focused on his immediate concern of bringing the 9th Frontier War to a rapid and successful conclusion and as he journeyed south the thought of war against the Zulu nation, and the road that would take him to Ulundi, must have been far from his mind.

Chapter 2

A Troubled Frontier

E arly European contact with Southern Africa focused on the area around what is now Cape Town. The first mention of the Cape in European texts was in 1488 by the Portuguese explorer Bartolomeu Dias, who first reached the area and named it *Cabo das Tormentas*, or 'Cape of Storms'. King John II of Portugal renamed the area *Cabo da Boa Esperanca*, the Cape of Good Hope, for it was considered to be a possible sea route around Africa to India and the Far East, as it indeed turned out to be. Another Portuguese explorer, Vasco da Gama, recorded his passage round the Cape in 1497.

By the sixteenth century French, Danish, Dutch and English, but mainly Portuguese, ships regularly stopped over at the Cape in Table Bay on their route east. They traded tobacco, copper and iron with the local indigenous tribes of the region, in exchange for fresh meat and vegetables and water barrels were refilled before their long and arduous journeys were continued. As the Dutch East Indies flourished the visits of Dutch vessels to Table Bay became more frequent and the Dutch East Indies Company decided that a permanent settlement needed to be established there. In 1652 the Dutch agent Jan van Riebeeck took possession of Table Bay as a staging post for Dutch ships travelling from Holland to the port of Batavia, modern day Jakarta, the entrepôt for the growing Dutch Far East empire. Not only were the Dutch able to stock up on fresh provisions but crews were able to gain some much-needed land rest before continuing their voyages. The Dutch were also keen to prevent the British from acquiring a physical foothold on the Cape and the Fort de Goede Hoop was built soon after van Riebeeck arrived.

Although the Dutch viewed the Cape very much as a staging post, rather than a commercial settlement, money was to be made. Into the eighteenth century British, French and even American ships were regular callers at the Cape and the Dutch charged higher rates to these vessels for the right to drop anchor and obtain provisions. This income was then used to subsidize the Dutch East Indiamen when they called. As the number of vessels increased so did the demands on the colony. Too few Dutch had been enticed to emigrate to the Cape to support an industry centred on supplying visiting ships. The Dutch turned to the indigenous peoples, the Khoikhoi (otherwise known as Hottentots or Bushmen), who were an ethnic grouping of the San people found today in the Kalahari Desert, for the necessary labour. Much to the disgust of the Dutch the Khoikhoi proved reluctant labourers. Regular work and settlements were not part of the Khoikhoi culture, for they had for centuries lived a nomadic subsistence life, grazing sheep and cattle on the lush grassland of the Cape. In what was to become a pattern of how first the Dutch and Boers and then the British dealt with and treated the indigenous tribes, the Dutch initially traded amicably enough with the Khoikhoi with brass, iron and ornaments exchanged for meat. However, as the Dutch spread out from Table Bay in search of more arable land, they impinged on traditional grazing and claimed right of ownership on common lands. Tensions increased and by the late seventeenth century the Dutch were using all their technological advantages to expel, imprison and exterminate the Khoikhoi. The Dutch colonists, spreading out as free burghers, took the best lands to grow crops and grapes whilst stealing livestock in huge numbers from the Khoikhoi. Without large tracts of land, the Khoikhoi culture wilted, their economy collapsed, the various chieftains imploded and the language began to fade. Disease, particularly smallpox, was brought to the Cape on Dutch ships and with no natural resistance the indigenous peoples of the Cape died in droves. It is estimated that between the mid-seventeenth and the start of the nineteenth century, the Khoikhoi population fell from 200,000 individuals to less than 20,000, mainly due to the collapse of their economy, way of life and disease.[1]

In need of labourers, van Riebeeck petitioned the Dutch government to allow him to enslave the reluctant Khoikhoi, but this request was refused. He thus turned to other sources and in 1658 slaves were brought in, mainly from the Dutch East Indies with Indonesia, Sri Lanka and Goa providing most of these, but slaves also came from Zanzibar, Madagascar and Mozambique. Over the next 150 years it is estimated that some 63,000 men, women and children were sent to the Cape in bondage.[2] These individuals, along with Dutch immigrants and their descendants, developed a small but thriving colony over these years and although the economy remained focused on supplying vessels, it broadened as the burghers fanned out further into the hinterland. Although there was no plantation economy, as in the West Indies, life was undoubtedly brutal for many slaves and punishments severe and indeed sometimes barbaric. As the years passed, Cape Town developed with many fine whitewashed Dutch stone buildings, parks, paved roads and streets constructed. It had undergone a major transformation from its early days of inns and brothels serving the sailors of the passing ships. By the 1790s the Dutch had created a self-contained colonial backwater that featured little in European thoughts.

All this was to change with the declaration of war between Britain and Revolutionary France in 1793. The French decided that one opponent was insufficient and also declared war on the Dutch. The British Secretary of State for War, Henry Dundas, 1st Viscount Melville, quickly realized the strategic importance of Cape Town. Any French conquest of Holland would also likely bring with it control of the Dutch colonial outposts and Dundas wasted no time in petitioning the Foreign Secretary, Lord Granville, as to the likelihood of British troops being available to secure the Cape. Others, such as Sir Francis Baring, founder of Barings Bank, made clear their concerns that if the French gained control of the Cape then British possessions in India could be threatened. In January 1795, the French invaded Holland and Captain John Blankett of the Royal Navy wrote to Evan Nepan, Under Secretary of the War Department, with a briefing on the likely loss of the Cape to the French:

> Whatever tends to give to France the means of obtaining a footing in India is of consequence to us to prevent, it would be idle in me to say anything more to point out the consequences of the Cape than to say that what was a feather in the hands of Holland, will become a sword in the hands of France.[3]

Similarly, Captain Robert Percival wrote, 'For the purposes of defending our own foreign possessions, or keeping our enemies in check, no station can indeed be found comparable to the Cape of Good Hope.'[4]

For reasons of trade and the defence of India, Cape Town could simply not be allowed to fall to the French. The British government sanctioned a pre-emptive assault upon the Dutch possession and on 11 June 1795, Admiral Keith Elphinstone and Major General James Craig sailed into False Bay with a force of 1,200 infantry. The Dutch were anxious to spare Cape Town from assault and swiftly surrendered under very favourable terms, perhaps thinking that this was an occupation of necessity and once war with France was over the colony would return to its former owners. The British took over responsibility for around 20,000 Dutch-Afrikaans, over 25,000 slaves and 15,000 Khoikhoi and a few thousand Bantu-speaking locals. The new British colony was the run by a military governor, Lord Macartney, who in writing to Dundas in July 1797 was rather sanguine about whether the British should maintain a long-term presence at the Cape. Whilst recognizing the colony's geographical and strategic importance, he felt that it would be unlikely to offer an abundant source of revenue and its maintenance would not come cheap for to deter a French attack would require the presence of a sizeable military force. The Dutch had always run the colony at a loss, and it seemed that the British must be prepared to do the same.

Yet, as the French war progressed, the apparent threat to the Cape seemed to recede. Napoleon's invasion of Egypt in 1798 led British strategists to think that it was now Malta, rather than distant Cape Town, that was the focus of French designs. With the fall of the Pitt ministry in 1801, the Cape lost its greatest defender in Henry Dundas and the new Secretary of War and the Colonies, Lord Hobart, was decidedly unenthusiastic declaring, '... he had scarcely ever met with one person who did not consider the Cape a burden rather than an advantage to this country ... the expense of it has been enormous, its revenue did not pay its civil establishment, it was a peculiarly expensive station for ships'.[5] For those in government keen to reduce this burden, peace with France came at an opportune moment. The resulting Treaty of Amiens of 1802 handed back the Cape Colony to Holland (known as the Batavian Republic at this time). However, within a year the fragile peace between Britain and France was lost and in May 1803 the two old protagonists were at war once again.

In light of renewed hostilities, the government of Henry Addington received much criticism for allowing the Cape to be surrendered so easily and once again calls were made to recognize the strategic importance of returning the Dutch colony to British control. In July 1805 rumours that a French fleet was readying to sweep into Table Bay prompted action. William Pitt, now back in office, seized the opportunity and in the autumn two separate fleets departed from Falmouth and Cork carrying 6,650 troops to Southern Africa. They rendezvouzed at Madeira, and it was here that Commodore Sir Home Popham took command of the combined fleet. Popham anchored off Robben Island and on 6 January 1806 General Sir David Baird led the Highlanders of the 71st, 72nd and 93rd Regiments ashore.

The weather was atrocious, and both the ships and the landing craft were tossed around in the violent surf of Losperd's Bay, 30 miles north of Cape Town. Within moments, landing craft were upturned and many Highlanders were thrown into the sea, the first British casualties of what was to become a century of pain and death for thousands of the British soldiers in Southern Africa. Forty-one Highlanders weighed down with equipment drowned and many others dragged themselves soaking from the water to collapse with exhaustion on the shore.

In was an inauspicious start to the campaign and further hardships were to follow. The British now faced a challenging trek through the bush, manhandling cannons until they were opposed by a mixed force of Dutch, French and German mercenaries, and a slave and volunteer militia. The commander of the force, Lieutenant General J.W. Janssens, had planned to oppose the British landings but arrived too late. As Janssens' army of 2,049 men marched through the bush, Baird hurried his men forward and they were able to gain the slopes of Blaauwberg Mountain before the Dutch could reach this high ground. On the morning of 8 January 1806, Janssens drew his force into a line across the veld to oppose the British. The Battle of Blaauwberg, or the battle of Cape Town as it is sometimes known, began at sunrise with an exchange of artillery fire, as well as supporting fire from three Royal Navy ships. This was followed by an unsuccessful charge of Janssens' militia cavalry as well as musket volleys from each side, which claimed several lives. The Dutch centre was weakened when one of the mercenary units fled the battlefield and a well-timed bayonet charge by the Highlanders on the enemy's right flank won the day and forced Janssens to withdraw. Although a brief affair of less than an hour, the battle had been a bloody one. The Dutch suffered 353 casualties, whilst 212 men from Baird's force of 5,399 were killed or wounded.

British forces reached the outskirts of Cape Town on 9 January. To spare the town and its civilian population from attack, the commandant of Cape Town, Lieutenant Colonel Hieronymus Casimir von Prophalow, sent out a flag of truce to the encircling British. He handed over the outer fortifications to Baird, and terms of surrender were negotiated later in the day. On the signing of the articles of capitulation, General Baird announced, ' ... that being in complete possession of the Town and principal Places, I am fully entitled to consider the whole of this Settlement as completely subject to His Majesty's Authority'.[6]

The terms of the capitulation saw Janssens and the Batavian officials and troops sent back to the Netherlands in March. The British forces occupied the Cape until 13 August 1814, when the Netherlands ceded the colony to Britain as a permanent possession. The Union flag would fly over the Cape Castle for another hundred years and in that time the British would face conflict against both indigenous tribes and the Boer settlers. The Xhosa were part of a large migration of Bantu peoples, which included the ancestors of the Zulus, from the equatorial west coast of Africa that travelled south-east, possibly via the Congo River. Archaeological finds and supposition suggest that, over several thousand years, the progressively migrating Bantus lived an essentially nomadic life centred on cattle. After journeying south of the Congo, they then headed south and east around the Kalahari Desert towards the area known as the Transvaal and Natal, until eventually reaching the east coast, probably in the early sixteenth century. One group, the Nguni people, comprising some 200 separate clans, detached themselves from the main Bantu group and established a presence in the unexplored coastal area on the eastern side of the Drakensberg Mountains bordering the Indian Ocean. These clans would later unite to become the Zulu nation under the first king, Shaka.

The remaining Bantu peoples continued their onward migration as it was this group which became known as the Xhosa. The Xhosa were well established to the north, along the banks of the Great Kei River, by about 1675. Yet, the Xhosa had not lived harmoniously together. In about 1750, in what appeared to be a power struggle, the lineage split into two rival groupings, of which one, in 1782, split further. These three divisions were geographically separated, each with their own chiefs, and sub-chiefs. To add to the complexity, chiefs were often referred to by their clan names. The Gcaleka were found east of the Kei River, whilst the Ngqika were located between the Kei and Great Fish rivers and the Ndlambe were west of the Great Fish River in an area known as the Zuurveld. This area was shared with other Xhosa-speaking chiefdoms, the largest being the Gqunukhwebe and included a number of peoples of Khoikhoi origins. Indeed, the indigenous Khoikhoi people in the Zuurveld were absorbed into the Xhosa over a number of decades, losing their independence and identity as they had in the Cape.

The Xhosa's economy centred on cattle and, although their nomadic life was now over and settlements had been established, the search for good grazing land made the Xhosa edge further westwards from the mid-eighteenth century onwards. By coincidence, it was at this time that the Cape whites, specifically the Boer burghers of largely Dutch and German descent, were moving east out from the Cape in search of arable land both for grazing and crop production. In 1769 Cape whites explored to the north-east and made their first contact with the advancing Xhosa people approaching from the Eastern Cape area, with both sides meeting on opposing banks of the Great Fish River. Relations with the Xhosa began amicably with both appreciating that trade between the two groups was mutually beneficial; animals and their products were exchanged by the Xhosa for Dutch manufactured goods, iron and even alcohol. However, the relationships soon turned sour as both groups realized that they were in direct competition for land.

Whilst the early contacts were largely peaceful there were the occasional flare-ups of bloody violence. Isolated incidents usually happened when small parties of trekboers (as the more adventurous and enterprising itinerate Boers were labelled) strayed too far into territory that the Xhosa considered their own. An example occurred in 1737 when a party of elephant hunters led by Hermanus Hubner ventured across the Kei River and were slaughtered to a man. After the first significant contact in 1769 more trekboers ventured east towards the Kei, over 400 miles away from the Cape and effectively out of the control of any form of governance from the Dutch military and political authorities. These settlers, who never numbered more than 1,000 individuals in these early years, were able to enter into tentative agreements with the Xhosa over trade and effectively imposed their own rules over land rights, which was bound to result in conflict. The growing tension was most apparent in the Zuurveld region, which had fertile soils for crop growth as well as all-year-round grazing. Yet, the area was relatively small and with the arrival of the Boers, seeking land which the Xhosa had already occupied, competition and conflict over resources was inevitable. By the early 1770s some Boers had already settled in the valley of the Fish River, directly contravening the dictates of the authorities in the Cape. For example, men such as Willem Prinsloo, who was the patriarch of three families that established themselves as a feudal destiny on the upper reaches of the Great Fish River, considered it his right to expel the Xhosa from what he considered to be his family's land and was prepared to use all means to achieve his goal.

It is worth considering the military structure and tactics of the Xhosa. Unlike the Zulu nation, which was built on conquest and maintained a warlike reputation, even to this day, the Xhosa held that honour did not have to centre upon military prowess. An individual's reputation could be enhanced as much by cultivating domestic virtues such as running a prosperous homestead as it could be by heroism in battle. Men were judged by their courtesy and social behaviour. Yet they expected the same of others and would take quick offence to slights or dishonesty, particularly in matters of trade. In early contacts between Xhosa and Boers, those Boers who tried to cheat the Xhosa were soon ostracized from future trades. Yet, many Boers failed to realize that essentially Xhosa culture was based on honour and simply saw them as a hinderance to their own advancement, to be dealt with and exploited how they saw fit.

From an early age, Xhosa boys would accompany warriors on large hunting drives, which formed the basis of their military training. Their prey would be encircled and often the younger men would be initiated by killing the animal, which ranged from antelopes to even lions, and these beasts were despatched by the hurling of spears. Further training was in the form of bouts of stick-fighting and often those involved would acquire wounds and scars during the fierce encounters, and these would be 'worn' with pride. Even death was not uncommon during these tough 'training' sessions. Once initiated, the boys became men and were on constant call to serve their chief in battle as required.

It was not until the nineteenth century, and largely against the British, that the Xhosa were able to gain ready access to firearms and horses. Until this point the battlefield weapon was a spear, up to 5ft long, with an iron blade. There were eight separate types in the Xhosa arsenal, each with specific names. Some had barbed or serrated blades, used mainly for hunting, but all were thrown with a sharp flick of the arm which imparted a quivering motion through the air that improved accuracy in flight and penetration of the victim. The warriors might also carry broad-bladed stabbing spears for close-contact fighting as well as a knobkerries for smashing skulls, although close-quarter combat was rare. Oval shields, made of stretched cowhide, were carried until the early nineteenth century. The warriors soon discovered that such shields offered no protection against British bullets and also hindered their passage through the bush, so these were discarded.

Unlike the Zulu nation, the Xhosa had no centralized military system, nor did they have a regimental one. Throughout the eighteenth and into the nineteenth centuries the various Xhosa tribes, and within them sub-chiefs, expressed a nominal authority to the Xhosa paramount chief. Whilst both the Boers and the British became frustrated for not having a single Xhosa chief to negotiate land and political settlements with, the Xhosa themselves, whilst not always agreeing to fully accept the authority of the paramount, would normally honour their commitment to him if called for military service. As soon as the paramount issued the phrase, 'the land is dead', then all chiefs would know that war was imminent, and warriors were called to arms. Although no chief could compel men to muster at the paramount's Great Palace, the strict code of honour meant that non-adherence was unlikely. Even so, it was still for the paramount to justify the need for war and explain his reasoning behind asking the warriors to fight. Once war had been decided upon then the army would be organized along clan-related lines and divided into two divisions, one composed of royal clans and the other of commoners. Like the Zulu army, the Xhosa advanced quickly with no commissariat, apart from a few cattle driven to be slaughtered en route. With just a small amount of roasted mealie carried by each warrior, the Xhosa army relied on foraging and raiding for its subsistence and hence campaigns were usually short-lived. Indeed, much of Xhosa warfare can be viewed as large raiding parties in which once their objective had been achieved, the warriors would return to their families and livestock. Sanctuary would be sought in forests and mountains to avoid their enemy's retribution. Unlike the Zulus, the Xhosa avoided the offensive pitched battle wherever possible, but like the Zulus the Xhosa would try to encircle their enemies. The 'centre', composed of young warriors, would rush at the enemy whilst two wings of veteran warriors would endeavour to outflank and surround the opposition. A reserve body was held back to offer protection for the rear and could rush forward if needed to provide support to an advance or plug holes in defence.

From 1780 until 1878 the Xhosa were engaged in nine separate frontier wars. The first two were solely against the Boers and as the nineteenth century progressed the Xhosa clashed more frequently with British settlers, colonial militia and British regulars. The start of the First Frontier War began with what appeared to be an innocuous raid by warriors who went after sheep belonging to the Prinsloo clan. This raid in late 1779 justified a revenge attack in April of the following year. A large number of burghers, under the command of Josua Joubert, led a commando raid against the Xhosa across the Great Fish River and indiscriminately killed any Xhosa who were found between there and the Keiskamma River and captured over 8,000 head of cattle. In May, a second commando, led by Adriaan van Jaarsveld, again raided across the Fish River. The Dutch governor, Baron Joachim van Plattenberg, decided to give these raids his sanction for he was keen to see an agreement with the Xhosa for official recognition that the Fish River would now be the boundary to keep the feuding parties apart. On 5 December 1780, the governor declared an official commando, thus allowing for government munitions to be made available and the offensive began in May 1781. The commander of this enterprise to push all Xhosa back across the Fish River was van Jaarsveld.

The Xhosa used all their traditional knowledge of bush fighting to ambush and then melt away, avoiding pitched battles wherever possible, weary of the firepower from their foe's muskets. The Boers, frustrated by such tactics and struggling to manoeuvre through the thick terrain, resorted to deception. After a month of ineffective fighting van Jaarsveld persuaded members of one Xhosa clan to meet for a parley. With over a hundred warriors assembled, van Jaarsveld laid tobacco on the ground for the Xhosa to pick up. As the unsuspecting warriors bent down to collect the offering van Jaarsveld ordered his men to open fire and the resulting massacre became burnt into the Xhosa memory for years to come. With one clan decimated, van Jaarsveld led his commando in a series of attacks upon other Xhosa, although the theft of cattle seems to have been as central to van Jaarsveld's aims as much as defeating the enemy. By July van Jaarsveld had acquired over 5,000 head and had come to realize that he had insufficient men to drive all the Xhosa across the Fish River, and with this the First Frontier war petered out. However, although it had finished in something of a military stalemate, the war had defined, in Boer minds at least, that the Fish River would be the natural boundary between the Xhosa and European settlers.

An uneasy peace prevailed for over a decade, although during this period the white settlers made no secret of their disdain for the Xhosa and their designs on Xhosa lands. It was not until 1793 that fresh conflict led to the Second Frontier War, and trouble was sparked by a severe drought which put further stress on grazing land. Alongside this, the paramount chief of the Ndlambe, to the east of the Great Fish River, put pressure on those Xhosa, the Gqunukhwebe, west of the river to return and recognize him as their chief. This they refused to do and instead ventured further west into the Zuurveld region, overrunning settler farms, to the anger and indignation of the Boers. Under the leadership of Barend Lindeque, the Boers, without consulting the authorities in Cape Town, approached the Ndlambe paramount to form an alliance against the Gqunukhwebe. The chief readily agreed and on 18 May 1793 a combined force attacked the Xhosa in the Zuurveld, around Bushman's River, seizing 1,800 cattle and killing many. However, several thousand Ndlambe warriors had crossed the Fish River and the sight of these men panicked many of the settlers who fled westwards. The remaining Gqunukhwebe seized their opportunity and burnt 116 of the 120 homesteads in the Zuurveld and drove off 50,000 head of cattle and 11,000 sheep. Humiliated and frightened, many of the settlers never returned but those who did raised another commando force in August 1793, determined to regain their lost stock and push the Gqunukhwebe back across the Fish River. Although 8,000 cattle were retrieved, the commando was simply not large enough to force all the Xhosa out of the Zuurveld and by the end of November the Boers recognized that they would not retake all their lost animals and that many Xhosa would remain living to the west of van Plattenberg's Fish River boundary line. Deep hatred remained between the Xhosa and the Boers and political leadership was lacking in resolving the various disputes and overcoming intransigence.

This absence of political willingness to manage the issues surrounding the disputed lands coincided with the upheavals in the Cape at this time, with the British determined to seize the area from the Dutch to deny it to the French. In November 1798, Major General Francis Dundas (no relation to the Secretary of War) arrived in Southern Africa to become acting governor of the Cape. He was almost immediately embroiled in a rebellion of Boer settlers in the disputed lands of the Eastern Cape, led by Coenraad de Buys, whom historian John Laband describes as an 'irrepressible troublemaker'.[7] Dundas was forced to despatch British troops, under the command of Brigadier General Thomas Packenham Vandeleur, to quell the uprising around the town of Graaf-Reinet. Troops arrived there in March 1799 and after a brief pursuit the leading rebels surrendered without a fight. Dundas now could not resist the opportunity to seize a political and military settlement and, with British troops near the Zuurveld, he decided to resolve the Xhosa issue and ordered Vandeleur to push the remaining Xhosa back across the Great Fish River. Thus, for the first time British regulars fought the Xhosa in what became known as the Third Frontier War, which rumbled on until 1803.

At first Vandeleur and his men struggled to overcome the difficult and alien terrain over which they had to fight and the hit-and-run ambush tactics of the Gqunukhwebe Xhosa. The British had many local defeats, including a bloody incident in which the Xhosa wiped out a British patrol of twenty-one men. Frustrated at failing to vanquish the Xhosa, Vandeleur pulled his men out of the bush and retired back to Fort Frederick at Algoa Bay. Here in a fit of pique he declared that fighting the Xhosa '... in the midst of impenetrable thickets adds little lustre to British arms'.[8] He would not be the last British officer to share this view. Vandeleur sent the majority of his command back to the Cape and the local Khoikhoi, allied to the Xhosa, saw this as a chance to gain revenge on the Boer settlers, many of whom had earlier enslaved them. The frontier was aflame once more and Dundas himself was forced to lead 500 British troops back to the area to restore order. The brief return of the Cape to the Dutch in the Treaty of Amiens allowed Dundas to wash his hands of the problem and left the Boer commandos to tie down the Xhosa. Bitter but ineffective bush fighting continued until 1803. The Dutch ignored the fact that the Fish River boundary remained a fanciful settlement, with Boers, Khoikhoi and Xhosa still uneasily inhabiting the Zuurveld. The Xhosa had prevailed against both the Dutch and British in this Third Frontier War.

British victory at the Battle of Blaauwberg in 1806 settled ownership of the Cape for over a hundred years and meant the subsequent Frontier wars would be a British affair. It was not long before further conflict, in the shape of the Fourth Frontier War, occurred. Initially the young new British governor, the Earl of Caledon, aimed for a conciliatory approach with both the Boer settlers and the Xhosa west of the Fish River, and despatched Lieutenant Colonel Richard Collins to the eastern frontier on a fact-finding mission. Collins was heavily influenced by the burghers who stressed that since the British humiliation of the Third Frontier War their standing was low amongst the Xhosa who were ready to exploit any perceived weaknesses. Collins delivered his findings in August 1809 and in it he stressed that it was imperative that contact between the settlers and the Xhosa in the Zuurveld had to be avoided. The only logical way to do this was to force the Xhosa back across the Fish River and that this natural boundary had to be honoured and enforced. Caledon was far from convinced, knowing that such action would certainly involve British troops once again in conflict with the Xhosa. Yet, Caledon's replacement, Sir John Cradock, had no such qualms and soon after his arrival in September 1811 he was considering military options against the Zuurveld Xhosa.

Cradock invested a hero of Blaauwberg, Lieutenant Colonel John Graham, with civil and military powers in the eastern district and instructed him to use all means to evict the Xhosa from the Zuurveld. By December 1811, Graham had assembled a force of 900 regulars, supported by around 450 mounted burghers and instructed that no mercy was to be shown to the Xhosa. All males were to be killed without question, even if they were found in their homesteads, and Xhosa settlements in the Zuurveld were to be destroyed. In a series of column sweeps through the bush Graham's force at first experienced the usual frustration of trying to locate the Xhosa whilst avoiding ambushes. Again, the Xhosa achieved some local successes, but they were soon overcome by the brutality of the British and Boer assaults. In the bush it was frequently impossible, if not inconvenient, for Graham's forces to distinguish between the hiding Xhosa and as a result women and children were also killed. The Xhosa were overwhelmed and shocked by the intensity and ferocity of the fighting and by January 1812, the leading chiefs, the Ndlambe paramount amongst them, led their followers back across the Fish River. To further strengthen the boundary Cradock ordered the construction of twenty-six posts at strategic points along the river and the troops manning these stone-built shelters were given orders of shoot to kill if any Xhosa were spotted infiltrating back. Although the posts did stop the Xhosa from returning en masse, they did not prevent Xhosa raiding parties seeking revenge against settler farmers and the Boers lived in fear. The Fourth Frontier War had been on a different scale and intensity to the previous conflicts and ruptured the ties of labour and commerce that had tentatively allowed the settlers and Xhosa to coexist as reluctant neighbours. The British had introduced a cruel form of warfare which would characterize future conflicts and they had categorically marked and enforced the Fish River as the boundary between the Cape and the Xhosa.

In April 1814 Cradock was succeeded as governor by Lord Charles Somerset. Somerset's early months were typifed by the suppression of a Boer revolt, the Slachtersnek Rebellion, in the Eastern Cape, around the town of Graaf-Reinet. Although no British troops were involved in the capture of the Boer rebel leaders, British justice certainly was. Somerset did not hesitate to support the use of capital punishment and five of the ringleaders were subsequently hung. This act alone ensured that British administration and the rule of British law were accepted on the eastern frontier. With the Boers pacified, Somerset now turned his attention to the Xhosa. He considered that he had only two options: either the British could conquer the Xhosa entirely and make them a subject people or the Xhosa could be firmly excluded behind a set border. Either option would require far more troops than Somerset currently had at his disposal and indeed, over the next few years, the Cape garrison was reduced in number, in line with a general retrenchment of the British army after the Napoleonic Wars. Rather than being able to dictate a frontier policy, the British would be led by the internal politics of the Xhosa.

Realizing the weakness of the military position, Somerset set about improving and extending the line of fortified posts established by his predecessor and began a diplomatic initiative. One of the common features of British/Xhosa relations was the British misconception that one chief alone could speak for the Xhosa nation. Somerset fell into this trap and first tried to charm and then later harangue chief Ngqika to guarantee that the Xhosa raids across the Fish River into the Zuurveld would cease. Ngqika, knowing that he was powerless to stop the raids in their entirety, nevertheless accepted responsibility for future Xhosa behaviour. By doing so Ngqika's prestige and authority plummeted and many of his followers deserted him. His rival Ndlambe took advantage of the internal turmoil and in 1818 he decisively defeated what remained of Ngqika's supporters in a pitched battle. Confident in his position, Ndlambe decided to now take the war to the British and in January 1819, he and his warriors crossed the Fish River once more and raided into the Zuurveld, to begin the Fifth Frontier War.

The British were taken by surprise by the ease with which Ndlambe skirted around their defensive posts and raided farmers, seizing cattle and firearms, and forcing the settlers to flee. Somerset ordered British troops from the Cape to join a Boer commando to push the Xhosa back. The British, under the command of Colonel Thomas Willshire, arrived on the frontier in late March 1819, only to discover that the Xhosa had already left the Zuurveld. This was a ruse for instead of the Xhosa disbanding, Ndlambe had massed his warriors in the bush away from British and Boer eyes and, on 12 April 1819, up to 10,000 Xhosa warriors attacked the British garrison at Grahamstown. Neither Somerset nor Willshire ever considered that the Xhosa would dare target their headquarters in the Eastern Cape. However, Willshire quickly rallied and led a superb defence of the barracks and the town with just 350 men, many of them veterans of the Napoleonic Wars. The resulting British victory demonstrated that up against disciplined troops, fighting behind defensive positions, with controlled musket fire and artillery support, the bravery of the Xhosa was simply not sufficient to gain a victory. For the loss of only 2 dead, the defenders inflicted a crushing defeat upon the Xhosa, with estimates of their casualties varying between 500 and 2,000 dead.

In July Willshire took to the offensive and with three converging columns he swept across the Fish River into Ndlambe's territory. The campaign was another brutal one, with no quarter being given by the British, and women and children were again victims of British shot and bayonets. The Xhosa achieved some local successes, and the winter weather slowed the operation, but the outcome, once the British decided upon a policy of crop burning and the destruction of Xhosa settlements, was inevitable. With famine threatening, Ndlambe was forced to negotiate with the British. The terms of the final settlement saw the restoration of Ngqika as the paramount chief and the annexation of the territory between the Fish and Keiskamma rivers as a 'neutral belt', to be enforced by a new line of defensive posts, which included the construction of the more substantial forts of Willshire and Beaufort. With the border now secured, Somerset turned his attention to bringing settlers back to the Zuurveld and into the ceded territory and aimed to encourage a restoration of trade between the Xhosa and the settlers. Somerset was under no illusion that taming the Xhosa would take time, but he was hopeful that the complete British military victory had taught the Xhosa that their future had to be driven by co-existence.

The 1820s was a period of relative peace and prosperity on the frontier. British settlers, with financial support from the government and material support from Cape Town, arrived to take on farms in the Zuurveld. Many of the settlers had little or no farming experience and struggled in their new ventures. To add to their difficulties, the decade was marked by drought which resulted in crop failures. The more enterprising settlers moved to stock farming with merino sheep, introduced with Somerset's support in 1827. Over the next decade wool became the Cape's biggest export. Around half of the original 2,000-plus British settlers were artisans and these individuals soon turned away from the land and established themselves in business in the growing towns of the region, such as Albany and Bathurst as well as Grahamstown. With the encouragement of these new immigrants, the colonial government relaxed border control measures and by the end of the decade British traders and missionaries were regularly crossing into Xhosa territory and the Xhosa were introduced to new commodities and beliefs. Similarly, Xhosa men would venture into the Zuurveld to work on settler farms for several months at a time. In addition, the Xhosa accepted refugees from the east. The Mfengu had been displaced by the advancing and expanding Zulu nation. They sought sanctuary in Xhosa lands and although the Xhosa were not hostile to these new arrivals, the Mfengu had a low status in society. This made them particularly susceptible to the practices of both missionaries and traders and the presence of the Mfengu would later threaten the very existence of Xhosa society.

It is not to say that the decade was not without conflict and violence. The presence of large numbers of sheep was just too tempting for some Xhosa and there was an increase in border raids by the Xhosa in which stock was taken. However, there were serious acts of violence in the Ceded Territory and one of Ngqika's sons, Maqoma, was at the centre of the disturbances. Maqoma had been expelled from the territory in 1819, but in 2 years he had returned and established a semi-autonomous chiefdom with around 16,000 followers, many of these disaffected adherents of his father. Maqoma became the most important chief to the west of the Kei valley. The authorities wished to both restrict his growing influence and to punish the Xhosa for their stock raids and Colonel Henry Somerset, son of Governor Somerset, was appointed in an act of nepotism as commandant of the eastern frontier.

Colonel Somerset was the leading advocate and proponent of what was known as Spoor Law, whereby the British claimed the right to raid Xhosa settlements to regain stock and punish Xhosas who had raided into settler territory. In December 1823 Somerset led a 200-strong commando force against Maqoma in the Kat River valley, achieving complete surprise. Somerset and his men rampaged across the valley, rounding up 7,000 head of cattle and indiscriminately killing men, women and children. Of the 7,000 cattle, 2,000 were given to the settlers as compensation for their earlier losses, whilst Somerset returned the balance to Maqoma on the understanding the chief pledge that his followers would desist from further raids.

Somerset's reprisal system continued to be used for the rest of the decade and its overwhelming force largely kept Xhosa raids in check. However, such punitive methods caused huge resentment amongst the Xhosa and it inflamed a strong sense of revenge in Maqoma's heart. Added to this, the government, and in particular Andries Stockenstrom, commissioner general of the eastern districts, now encouraged settlers into the Ceded Territory, along the Upper Great Fish River and the Koonap River to its east. These included Khoikhoi and people of mixed race. It was Stockenstrom's dream that the Kat River Settlement would be established within the choicest lands of the Ceded Territory, and this would become a prosperous community of small-scale farmers, both white and coloured.

The paramount Ngqika died in November 1829 and with his eldest sons, Tyhali and Maqoma, rivals for the throne, internal conflict was avoided when the youngest son, the lame Sandile, was proclaimed the new chief. However, at just 9 years of age Sandile required a regent and Maqoma was appointed. In what was viewed as a provocative step by the authorities, Maqoma established Sandile's Great Palace near the boundary of the Ceded Territory. Tensions continued to rise as Stockenstrom was unable to control Somerset, who was set on continuing his reprisal raids into the Ceded Territory and other Xhosa lands. To Stockenstrom it appeared that Somerset was deliberately trying to provoke the Xhosa into attacking the colony. This view was enhanced when Somerset appeared to directly target the communities of such peaceful chiefs as Tyhali and Hintsa. For the Xhosa these attacks upon the chief and the disdain shown toward men of such high rank by the colonists pushed them towards retaliation.

In 1832 Somerset went home on leave to settle his father's estate but resumed his command in early 1834 and, with the newly arrived governor Lieutenant General Sir Benjamin D'Urban's tacit support, he returned with renewed vigour to his task of ridding the Ceded Territory of both Maqoma's and Tyhali's communities. Somerset's patrols rode over the frontier burning any Xhosa settlements and eradicating any opposition. Whether D'Urban, distant as he was in Cape Town, was aware of the level of brutality or not, he was certainly not informed that such continued harassment was forging a sense of solidarity amongst all the various factions of the Xhosa who were being driven to resist. Yet, the British were so complacent that only 755 British soldiers was stationed along the border in late 1834. In December one of Somerset's patrols wounded Xhoxho, a half-brother of Maqoma, sparking widespread anger amongst the Xhosa. Maqoma, who was to become the figurehead of the resistance, realized that the time had now come to act.

On 21 December 1834 the opening moves of the Sixth Frontier War began. Maqoma had managed to assemble up to 10,000 warriors and with these men a series of raids was launched into the colony on a 90-mile front, from Winterberg in the north down to Algoa Bay. Avoiding mass attacks upon defensive positions, the raiders advanced in numerous small groups, easily bypassing the chain of fortified posts and patrols to rampage through the border district. Over-run, the British pulled back and withdrew from many of their fortifications, including the key stronghold Fort Willshire, which was looted and burnt.

Between the beginning of the invasion and 12 January 1835, 456 farmhouses were besieged and burnt to the ground. Thirty-two settlers and around eighty Khoihkoi servants, who attempted to defend their employers, were killed. Unlike the British, the Xhosa never harmed women and children. Missionaries were also untouched, but thousands of colonists were left homeless and landless almost overnight. They became refugees in frontier villages and towns, such as Fort Beaufort, Bathurst and Grahamstown and in each barricades were erected and manned by the terrified inhabitants. The triumphant Xhosa returned to their territories with a huge bounty of 5,700 horses, 115,000 cattle and 162,000 sheep.

It took a week before news of the Xhosa incursion reached Cape Town and although taken by surprise, and with only 1,600 British troops in the whole colony, Governor D'Urban reacted by immediately despatching Colonel Harry Smith, a veteran of the Napoleonic Wars, to assume command of military operations on the eastern frontier. Smith possessed an energy that verged on manic. It could be argued that his extensive combat experience had perhaps unhinged him for he was to demonstrate a level of brutality and determination in this and subsequent commands that brought condemnation from many of his contemporaries. Yet, there is no doubt he was able to rally men to his side and at this critical moment for both settlers and the British alike he rose to the challenge.

On his arrival in Grahamstown, Smith found chaos, fear and confusion, even though the Xhosa had already begun a withdrawal back across the Fish and Keiskamma rivers with the stolen stock. Maqoma's ambitions had been strictly limited. He knew that he had neither the men nor the weapons to fight a prolonged war and that the British would only get stronger. The aim of the invasion was to strike a destructive blow, the shock of which, it was hoped, would force the British to negotiate a fair settlement for the many

Xhosa grievances. Smith thought otherwise and after restoring morale he was able in just a few days to assemble a force of 400 mounted volunteers who rode east from Grahamstown to destroy the homesteads of chiefs Nqeno and Tyhali. Smith also ordered Somerset to clear the road to Port Elizabeth to ensure that supplies could be sent there from Cape Town and then on to the frontier.

When D'Urban arrived in Grahamstown on 20 January he found order restored and he used the next weeks to muster a large force to take the offensive to the Xhosa. In the meantime, Smith continued to lead mounted assaults into Xhosa territory, and his force included a newly raised battalion of Khoikhoi volunteers. In early February Smith attacked the last of the Xhosa occupying the Great Fish River bush, killing around 75 individuals, and capturing 2,000 cattle. In late March Smith was out again, this time attacking the Amathole Mountains, where Maqoma had sought refuge. Although his force captured 1,200 cattle, this sortie experienced great difficulty in crossing the rugged terrain of mountains, valleys and bush and did not locate Maqoma or his followers. Indeed, in later wars this area would long remain a sanctuary for the Xhosa.

By the end of March D'Urban had assembled a massive force with which to launch an offensive of revenge against the Xhosa. He had nearly 400 British cavalry, with an additional 1,600 mounted troops from the settler community. There were over 1,500 British regular infantry and Smith was able to include his Khoikhoi battalion which had already demonstrated their fighting ability. D'Urban divided his troops into four separate supporting columns with the aim of converging on Maqoma's stronghold in the Amathole. Maqoma realized that he had to evade such a large force if he was to survive. He thus resorted to the usual ambush tactics of the Xhosa and the terrain not only favoured such an approach but allowed his warriors to disappear into the bush. D'Urban's plan became bogged down in the Amathole and he quickly decided that he needed to change tactics. Leaving two columns in the area to continue to pursue and harass Maqoma, he switched the rest of his command against the chiefs of the Ciskei region to the north and in particular the lands of Hintsa, the paramount chief of the Gcaleka Xhosa. By the end of April, facing overwhelming British force, Hintsa, accompanied by his son Sarhili, entered the British camp ready to sue for peace. Here he came face to face with Smith who was in no mood to give Hintsa any respect for his high rank and roundly condemned the Xhosa for starting this latest conflict. Smith decide to hold Hintsa hostage on demand of the repatriation of 50,000 cattle and the surrender of Maqoma.

On 10 May 1835, in the presence of Hintsa, D'Urban proclaimed that the British would seize a huge area of Xhosa land between the Keiskamma and Kei rivers and it would be named the Province of Queen Adelaide, after the consort of King William IV. It would be administered from a site on the Buffalo River and this, in honour of the king, would be named King William's Town. D'Urban's strategy for securing the colony against further raids was to make the frontier safe via the mass expulsion of the Xhosa from this area. In his words, the intention was to 'provide for the future security of the Colony ... by removing these treacherous and irreclaimable savages to a safer distance'.[9] Once again, the frontier had been effectively pushed back. As an inducement to accept his terms, D'Urban ordered that Hintsa accompany one of Smith's patrols which set out to capture some of his people's cattle. Seizing a potential opportunity to escape, the chief galloped away from his escort as they neared the Nqabara River. Smith himself pursued the fleeing Hintsa and shot him twice. The chief sought refuge in the river, but there he was found and executed by a member of the escort. Hintsa was stripped of all ornaments and his corpse was desecrated with both ears and several teeth taken as souvenirs. Such a barbaric act, and effectively the assassination of a paramount chief, demonstrates that the British viewed their Xhosa foes with contempt and even hatred.

In the Amathole the British continued their futile pursuit of Maqoma, who still cleverly avoided pitched battles. Indeed, the Xhosa here continued to have small successes, particularly against the slow-moving British supply trains. Realizing that British regulars, as well as the settler volunteers, were proving useless at bringing Maqoma to heel, Smith, now in overall command with the return of D'Urban to Cape Town, deployed his Khoikhoi troops, as well as the Mfengu, now happy to accept British pay and keen to fight against those who had once welcomed them as refugees. These auxiliaries were better able to seek out the enemy in the bush and, as important, did not view the terrain as an alien environment. Smith also changed his tactics and rather than using large columns of troops he sent in small patrols of 30–100 men, mostly of these auxiliary troops, led by British NCOs and officers. Their primary role was to destroy Xhosa food stores, thus depriving them of supplies to carry on the fight. This tactic, and the brutality the British allies inflicted upon Xhosa woman, gradually wore down Maqoma's resistance.

The war was concluded, however, only when, under pressure from London to bring the expensive war to an end, D'Urban began negotiations.

On 15 August 1835 the two delegations met to begin several weeks of wrangling, but eventually a compromise was reached. D'Urban recognized that the Xhosa living between the Keiskamma and Kei rivers would be allowed to remain, but in return the Xhosa accepted British suzerainty. The prominent chiefs were allocated land by the governor and the British recognized Maqoma as the senior chief. The chiefs were responsible for controlling their people's behaviour, but each had to report to a resident agent appointed by the British. With this agreement the bitter and bloody war was concluded. D'Urban now, like his predecessors, encouraged British and Boer settlers into the area knowing that future conflicts could only be contained by assimilation. In this he was wrong for the Xhosa had been left in a pitiful state by the war and resentment and revenge was always close to the surface in their dealings with the British.

The governor's plans to allow a mass settlement of white farmers into the new territory of the Province of Queen Adelaide were thwarted not by the Xhosa, but by the home government. Within Britain there was a groundswell of anger at the manner the indigenous peoples of the empire, and in particular the Xhosa, had been treated. In Parliament a Select Committee was appointed to report on 'Aboriginal Tribes'. The committee recommended greater rights for indigenous peoples and that their administration should be removed from settlers. In government, Lord Glenelg, Secretary of State for War and the Colonies, wrote a scathing letter to D'Urban which squarely laid the blame for the latest war on the governor's unjust treatment of the Xhosa. The minister also ordered the immediate retrocession of the province, and this did indeed happen in February 1837. In addition, Glenelg encouraged Andries Stockenstrom out of retirement to become lieutenant governor of the Eastern Cape.

Following such criticism D'Urban was replaced by Sir George Napier, who remained governor until 1844. Napier supported Stockenstrom's policy of appeasement towards the Xhosa, but these plans were thrown into jeopardy by the actions of Boer settlers. The Boers had been frustrated by what they perceived to be the leniency shown towards the Xhosa by the British. In addition, many felt that although they had answered the call to arms during the recent wars, the British had treated them with disdain and failed to financially compensate them sufficiently. Furthermore, there was a sense of alienation that their language and culture was being lost. All this resulted in what became known as the 'Great Trek' in which thousands of Boer families, and their servants, headed for the interior, where free of British influence they were able to build and regulate their own society. Within the Eastern Cape districts up to 20 per cent of burgher inhabitants joined the Trek.

Xhosa and Mfengu from the Ceded Territory were used by the remaining farmers to remedy labour shortages, but soon stock theft once again became an inflammatory issue, with many settlers blaming the transient workers for the losses. Tyhali, who had done so much to repress cattle raiding, died in 1842 and Stockenstrom, who had unsuccessfully attempted to reduce the tensions between the settlers and the Xhosa, was forced to resign because the governor recognized that Stockenstrom's unpopularity amongst the white community had become part of the wider problem. His attempts to introduce a treaty system, which acknowledged chiefs as sovereign rulers via proper treaties with law enforcement through diplomatic means, had been largely welcomed by the Xhosa at least as a means of official recognition, but had been viewed with disdain by the settlers.

Tensions were also running high amongst the Xhosa themselves. Maqoma's regency of Sandile had ended with the young chief's rise to maturity and although Maqoma attempted to maintain his power, he was frustrated and the Xhosa as a whole lacked leadership. Further to this, relations between the Xhosa and the Mfengu frequently erupted in violence. Napier returned to Britain knowing that although a renewed war on the frontier was unlikely, he had failed to restore any sort of harmony. British policy changed with a new government under Sir Robert Peel and a new governor, Sir Peregrine Maitland, who would take a much firmer stance towards the Xhosa. In September 1844, he announced to the summoned Xhosa chiefs, although pointedly not Sandile or Maqoma who Maitland was trying to undermine, that the governor's words ruled supreme and that Stockenstrom's treaty system was effectively over. Maitland would allow white settlers to cross over the border and if their livestock went missing, then they could insist on compensation from the Xhosa. This, of course, had been the root cause of earlier conflicts.

By March 1846 Maitland's more aggressive attitude towards the Xhosa had increased tensions so much that when a Xhosa named Tsili was arrested for stealing an axe from a shop in Fort Beaufort the brutality quickly escalated into yet another frontier war, the Seventh, or the War of the Axe.

The thief was arrested and sent for trial in Grahamstown. En route the escort was attacked, killing one Khoikhoi policeman, and Tsili escaped. The British demanded that Sandile hand over the fugitive, but with relations now so fractured the chief refused to comply and on 1 April Maitland declared war. The first clashes of this new conflict went the way of the defenders as again the British, under the command of Somerset, attacked the Amathole Mountains in three slow-moving converging columns. Although the rendezvous of the columns at the town of Burnshill met no resistance, it was when the British fanned out in search of their enemy that the Xhosa struck. For the first time the use of firearms by the Xhosa became a feature of the war, although their flintlocks were of inferior quality to those utilized by the British. The Xhosa, under Sandile's command, used cattle to entice the British to charge into the bush where they could be overcome. They then turned to attacking the vulnerable British supply trains as they attempted to deliver provisions to the force at Burnshill. So successful were the Xhosa tactics that they compelled the British to abandon scores of wagons with all their stores, and lack of food forced Somerset to lead a fighting withdrawal out of the Amathole.

Sandile's victory encouraged other chiefs to take up arms with fighting breaking out all along the frontier and the Xhosa storming through the Zuurveld, regaining long-lost lands, and even threatening Port Elizabeth. Grahamstown was overwhelmed with settler refugees. Sarhili was a notable exception for he gave only passive support to the resistance, allowing his lands to be used as a sanctuary where the fighting chiefs could send their cattle safe from British reprisals. The war entered a second phase when on 28 May an 8,000-strong Xhosa army, forgetting the lessons of previous wars, attacked the strong British position of Fort Peddie. Predictably the attackers were driven back, although the fort remained besieged. Somerset led a relief column to Fort Peddie and although the Xhosa ambushed it, the British had enough firepower to beat off the attack and arrive at their destination. John Percy Groves, a young officer with Somerset's relief column, wrote of the ferocity of a Xhosa attack as the column tried to edge its way to Fort Peddie:

> … for the space of six or seven minutes there ensued a regular melee; the troopers, urging forward their half-maddened steed, wielded their sabres right manfully, and slashed and thrust at their opponent, who in turn offered a stubborn resistance, striving to drag the soldiers from

their saddles, and stabbing furiously at the horses' bellies as they were ridden down; until at length the escort cut their way right through the black shining wall of human flesh and rode onwards ...[10]

Once he had resupplied the fort Somerset returned to Grahamstown and en route stumbled upon a large force of Xhosa out in the open, and with colonial mounted infantry and the 7th Dragon Guard he led them in a charge. Unable to defend themselves or flee, the Xhosa were brutally cut down, with over 300 killed. These two defeats forced the Xhosa back onto the defensive and Maitland quickly took the offensive, with over 3,000 regulars and nearly 5,000 Mfengu and Khoikhoi auxiliaries. Yet, despite the available manpower, Maitland's offence achieved little and fighting in the Amathole remained as difficult as ever.

By July the war began to peter out as the Xhosa retired from the conflict to tend to their fields, knowing that if crops were not planted and cultivated then famine would be the result. Maitland was knocked off guard and something of a stalemate emerged. Maqoma, who had actively discouraged his warriors to fight, was desperate for peace and in October he and many of the chiefs west of the Kei approached the British seeking terms. Sandile also sent out peace-feelers and as a gesture he finally relinquished the offending Tsili to British justice. Although the war rumbled on into 1847, Maitland was recalled to London to answer criticism of his handling of the war, and its cost. His successor was Sir Henry Pottinger, who arrived with the additional title of High Commissioner for Southern Africa, as well as Governor of the Cape, for the British government had moved to a new policy of conceding representative government to the colony with an elected House of Assembly. The High Commissioner now had the authority to intervene in all areas of Southern Africa if he felt British interests required it.

Pottinger had also been briefed to end the war as soon as practical by proclaiming British sovereignty up to the Kei River and subjugating those Xhosa between that river and the colony. Yet, when he arrived on the frontier in August 1847, he found the Xhosa peacefully cultivating their crops and unwilling to either fight or listen. He concluded that the only option to bring the Xhosa to the negotiating table was to relaunch hostilities and on 29 September the British, again with colonial and native troops, entered the Amathole. Pottinger concentrated British efforts on the destruction of Xhosa foodstuffs and within a month Sandile was accompanying British troops to Grahamstown to discuss, as he thought, peace terms. Yet, as soon as he arrived Sandile was imprisoned and with Maqoma also in captivity the British could now dictate terms. Somerset continued in the field to intimidate those still offering resistance but by December the last of the chiefs surrendered. The Xhosa people were now in a wretched position, starving and many destitute. It was even said that the warriors were so hungry that they had been forced to eat the leather from their shields. All resistance had been crushed and the British could now dictate their terms.

Pottinger's time in Southern Africa had been brief for he was destined for service in India. He was replaced by Sir Harry Smith, who after distinguished action in the First Sikh War of 1845–6 returned to the Cape where he was keen to continue his crusade against the Xhosa. First though he had to formally conclude the Seventh Frontier War, which he did in the most dictatorial fashion. Smith, with his usual homage to grand theatre, summoned the various Xhosa chiefs to King William's Town to hear him pronounce his decision as to the future of the frontier. To the stunned amazement of the chiefs, Smith proclaimed that all the Xhosa would be expelled from the old Ceded Territory, which was to be called Victoria East, whilst the lands north of the Amathole would be renamed Victoria North. In addition, the former Province of Queen Adelaide would be reinstated as a dependency of the British Crown and would be known as British Kaffraria. The Xhosa would be permitted to remain in this area as long as their recognized Smith as their supreme chief. Smith then insisted that all the chiefs showed their acceptance of these new terms by walking one by one up to him to kiss his boots in homage. In a later ceremony, and again in front of the chiefs, Smith ripped up sheets of paper to illustrate that all previous treaties were no more. Beaten, famished and demoralized, the Xhosa meekly accepted their fate.

Over the next years Smith's legendary energy drove forward his plans. Where once Maqoma and Sandile had lived, flourishing settler sheep farms covered the land, and many Xhosa chose to reside and work on these farms. At the heart of Smith's mission was one of 'civilizing' the Xhosa and this sort of integration was exactly what he had envisaged. Within the new administrative area of British Kaffraria the land was mapped out by surveyors. Each chief was given up to 800,000 hectares and settlers' farms were allowed inbetween each of these allotted Xhosa lands, to restrict any future convergence of Xhosa power. As far as funds allowed Smith also increased the number of military forts in Xhosa areas and encouraged former soldiers to settle in six 'military' villages in the foothills of the Amathole as a buffer against Sandile. The only area within the old frontier districts that retained any semblance of autonomy was the Kat River Settlement, which became something of a haven for displaced Xhosa. It was not long before those on the fringes of the settlement were complaining that their livestock was disappearing at the hands of rustlers and there were petitions to the government to end the area's self-governing status. Tensions rose further at the end of 1850 when the police entered the area and expelled many of the dispossessed, burning what pitiful shacks they had managed to assemble.

The Xhosa were now so aggrieved and humiliated, and feeling that their way of life was under terminal threat, war seemed their only option. By late 1850 weapons were stockpiled and Maqoma was elected as the military leader of what became the Eighth Frontier War, which lasted from December 1850 to March 1853. Smith became aware of the growing threat and summoned Maqoma to a meeting at Fort Cox, near the Keiskamma. Smith employed his usual bullying tactics on the chief, but Maqoma was not to be intimidated and was even insolent towards Smith. Realizing that another Xhosa rebellion was close, Smith decided to launch a pre-emptive assault.

Thus, on Christmas Eve 1850, 600 troops left Fort Cox and marched into the Amathole with orders to arrest Sandile. Maqoma ambushed the column in a gorge on the Keiskamma River and the British were forced back, having sustained many casualties. The next day Maqoma went on the offensive and overwhelmed three of the military villages on the Tyhume River. Maqoma then turned his attention to the principal British forts between the Amathole and the Kat River and Smith found himself besieged in Fort Cox. Somerset led two unsuccessful attempts to rescue Smith, but both were met by determined resistance and beaten back. After a week, Smith resorted to a mad dash out of the fort and after evading several ambushes reached the sanctuary of King William's Town.

Maqoma's initial spectacular successes encouraged further rebellion and the British were shocked when even the Kat River Settlement rose in revolt. The rebellion there was led by Hermanus Matroos of Khoikhoi descent. Yet, again, success bred over-confidence and when Matroos and Maqoma combined forces in a night-time attack upon Fort Beaufort it was poorly co-ordinated and easily beaten back. Matroos was killed in the ill-fated assault and his body was put on display by the British. Robert Godlonton, one of the spokespersons for the settlers, wrote that the corpse was ' ... a warning to traitors, a spectacle full of encouragement for the honest, and instruction to all'.[11]

An attempt upon Fort Hare by Sandile also ended in failure. Here the British received assistance from 800 Mfengu who fought well against Sandile's warriors. The Mfengu would feature prominently in many of the engagements in this war and the next and were rewarded with cattle and land by the British. As the war progressed, the loyalty of many Khoikhoi troops was questioned and indeed some defected with their arms to the Xhosa, which raised the standing of the Mfengu amongst the British. There was one further Xhosa success in the opening stages of the war. Fort Armstrong, which was strategically placed as it protected the supply route in the area, was lost to the British when the garrison of largely Khoikhoi militia mutinied. Yet, this was to be the high-water mark of Xhosa success for other attempts to take British towns or forts were beaten back and gradually Smith was able to turn the tide.

Smith's first counter-offensive was launched in British Kaffraria. A series of column marches first relieved the besieged Fort Cox and later drove the Xhosa out of the territory to seek sanctuary in the Amathole. The Xhosa had bravely attempted to resist Smith's troops, but the effective use of artillery had dispersed any efforts to concentrate forces. The rebellion in the Kat River Setttlement was similarly extinguished and Smith felt the war would soon be drawn to a successful conclusion, yet he had underestimated the resourceful Maqoma. He continued to resist from the Waterkloof Highlands, north of Fort Beaufort, between the Kat River in the east and the Koonop River to the west. An area of just 60 square miles, the terrain was even more impassable for British troops than the Amathole. Here, with just a few hundred warriors, Maqoma fought off repeated attempts by Smith to dislodge him and he could use this location to raid nearby settler farms. The height of Maqoma's success was when he ambushed and beat back two British columns, led by Somerset and Lieutenant Colonel Fordyce respectively. On 6 November 1851, Fordyce was killed by a Khoikhoi sniper allied to Maqoma and once again the British were forced to withdraw. Maqoma had completely outmanoeuvred the British, repeatedly enticing them into ambushes and his skill as a military leader has remained a feature of Xhosa oral history ever since. Chief Ntsele, writing in 1991 of Maqoma, stated, 'Maqoma was a hero and a master of tactics in war. Even though we had no guns and canon he was able to defeat trained and skilled British soldiers … When the British army came Maqoma killed them like flies. Maqoma confused them although he was not educated.'[12]

In early 1852, Smith received the devastating news from London that he was to be replaced by George Cathcart. Smith's lack of success against Maqoma and the high financial cost of the apparently never-ending war had sealed his fate. On his arrival Cathcart ordered hostilities to cease whilst he assessed his next move. Despite all Smith's efforts, Sandile was still resisting in the Amathole and Maqoma was ensconced in the Waterkloof. Cathcart decided to remove Somerset, accusing him of incompetence and profiteering, and he was replaced by Lieutenant Colonel William Eyre. Operations were renewed in June 1852 in the Great Fish River and Waterkloof regions. Eyre employed uncompromising tactics with no mercy being shown towards any Xhosa men who crossed his path. Many, rebels or not, were hung from nearby trees. In conversation with a fellow officer, Eyre outlined his determined and ruthless approach, 'Well, Sir, my idea is to destroy all the enemy without being killed myself or losing my men and shall continue that plan as long as I have anything to do with the war.'[13]

In addition, Eyre employed Mfengu auxiliaries out in front of any advance to seek out the hiding Xhosa. In a new level of brutality, the Mfengu, and some British troops, killed the wounded as well as women and children. This in turn resulted in retaliation from the Xhosa and any troops who were unfortunately captured by the Xhosa were frequently slowly tortured to death. Finally, Maqoma was forced to seek refuge in the Amathole and by October Eyre was able to confirm that the Waterkloof was clear of rebels.

Eyre now focused on the Amathole and throughout October and November he led a series of sweeps through the area in which a scorched-earth policy was deployed with the aim of destroying the last of the Xhosa food supplies. Crops were burnt, cattle seized and resistance in the area crumbled. With fighting effectively at end, and Sandile and Maqoma seeking refugee with Sarhili in Gcalekaland, Cathcart could claim victory. The last three great chiefs finally surrendered in February 1853 and on 9 March Cathcart met these and other minor chiefs at King William's Town where the governor was able to issue a proclamation of 'Royal Mercy and Pardon'. Cathcart and the British government, having won the war, had to now decide upon the peace.

Cathcart dealt severely with the Kat River rebels, removing them from their lands and giving possession to white settlers. Elsewhere he was lenient, fearing that harsh measures could lead to more instability and increase the risk of further conflict. Cathcart's successor, Sir George Grey, focused on a civilizing programme; bringing about a socio-economic integration of settlers and Xhosa, hoping that both would become interdependent of each other, for labour and trade. He aimed to transform the Xhosa into '... useful servant, consumers of our goods, contributors to our revenue; in short, a source of strength and wealth for this colony ...'.[14]

Yet, Grey's economic utopian vision was shattered by major upheavals amongst the Xhosa. A spike in smallpox cut through the physically weakened Xhosa and in 1853 contagious bovine pleuro-pneumonia (lung sickness) wrought devastation in the Xhosa cattle herds. Within 2 years around 5,000 head of cattle a month were being lost to this dreadful disease. For a society that placed such economic importance, as well as prestige, on their herds this latest calamity had significant consequences. In British Kaffraria alone death by smallpox and the loss of cattle resulted in forced migration, which saw the population plummet. In just one year, 1857, the number of Xhosa fell from 105,000 to 37,000 and by the end of the following year it had fallen by an additional 10,000 souls. Grey used this tragic opportunity to open the territory up to further white settlement and many of the remaining Xhosa were forced to work as labourers or domestic servants.

In addition to these momentous events, a prophetic movement spread across Xhosa lands from June 1856. A 15-year-old girl named Nongqawuse prophesied that in order to overcome the current disasters that were befalling the people they must purify themselves and this could only be done by destroying the remaining herds and planting no crops. Her beliefs rapidly gained adherents amongst the traditional people who were desperate to elevate their hardships, but both Sandile and Maqoma refused to comply. Yet, hysteria took over and soon most chiefs were unable to stop this mass act of self-destruction and for some, Sarhili amongst them, to have denied the prophesy would have courted personal disaster. By the time the cattle-killing frenzy had petered out up to 400,000 cattle had been needlessly slaughtered and the total tally of Xhosa who died of starvation in the resulting famine caused by the failure to plant crops was as many as 50,000 persons.

In the chaos, the British took the opportunity to imprison many of the Xhosa leaders. Maqoma was arrested in August 1857 and was sent to

Robbin Island where he died in 1873, some of his followers convinced that he had been murdered by the British. Over the next twenty years, various British governors used the upheavals to move more Xhosa off their lands, particularly Sarhili and his Gcaleka people who were moved beyond the Mbashe River where they lived a desolate existence. Not only were British settlers encouraged to absorb the Xhosa lands as their own, but the authorities also rewarded the Mfengu for their loyalty. In the former Gcalekaland the British created a new buffer zone of loyal Africans. In the space of just seventy years the British had undermined much of Xhosa culture and had deprived many of their lands. To the settlers and the authorities, the Xhosa now seemed a broken people who were increasingly dependent on an alien economic system which tied them to those that now farmed their lands. It appeared that all fight had now been extinguished from the Xhosa, but in this the white population was mistaken.

Chapter 3

Command at Last

In the years following the death of Maqoma the Xhosa tried desperately to retain some of their customs and way of life. Chief Sandile, ruling over an ever-decreasing kingdom, battled the demons of his own alcoholism to defend traditional values and he and other Ngqika Xhosa abandoned the Western clothing that they had adopted. Across the Kei River, the Gcaleka lived an unhappy existence with the now despised, and in their eyes treacherous, Mfengu and tensions would frequently result in blood being spilled.

Yet, the Xhosa way of life was to be further undermined by outside influences. In 1867 diamonds were discovered at the confluence of the Orange and Vaal rivers, deep in the interior, near the insignificant town of Kimberley. Over the next five years tens of thousands of white and black prospectors flooded to the area, all dreaming of riches. The new High Commissioner, Sir Henry Barkly, reacted quickly and Britain annexed the territory as the new Crown Colony of Griqualand West. Thousands of Xhosas were enticed to the area in search of any sort of work and soon money and guns were being sent to the Eastern Cape.

The economic dividend provided by diamonds led the government of William Gladstone to consider that the Cape was now well able to pay for its own administration and, crucially, its own defence. Added to this it was felt that the colony should be allowed responsible government, with a two-chamber parliament. This was instituted in June 1872 and John C. Molteno, a member from Beaufort West and thus someone who was well aware of the history of settler/Xhosa relations, was elected as the Cape's first prime minster in December 1872. From this point on the governor would be required to work alongside the colonial prime minister and his cabinet, who in turn had a responsibility to an elected assembly.

The colony was now an economic asset, and with a change of government to that led by the more expansionist Benjamin Disraeli Britain was now determined to assert its authority by creating a self-governing dominion.

To create such a system required that all the colonies of Southern Africa be brought into a confederation, including the Boer Transvaal and Orange Free State. This was not the only obstacle, for the Molteno administration saw no benefit to the Cape of being part of this imperial ideal and Molteno himself was deeply suspicious of potential British interference in his new government. Disraeli, and his foreign secretary, the Earl of Carnarvon, realized that to convince all parties that confederation would be to their benefit a diplomat of the greatest skill and experience would be required. They turned to Sir Bartle Frere who had gained a positive reputation following his long service in Indian administration and more recently as governor of Zanzibar, where he had made great strides in suppressing the slave trade from the Congo. Frere would soon by joined in Southern Africa by his old friend Frederic Thesiger and together their destiny and reputation would become intertwined.

Frere arrived in Cape Town on 31 March 1877 and was welcomed by Sir Arthur Cunynghame, General Command of British Forces in Southern Africa. In truth Cunynghame, who had been in situ since 1873, did not have much of a command with only three thinly spread battalions of British regulars. Frere immediately received a briefing from the General regarding the renewal of tension in the Eastern Cape which would eventually lead to the Ninth, and final, Frontier War.

Acts of aggression in the Eastern Cape between the Xhosa and Mfengu had been increasing significantly and these were amplified by a drought which hit the region in late 1877, resulting in crops failing and livestock dying. With such bubbling animosity between the two groups, it was to be a relatively minor incident that would be the catalyst for war. In August 1877, a group of Gcaleka men gatecrashed a Mfengu wedding feast and began helping themselves to beer. These men were bitter that the Mfengu festivities were being held on former Xhosa land and drink-fuelled tempers soon turned to violence in which one of the unwelcome guests was killed. The Gcaleka could not allow such an act to go unpunished and a retaliatory raid was launched in which more blood was spilled. For the rest of the month and into September further raids and clashes continued, with bloodshed on both sides. Frere, realizing that he needed to be close to the disputed areas, arrived in King William's Town and based himself with Cunynghame and the officers of the 1st Battalion of the 24th Regiment in the barracks. In an effort to lessen the tension, Frere attempted to visit and speak directly to

Sarhili, but the chief refused to admit him. So, in an attempt to make the British position clear, Frere wrote to Sarhili and told him to, '... warn your people that if they do not in future obey your orders and abstain from making wars or raids and from all wrong-doing towards the Fingos [Mfengu] and all others, the Government will take matters into their own hands and very severely punish all the guilty'.[1]

Sarhili tried to lessen tensions but admitted to the British agents that he was powerless to stop his people moving towards war. Finally, realizing that conflict was inevitable, Sarhili gave in and declared that, 'I intend to fight the English. I am in a corner. The country is too small, and I may as well die as to be pushed into a corner.'[2]

In addition, envoys had travelled between the two Great Palaces of Sarhili and Sandile and it was clear to the British agent, West Fynn, that a pact had been agreed between the chiefs to unite their warriors in an attack upon the Mfengu. On 29 September Fynn told Frere that the area was abuzz with rumours of an imminent attack, and this was confirmed by reports from both missionaries and traders that stated that warriors were flocking to Sarhili's Great Palace.

With war now inevitable, Frere held a meeting with Cunynghame and two members of Molteno's cabinet, John Merriman and Charles Brownlee, to establish the respective levels of authority in the forthcoming campaign. Determined to preserve the independence of self-government, the cabinet members strongly argued with Frere and the general. Eventually, a compromise was reached in which the general retained command of all troops, both British and colonial, but that in any forthcoming operations colonial forces would be exclusively used. This issue would later result in a breakdown in relations between Frere and Molteno that would have significant political repercussions.

Colonel Richard Glyn, of the 24th Regiment, commanded the British garrison in King William's Town, and with the compromise between Frere and Molteno agreed for the immediate future, he spread the British regulars in military posts on the Kei River to secure the frontier. Farmers and traders rushed to the main towns which were fortified with barricades. The first clash of the Ninth Frontier War occurred on 26 September, when a twenty-five-strong force commanded by Inspector Chalmers of the Frontier Armed and Mounted Police (FAMP), along with 1,000 Mfengu allies, led by colonial officers, intercepted a Xhosa force which he had witnessed attacking a Mfengu kraal (a traditional African homestead enclosed, usually, by a wooden fence) near Gwadana Hill, and by doing so the Xhosa had crossed into British territory. The resulting Battle of Gwadana was something of a farce, in which the carriage of the one piece of colonial artillery broke and Chalmers ordered a withdrawal in the face of the advancing enemy. However, the Mfengu panicked and fled, which in turn caused horses to bolt and in the ensuring confusion the Xhosa were able to close and seven of Chalmers men were killed.

A colonial force of 180 men of the FAMP and 2,000 Mfengu levies, under the command of Colonel Charles Griffith, a veteran of the Eighth Frontier War, brushed aside the setback of Gwadana and took the offensive. Griffith used the small post of Ibeka, just a few miles from Sarhili's Great Palace, as his base of operations. This choice was a deliberate provocation for Griffith knew that Sarhili's warriors could not resist attacking a position that was so close to the palace and that the Xhosa had become over-confident after their initial success. On 29 September 1877, the great war leader Khiva led 7,000 warriors in a traditional assault. Attacking in densely packed columns, the Xhosa were vulnerable to the artillery and rocket tubes of the defenders as well as the rapid fire from Snider rifles. Despite taking high losses, the Xhosa threw themselves at the post for two whole days, but when Griffith ordered his mounted men out from behind the barricades, the Xhosa broke and fled, and were ruthlessly pursued by the revengeful Mfengu who gave no quarter.

Griffith had inflicted a crushing defeat on the Gcaleka and Sarhili tried to open negotiations with the British, but Frere was now determined to annex Gcalekaland as his first act towards Southern African confederation. Thus, on 5 October, Frere issued a proclamation which stated that Sarhili must relinquish his chiefdom and forfeit his lands to the Crown. To reinforce his strong position, on 9 October Griffith's command marched to Sarhili's palace, burnt it to the ground and withdrew with a large herd of cattle. Ibeka was utilized as a rallying post for over a 1,000 white colonial volunteers, many of whom enlisted in the hope of gaining both land and cattle as a benefit of their service. The FAMP contingent increased to 500 men along with 6,000 African levies, mainly Mfengu, but also some Xhosa under Chief Ngangelizwe who decided to side with the authorities. With this force, Griffith led column sweeps through Gcalekaland destroying settlements and raiding cattle wherever they went for much of October and into November.

Yet, occupied as they were in acquiring livestock, the mixed force failed to capture Sarhili or his followers who fled into the Transkei. By 13 November, with his commissariat failing, Griffith called off the campaign, declaring victory and offering grants of land to settlers in the conquered land. On 1 December, Frere declared Gcalekaland a Cape magistracy and the war seemed to be effectively won.

However, the war was to receive a first spark. During Griffith's campaign some Gcaleka Xhosa had sought refuge west of the Kei, on Cape soil, with Chief Makinana of the Ndlambe Xhosa. Frere felt that the refugees must be disarmed and ordered the FAMP to target Makinana, who, learning of the approaching force, fled with his followers to the Ngqika reserve. Cunynghame now involved imperial troops and the reserve was cordoned off by a thinly stretched line of British soldiers. With the British so engaged, Gcaleka warriors hiding in the Transkei, led by Khiva, slipped south and, on 2 December, attacked FAMP forces near the settlement of Holland's Shop. Although the engagement was inconclusive, such a brazen attack shocked the local white inhabitants, and Griffith and his men, exhausted and overstretched, called for reinforcements. All the colonial authorities could provide was more Mfengu levies. Frere could no longer tolerate such a piecemeal and ineffective approach and took direct action. He appointed Cunynghame in direct command of colonial forces, which were pulled back to guard the Ngqika reserve and ordered the general to prepare imperial forces to march to the Transkei to deal with the Gcaleka once and for all.

Colonel Glyn, based at Ibeka, was appointed commander of the army of the Transkei and here he began to plan his offensive. Glyn received reinforcements; the 88th Regiment, which marched from Cape Town, and a Naval Contingent from HMS *Active* joined Glyn's command. Even with these additions, numbers were low, especially amongst mounted troops. An officer of the 24th, Lieutenant Frederick Carrington, was tasked by Cunynghame with forming a mounted infantry unit. Carrington was a natural leader and superb horseman, and he was soon transforming infantry volunteers from the 24th, the 13th and 3rd Regiments into a formidable, mounted infantry unit which would serve both Cunynghame and his replacement, Thesiger, with distinction as the Frontier Light Horse (FLH), or 'Carrington's Horse'.

Whilst Glyn was busy preparing his command at Ibeka, Khiva and a small group of his supporters slipped through the troops surrounding the Ngqika Reserve and brought a personal message from Sarhili to Sandile which begged that the two clans should unite against the British. Sandile was reluctant, but urged on by his son Mathanzima he gave his consent for war. On Boxing Day 1877 Sandile's warriors began to attack settlers and Mfengu alike. Cunynghame had arrived at Ibeka the day before and resolved that to prevent the Gcaleka and Ngqika joining forces Glyn should lead British troops on an offensive. Thus, on 27 December three separate columns of British troops set out on a sweep of Gcalekaland. Like Griffith before him, Glyn was equally unsuccessful in locating the enemy in any significant number. Indeed, the British had been duped, for whilst Glyn was pursuing an invisible enemy in the summer heat, Sarhili's warriors had slipped past his columns and crossed the Kei to join forces with Sandile's men of the Ngqika. The combined Xhosa force now concentrated in the densely wooded valley of the Tyityaba valley in the rear of the British troops. Glyn had no alternative but to withdraw back to Ibeka and prepare his exhausted troops to march west towards the enemy.

The panic caused by the new Xhosa threat saw settlers desert their homes and created huge political tensions. Molteno rushed to King William's Town and in a stormy meeting with Frere rejected Cunynghame's sole command of forces on the frontier. He insisted that colonial forces would retain an independent command and Griffith would again lead his forces against those Ngqika remaining on their reserve. This political wrangling would soon reach a firm conclusion, but not before the confused split of forces caused military difficulties.

Glyn and his troops were able to provide Frere with some good news from the Transkei. On 13 January 1878 a combined force of roughly 1,000 Gcaleka and Ngqika warriors attacked a British detachment, which included men of the 88th Regiment, on the River Nyumaga, 20 miles south of Ibeka. On learning of the presence of the Xhosa force, Glyn hurried his men on and arrived in the mid-afternoon with two companies of the 24th, along with a small detachment of FAMP and fifty men of the Naval Brigade, two 7-pounder guns and Mfengu levies.

Glyn adopted a formation that had been successfully used by the British throughout this last war. Infantry were placed in skirmish order on either side of the fixed artillery position. The FAMP and Mfengu were located on the flanks to prevent the force being enveloped by the traditional Xhosa tactics and this mobile force could be used for counter-attacks, as well as to plug any gaps the enemy might find. As one unit the force then advanced towards the Xhosa. The imperial infantry, armed with the new Martini-Henry rifle, entered into an unequal fire fight with the Xhosa, for many warriors possessed only ancient flintlock muskets, and were forced to utilize pebbles as ammunition. The warriors were unable to withstand the accurate and rapid fire and withdrew. Their retreat was turned into a rout as the Xhosa were pursued from the field by the Mfengu and FAMP. The Battle of Nyumaga had been the first time that British soldiers had stood against the Xhosa in the war and the troops had achieved a devastating victory. The following weeks were characterized by more fruitless patrols, intermixed with the occasional sharp encounters. With his troops becoming exhausted, Cunynghame ordered Glyn to return to Ibeka to refit and await further reinforcements.

Both Frere and Cunynghame hoped that the defeat at Nyumaga would neutralize the Gcalekas and with reinforcements due to arrive from England, the general now turned his attention towards the Ngqikas. As a precautionary measure Cunynghame chose to establish a forward base on the slopes of the prominent hill of Kentani, from which any Gcaleka movement away from the Kei River would be observed. The site also gave a view over the Mnyameni bush which was the likely route to and from the Transkei from the Tyityaba and Kei valleys. Two companies of the 24th under the command of Captain Russell Upcher were despatched from Ibeka to begin construction of the Kentani camp. Upcher's force also included 85 FAMP, 300 Mfengu and 25 sailors of the Naval Brigade. Upcher wasted no time in fortifying the position, which included the digging of rifle pits in advance of the camp. Mfengu scouts soon reported, to the disappointment of Cunynghame, that the Gcalekas had not dispersed as hoped but were in fact concentrating in large numbers in the Mnyameni bush. The British were daily receiving rumours that the Xhosa intended to launch a new offensive in the Transkei, with their objectives being either the positions at Kentani or Ibeka. Glyn considered that Upcher's command might be too weak to withstand an assault and he despatched Lieutenant Carrington with a detachment of fifty men of the FLH as reinforcements. In addition, Glyn decided to place a reserve of 200 men at an old mission station on the Tutura River, just 10 miles from Kentani, to rush to Upcher's aid if required.

Once committed to war, Sandile favoured a move to the Amathole Mountains which had in previous wars been a difficult area for the British to operate in. Yet, the aggressive Khiva persuaded Sandile to join forces with

Sarhili in the Transkei and for the combined armies to take the fight to the British there. When the two venerable chiefs met near the mouth of the Qolora River both must have known that even with their combined forces they had very little chance of defeating the British in the long term, but they hoped that if they could hit their enemy with a devastating blow then they might be able to negotiate a favourable peace from a position of strength. Sandile argued for an attack upon Mfengu villages followed by a withdrawal to the Amathole Mountains, but the senior Gcaleka warrior chiefs, Khiva amongst them, fought for an attack upon one of the British posts not only to strike at the heart of the British defences, but also to secure much-needed food, arms and ammunition with which to carry on the fight.

After some debate it was agreed that the combined Xhosa force would attack the Kentani post. As the battle neared, Sandile's old caution returned and he stated that the Ngqika would not take part in the attack on the British camp but that his forces would protect the flanks from any forces, Mfengu or British, that might try to offer support. So, at dawn on 7 February 1878, a wet, misty morning, it was three columns of Gcaleka warriors, of around 1,000 men each, that assembled to attack Kentani. Command was in the hands of Khiva and Sarhili's son, Sigcawu. Upcher was awakened at 5am with news from the Mfengu pickets that the Xhosa were advancing upon his command. The troops were roused from their slumber and the tents were quickly struck. In a pre-designed move, the imperial infantry were issued with seventy rounds per man and ordered to make their way silently to the newly dug rifle pits and conceal themselves there. As the enemy approached, the rain increased and soon the troops were drenched.

In a move that would be repeated against the Zulus the following year, Carrington led out his men of the FLH along with 'G' Company of the 1/24th as bait to entice the Xhosa warriors. Upcher feared that the enemy might decide to withdraw before becoming fully engaged and hoped that Carrington's force would provoke an attack. The FLH, as they moved along a ravine at the edge of the Mnyameni bush, chanced upon the leading Xhosa column and fired several volleys into the mass of warriors before retiring gradually back to the camp. This had the desired result, and the Xhosa column stormed forward out of the cover of the ravine and rushed towards the camp. When the converging mass of warriors were around 1,000yd from the camp the two 7-pounder artillery pieces of the FAMP opened fire, with apparent little effect upon the charging Xhosa. At around 800yd, the

Mfengu allies and the now dismounted FLH opened fire, but at this range the musket fire of the Mfengu and that of the Snider carbines carried by Carrington's men again seemed to have no noticeable impact on slowing the enemy's advance. The Mfengu now pulled back to the apparent safety of the camp, and this seemed to spur the Gcaleka on, who were now running at full pace. Suddenly as the warriors were slowed slightly by the need to cross a series of watercourses, white helmets appeared from the shelter of the rifle pits and within seconds the order 'Fire!' was shouted.

From the first disciplined volley from their Martini-Henry rifles, the men of the 1/24th wrought fearful carnage upon the Xhosa warriors. A Gcaleka who survived the turmoil later recalled that the volleys were like 'a sudden blaze' and that 'our men fell like grass'.[3] Amazingly under such intense fire the Xhosa stood their ground, but further advance was simply suicidal. Refuge was sought behind any available rock or bush, or even the bodies of now dead warriors. Smoke from the Martini-Henry fire drifted across the battlefield, and this combined with a damp mist that had descended meant that for a brief moment the British were unable to detect their targets. Many of the surviving Xhosa made the most of their opportunity, and crept unseen to within 100yd of the rifle pits, but then as quickly as it arrived the misty shroud blew away and the men of the 1/24th took full advantage and fired at the vulnerable and now visible targets. Their fire was combined with case shot from the artillery pieces and finally the defiance of the surviving Gcaleka broke and they fled, pursued by the revengeful Mfengu and the FLH, with Carrington at its head, reins in his mouth, revolver and sword in his hands. The warriors continued their flight to the banks of the Qolora, leaving many of their comrades hunted down and dead in their wake.

With the Gcaleka in retreat, Sandile's fighting spirit returned and he led his force of Ngqika forward. They were spotted on a ridge to the north-west of the camp and once again the British decided to send out a small force as a decoy to entice the Ngqika to attack. A troop of the FAMP and fifty soldiers from 'F' Company of 1/24th under the command of Lieutenant Atkinson set out, with the infantry lagging. The FAMP charged into Sandile's advanced guard and before the infantry could support them the Xhosa had rapidly moved around the flanks of the FAMP and cut off any retreat. Upcher immediately saw the danger and ordered a further troop of the FAMP to rush to support their colleagues and in addition the now-returned Carrington led his FLH in a gallop towards the danger.

The Ngqika used the terrain of the bush and broken ground to conceal themselves superbly and Carrington's men rode into a trap. They were forced to dismount and on foot attempted to reach the encircled FAMP, but with more and more Ngqika joining the fight, the FLH also became entrapped and had to resort to hand-to-hand fighting. Carrington was later to describe the ferocity of the encounter:

> I rode my horse and 4 scoundrels kept potting at me and at last hit my horse in the jaw and he spun round like a top. He was only 10 yds off so I potted him with my revolver. Another of my men had his horse shot dead under him. Another knocked out of line with a bullet in the hock. Another man shot thro' the thigh ... Sergt. Leslie was assegaied in the hand but knocked the fellow over with the butt end of his gun and then shot him.[4]

The infantry had more success and once again the fire from the Martini-Henry was devastating. Atkinson's men managed to turn one of the flanks of the Ngqika and relieved some pressure from the embattled troopers.

At this critical moment, help arrived from the detachment of soldiers that Glyn had positioned on the Tutura River, and who had received Upcher's early morning plea for assistance, covering the 10 miles in less than 3 hours. The presence of these extra troops saw Sandile's warriors hesitate. Carrington saw his chance and both the FLH and FAMP rushed at the enemy, causing them to withdraw in some disorder, leaving sixteen of their dead comrades behind. Yet, this Ngqika force was far from beaten and Sandile led them to the Amathole where they would continue to resist. The same was not true of the Gcaleka for their defeat at Kentani had been complete, with nearly 400 warriors dead, whilst the British lost 2 Mfengu allies. The fighting spirit of the Gcaleka was shattered and Sarhili fled to Bomvnanland to seek sanctuary. Furthermore, the aggressive Khiva was killed in a skirmish on 15 March and with his death the Gcaleka were effectively knocked out of the war. The Ngqika would now have to fight on alone.

Whilst Glyn's troops had been achieving a crushing victory Frere and Cunynghame had been involved in a different kind of battle. Throughout January relations between these two men and Prime Minister Molteno and his 'Minister of War', Merriman, had become increasingly strained. The main areas of disagreement centred on Molteno's unwillingness for his government to contribute to the cost of imperial troops, specifically the recently arrived reinforcements of the 90th Light Infantry, and the demand that colonial forces should be under the direct control of Merriman. Frere was also outraged by the recent operations of colonial troops under the command of Griffith and Commandant Frost respectively in which reports of atrocities against Xhosa men, women and children suggested that these operations were little more than brutal acts of vengeance. Frere was determined to wrestle back control of colonial forces and was appalled when Molteno stated that he intended to place all colonial troops under the command of a commandant general who would be responsible solely to Molteno's ministry.

Frere summoned both Molteno and Merriman to King's William Town on 31 January 1878. The meeting was a stormy one in which no agreement was reached. Frere spent the night collecting his thoughts and the following day again called for a meeting and again nothing was achieved, apart from an increase in discord. Now determined to resolve the matter once and for all, Frere convened one last meeting and in the presence of Cunynghame he accused Molteno and his ministers of trying to create an illegal dual command and this left the High Commissioner with no choice but to accept the resignations of the prime minister and those ministers who supported his stance. Molteno scorned Frere's resignation proposal and then suggested Frere could always dismiss him. Exasperated, Frere accepted the challenge and four days later Molteno and Merriman, along with Charles Brownlee, were summarily dismissed.

The sackings caused surprise rather than outrage in the Colony and Lord Beaconsfield's (Disraeli) government later endorsed Frere's direct action. Frere wasted no time in appointing a prominent eastern province politician, J. Gordon Sprigg, as Molteno's successor. Although Sprigg was to be no 'puppet' appointment, Frere at least knew finally he had a colleague with whom he could have a sensible debate about military matters as well as someone who did not possess a closed mind regarding the possibility of confederation.

Cunynghame was personally delighted by the political demise of Molteno and Merriman, both of whom had opposed the general at every turn and the three men's relationship had been poisonous. Indeed, Cunynghame described Merriman as '... a man of active temperament, unbound ambition, strong in faith in himself, not over-courteous in manner or conciliatory in disposition, most difficult to reason with …'.[5] However, there was to be one more casualty of this 'political war' and that was to be the general himself.

With victory at Kentani and political success against Molteno and Merriman Cunynghame must have felt that he was now able to wind up the war in a fitting manner before his term of command came to an end. His joy, however, was short-lived. There had been questions raised about Cunynghame's military ability. Although his actions in the Transkei were considered adequate, there was some disapproval of his early handling of the war, particularly how he had failed to control the movement of warriors in the Ngqika Reserve and had permitted Khiva to raid south through the Transkei. Yet, the biggest criticism of Cunynghame was his inability to work with colonial forces and politicians and his somewhat high-handed approach towards them and his own subordinates. Cunynghame had not won the hearts of the colonists. His criticism of the colony's defensive arrangements and his occasional tactless utterances had not been forgotten. With a sacrifice required to perhaps appease the new Sprigg ministry, it was decided that Cunynghame's tenure must come to an end. Just days before the Molteno ministry was dismissed the Duke of Cambridge had drafted a letter to Cunynghame which stated:

> … because of the want of cordiality existing between you and the Ministry … the Secretary of State for War has deemed it advisable … that another General Officer should at once be appointed to the Command of the Troops in the Colony, and I have therefore to request that you will be prepared to hand over your duties on the arrival of your successor, Lieutenant-General (Local Rank) The Hon. F.A. Thesiger, C.B. who will leave this country immediately.[6]

It is not clear if Frere and Cambridge had been in correspondence about Cunynghame's replacement, but the High Commissioner must have been both pleased and relieved that his old acquaintance from Bombay, Frederic Thesiger, was soon to be joining him. By the time the duke's letter reached Cunynghame Thesiger was nearing Cape Town.

The press reaction to Cunynghame's dismissal was one of silence and this was perhaps condemnation in itself. Lieutenant Coghill though was at least one officer who was genuinely distressed at Cunynghame's departure and believed that the retirement was the result of political pressure. Coghill wrote that the General 'had not made a single mistake' and that all his operations have been 'thoroughly successful'.[7] This might have been overstating it, but it was largely due to Cunynghame's agitation and his cantankerous nature that the colony had not found itself completely defenceless when the Xhosa first attacked. The preparations for the second Transkei offensive had been well planned and had achieved the desired result with the Gcaleka knocked out of the war. British troops had cleared Gcalekland in a shorter time than the colonial forces and had won a major battle against a powerful Xhosa force.

Cunynghame's retirement was represented as a promotion; he was given the unemployed rank of full general and on his return to England wrote the story of his Southern African command in which his chagrin is all too apparent. Thesiger must have been delighted when he was informed by Cambridge in January that he would assume his first operational command and that he would be working alongside Frere. It did not take long for the appointment to become known in army circles and in a letter dated 28 January 1878, writing from his command in Ireland, General Sir John Michel, who had fought in the Eighth Frontier War, was keen to share his concerns and offer advice to Thesiger from the experiences he had gained whilst fighting the Xhosa. Some of Michel's musings were about the logistics of any operations, such as not taking tents west of the Kei and that 'no man should carry anything except a haversack containing biscuit, a towel, and if on long patrol a pair of boots, and again a great coat or blanket. Of course, a water bottle and his mess tin.' Others were of an operational nature, which included that all Mounted Infantry 'should be armed at first with carbines for short range, and when good horsemen with revolvers. These latter are absolutely necessary to close fighting in the bush. Swords to be utterly abolished as never used as a weapon which would entirely take away from the power of moving in the bush which is a daily necessity.'[8]

Michel was also firm in his view about staff officers, 'Do not hamper yourself with staff, they are useless, as Colonels of Regts., do all the work.' These lines would have played into Thesiger's mindset for he was person who did not naturally delegate and indeed in the following conflict with the Zulus his lack of staff officers has been considered a major factor in some of the general's failings in the campaign. Michel also issued Thesiger with a warning, 'Yours, my dear Thesiger, is a command of great danger to your reputation. The two best Generals, Sir P. Maitland and Sir H. Smith, were dismissed, that is superseded, both most unjustly. I shall earnestly trust you may have better fortune, and I shall not forget to put in my voice if I find events placed to your discredit.'[9]

With these words surely troubling his mind, Thesiger boarded the mail steamer *America* to sail to the Cape. Two of his fellow passengers onboard were Colonel Evelyn Wood VC and Major Redvers Buller. Wood's regiment, the 90th, was already in Southern Africa and he expected to assume command when the regiment's current colonel, Palmer, retired in April. Wood was a veteran of the Crimean War, the Indian Rebellion and had served as Sir Garnet Wolseley's second in command during the Asante Expedition of 1873–4. He was renowned for his bravery, his leadership of men and his ability to endure anything a campaign could throw at him, including wounds or illness. Buller was also a veteran of the Asante War and was one of five senior officers who had been selected for special service in Southern Africa. Buller was later to succeed Carrington as commander of the FLH. Wood and Buller would not only distinguish themselves in the Eastern Cape but together would be the two officers Thesiger would rely upon most after the debacle of Isandlwana. Thesiger had certainly taken Michel's advice about the size of his staff and the small number chosen came from amongst those who had served under him at Aldershot. Thesiger's deputy assistant adjutant general at Aldershot, Major John North Crealock, became his military secretary whilst his two ADCs, Captain Matthew Gosset and Lieutenant William Molyneux, had also served at Aldershot.

Also onboard the *America* were 190 new recruits who were to make up the draft, largely in The Buffs, but also in the 88th Regiment (Connaught Rangers), and these men were destined to serve in both the Eastern Cape and Zululand. Thesiger was not impressed and soon discovered that many had under four months' service and nearly a third had not completed the musketry course. Thesiger felt compelled to write to the adjutant general on 15 February to voice his concerns and asked that Cambridge should be informed of the situation:

Thus, in a detachment of 190 men, 116 are absolutely untrained for all practical purposes of active service and, in the event of their Battalions being in the Field, would be likely to prove a source of embarrassment instead of one of strength. I would venture most earnestly to request that, should it be found necessary to furnish reinforcements for active service in South Africa, none but those who have completed a course

of both recruits and musketry drill be permitted to embark. Success in
the fighting peculiar to the Cape would seem to depend in a greater
measure upon the conduct of individuals than in moispatchsed warfare,
and it is not fair upon the recruit or his commander to place him in a
position for which he has not received the preliminary training.[10]

Despite Thesiger's clear frustration, if not anger, at the quality of these
soldiers, he would have little choice but to accept troops of equally limited
training when he called for urgent reinforcements after Isandlwana. In
the continued conflict against the Xhosa, though, Thesiger was fortunate
in that one experienced regiment had arrived, the 90th, and although the
2/24th, serving alongside its senior battalion for the first time in decades,
comprised short-service recruits with limited training, these men were to
equip themselves well as the general's other additional reinforcements. When
Thesiger arrived in Cape Town in late February he was assured that the
Ninth Frontier War was practically over, and he received the same assessment
when he arrived in King William's Town by special train on 4 March 1878.
Aware of the damage done by Cunynghame and Merriman's bitter quarrels,
Thesiger devoted himself to a charm offence to try and restore relations
between colonial and imperial forces. Writing to Commandant Griffith,
Thesiger wrote, 'I was sorry to find on my arrival at the station yesterday,
that I should not have the benefit of your advice and experience. My great
object will be to assist the Colony in every way that lies in my power. I am
anxious to give the Colonial troops every help that they may require.'[11] The
colonial officers must had been relieved to hear such words.

In his first despatch from Southern Africa to the Secretary of State for
War, Frederick Stanley, Thesiger demonstrated that he had clearly drawn the
wrong conclusion as to the threats he now faced, 'I found that the impression
existing here among many Officers, both Military and Civil, was that in the
disturbances had passed the critical stage, and that, owing to their losses
in the field, and want of supplies, both Gaikas [Ngqika] and Gcalekas will
offer no resistance.'[12] Yet, already there were worrying signs that the conflict
would be a prolonged one.

One of Cunynghame's last acts was to send the newly arrived 90th
regiment to Fort Beaufort, along with 'C' Company of the 1/24th under
the command of Captain William Mostyn. Alarming reports continued to
be received about a possible uprising of Xhosa, under the leadership of Tini

Maqoma, son of the legendary Maqoma. The area around Fort Beaufort, the western Amathole Mountains, had been the chosen fighting terrain of Maqoma, Sandile's half-brother, during the Eighth Frontier War. After this conflict the Xhosa had been forcefully removed from the area by the British. Over time many Xhosa had stealthy returned and Tini had acquired a sizeable following. By early February information was received that armed gatherings at Tini's homestead were becoming frequent and there were reported incidences of cattle theft from white settler farms. Added to these concerning reports was that Sandile's stepson, Mathanzima, had led a force that attacked a detachment of colonial volunteers in the Thomas River valley, which was the northern route into the Amathole Mountains. This raid seemed to suggest that the Ngqika intended to head towards the Amathole Mountains to join forces with Tini.

Colonel Palmer wasted no time in taking the offensive against Tini Maqoma and his followers. Although Thesiger had been unable to meet Palmer before he began his own operations in the Pirie Bush, he ordered the colonel to take action in the Kroome Heights, to the north of Fort Beaufort and to clear the Waterkloof and Schelm Kloof of all Xhosa found there. Palmer led his men in a series of operations from 3 March onwards, initially in the Schelm Kloof. His men encountered little resistance and drove the Xhosa before them. Having cleared the area of warriors and leading many women and children out of the conflict zone, Palmer built five small posts to dominate and ensure that the area remained pacified. The colonel now turned his attention to the steep-sided and heavily forested Waterkloof valley, an area defined by a north–south ridge known locally as 'Iron Mountain'. Palmer placed one company of the 90th, along with some burghers, near this spot and ensured that any passes in the area were patrolled by native police. With these dispositions, Palmer now led his main force into the Waterkloof, proceeded by native police, with Mfengu protecting each flank. In the rear were mounted colonial volunteers and two companies of the 90th, which Palmer held as a reserve to move forward as required.

The advanced colonial troops were soon engaged, and Palmer sent the Mfengu and a company of the 90th forward to support. In the official history of the 90th Regiment the operations were recorded thus:

> ... company of the 90th Light Infantry occupied Batho's farm (a strong position at the foot of the Iron Mountains) with a force of

220 Burghers placed along the line of Meyer's Kloof on the south-west, and two guns on the eastern ridges, while the two most important passes were occupied by native police. The main body commanded by Colonel Palmer entered the pass from the south-west, with police in advance, flanked by Fingoes [Mfengu] in the bush on either side, and followed by the mounted Burghers. The Fingo [Mfengu] levy and native police held the pass until the artillery, two guns, and two companies of the 90th Light Infantry had passed through. On arriving at the other side of the pass, it was found that the Burghers were engaged; they were reinforced by the Fingo [Mfengu] levy, supported by 100 men of the 90th. As the Kaffirs [derogatory Victorian term for the Xhosa] retired, they came under the fire of the guns on the eastern ridges and are supposed to have suffered severely. An advance was made, and the Kloofs and bush of the Iron Mountain were swept clear of the enemy. Their cattle and large stores of provisions and blankets, found in the caves of the various Kloofs, were brought away by the troops. The success attending these operations had a most salutary effect on all the native inhabitants of the Stockenstrom district, who now gave up their arms and assumed a loyal and submissive tone.[13]

The sweep of Iron Mountain saw fourteen Xhosa killed, including one of Tini Maqoma's leading advisors, and cattle and provisions taken. Once the operation was completed, Palmer repeated his tactic and constructed and manned five more posts in the Waterkloof, to restrict the movement and return of the Xhosa and he was able to declare to Thesiger that the Kroome Mountain had been cleared of Ngqika. Mfengu levies could now be sent to support Thesiger's operations against Sandile.

To try to incept Mathanzima, Sandile and their warriors from reaching the Amathole Mountains, a colonial commando was hastily assembled, led by Griffith, but the warriors managed to elude all patrols. On 9 March, as Thesiger was enjoying a mess dinner in the King William's Town barracks he was handed an urgent telegram from Griffith informing the general that a huge body of Xhosa had slipped through the net of colonial troops and was heading for the Sidenge Range in the eastern Amathole Mountains. Within a matter of hours two companies of the 2/24th were despatched towards Fort Beaufort. Thesiger was rapidly changing his mind about the Xhosa threat and began to consider the need for additional British reinforcements.

Despite his quick action, Thesiger was unable to stop Sandile from reaching the Amathole Mountains. Sandile resolved that in the Pirie Bush, 20 miles south-east of King William's Town, he and his warriors could not only hold out against the British, but the terrain of the impenetrable bush would allow the Xhosa to inflict casualties via their usual tactics of hit-and-run ambushes. Of further concern for the British was that even the Ngqika, who had been peaceful for years working on white settler farms or even in government service, were, according to Captain Hallam Parr, Thesiger's military secretary, exchanging 'their clothes for a blanket, their pen for a rifle' and were joining Sandile in the Pirie Bush.[14]

Thesiger resolved to act decisively and by 18 March he had assembled a force of 3,000 colonial and British troops to converge on the Pirie Bush. The general's plan was remarkably similar to those that Cunynghame had employed before him. The force would be divided into three columns that would close in on the Pirie Bush in a sweeping pincer deployment, which it was hoped would drive the Ngqika out of the bush and then they could be tackled and destroyed.

Such a plan necessitated detailed coordination of the available forces and a high degree of cooperation between imperial and colonial troops. Unfortunately, these requirements were sadly lacking at the start of operations. Thesiger ordered Wood to throw a cordon of troops around the eastern Amatoles and for this he was provided with two companies of the 2/24th, about 200 mounted colonials, mainly farmers from around King William's Town, and several hundred Mfengu. With these men he was to push westwards, in the form of a 'game drive', from the Buffalo Ridge towards Thesiger who, with five companies of the 2/24th, had ringed the opposite edge of the Pirie Bush. It was a simple plan but any hopes that a coordinated movement of troops would be possible soon evaporated. Wood had received local intelligence that over 1,000 warriors, aware of the forthcoming operation, had taken the Gwili Heights as a commanding position from which to oppose Wood's moves. To reduce the risk of ambush Wood decided to begin his sweep early and on the evening of 17 March he led part of his command in a single-file night march to the summit. It took his men all night to cover the 7 miles and their approach was far from silent. When at dawn they reached their destination, Wood and his men found the summit deserted and despite the 360-degree view Wood saw no trace of the enemy. Unbeknown to either Wood or Thesiger, several colonial troops led by Commandant Edward Bradant had fallen for the oldest Xhosa trick of pursuing what appeared to be abandoned cattle to then fall into an ambush by hundreds of Sandile's warriors. Their plight had forced a further colonial detachment, led by Commandant Frank Steatfield, to divert to support their comrades. The cordon had already been shattered and Wood had little choice but to await events from the Heights. Meanwhile, Thesiger was waiting in impatiently for any sign of warriors fleeing the bush. By the evening it was clear that the whole operation had failed in its attempts to coordinate and had been something of a farce.

Thesiger was most certainly not pleased by such an inauspicious beginning to operations, but he had little option but to renew the 'drive' the following day. Events of the first day were largely repeated over the next three days and this was a time of acute frustration for Thesiger who not only failed to ascertain the whereabouts of the enemy, but also of his own troops. Although a large group of Xhosa women and children did emerge from the bush, very few warriors were seen, let alone captured as they were easily able to evade both British and colonial troops alike. Indeed, the colonials proved very reluctant to risk their lives in the alien environment that was the thick undergrowth of the Pirie Bush. For many of the newly arrived imperial troops the bush was a similarly daunting place. On one occasion, Thesiger had been waiting for 3 hours for any sign of an emerging foe, having sent troops of the 2/24th on a 'sweep'. A single shot rang out and a private stumbled out of the bush to be followed by several of his comrades, all desperate to accompany the wounded soldier back to the rear. The general sent for the company officers, and he castigated them before ordering the troops back into the bush. Thesiger did gain first-hand experience of the elusive nature of the enemy when on one occasion, having gained a vantage point, he was able to witness Wood's men break camp and continue their advance, only to then see warriors emerge from the bush behind them to take possession of the now-deserted camp!

During the four days of this fruitless operation, Thesiger's men experienced extreme weather, from freezing night-times and cold, early morning mists to driving rain and high daytime temperatures. This in combination with the fear of sudden attack from an elusive but deadly enemy mentally and physically exhausted all those involved. Thesiger himself spent most of the days in the saddle from 6am to 10.30pm. Wood was to later remark that, 'the apparent result of our operations … was not commensurate with the discomfort we underwent'.[15]

Thesiger had not heeded the advice given to him by General Michel about the ineffectiveness of the artillery and much effort was expended manhandling both artillery pieces and shells through the difficult terrain. Heavy shelling of the bush also had no perceived effect on the enemy or his ability to move unseen, and indeed on at least one occasion the British had manged to shell their Mfengu levies rather than the enemy.

Although Crealock claimed that 126 Ngqika had been killed in the ten days from 11–21 March, and that nearly 700 cattle had been taken, Thesiger concluded that the operation had not been a success. He had lost three officers, one private soldier and four Mfengu killed. Thesiger was also accurately aware that both Frere and the colony would be assessing his generalship. He knew that Cunynghame's rapid departure was as a result of colonial dissatisfaction and Thesiger, not wanting a similar end, realized that he must begin a new offensive as soon as possible. First, though, he had to address an immediate manpower problem for the burgher volunteers clamoured to return to their homes as the period of their military service was due to expire. Thesiger complained to Colonel Stanley, the Secretary of State, that, '... it will be understood that the difficulties of command is enormously increased, and the General himself placed in an embarrassing position, when, in the middle of serious operations, a considerable portion of the force declares its intention of leaving him for their homes'.[16] Thesiger was forced to return to King William's Town to secure Frere's permission to raise a fresh colonial levy, as well as securing additional Mfengu warriors who were more willing to enter the bush than their colonial and imperial counterparts.

Before his departure, Thesiger ordered that two important points should be addressed before he would return to renew operations. He realized that future operations would need to be better coordinated and he arranged for flag-signalling, semaphore, to be introduced between the various columns and units. In addition, Thesiger recognized that the existing two roads that ran through the disputed area, both of which journeyed north to south, were insufficient to enable his troops to move effectively and speedily. So, the general ordered that new roads, running east to west, be cut through the bush and the men of the 2/24th and the Mfengu levies worked frantically on this task. In writing to Stanley, Thesiger stated, 'The effect of these [roads] must, I consider, be looked upon as most important, as now for many years, should the rebels again take refuge in the bush, there will be no difficulty in dealing with them ...'.[17]

Thesiger renewed his operations in the Pirie Bush on 29 March with an attack upon a reportedly large number of Ngqika in the country between the Gozo Heights and McNaghten's Krans, west of Hayne's Mill. Once again, the general was to be frustrated for as the Thesiger's command advanced the Ngqika disappeared from sight. With intelligence now reporting that the Xhosa had moved to the large area of the Buffalo Poort, Thesiger was forced to postpone operations until additional Mfengu arrived from the Transkei. The second assault, which began on 5 April, saw the Mfengu attempt to drive the Ngqika through the bush from Mount Kempt to Hayne's Mill in an arc towards the general and his imperial troops. However, the Ngqika had used the delay between operations to once more slip away and the Mfengu drive served only to send some bush antelopes towards the British troops.

Despite this further setback, Thesiger did receive some welcome news. Siyolo, chief of the Ndlambe Ngqika found by the Keiskamma River, had decided to join Sarhili but had been defeated by colonial forces led by Commandant von Linsingen. On 5 April, Siyolo was leading his remaining 1,200 warriors towards the Amathole Mountains when he was caught in the open crossing the Debe Nek by a force of the FLH, led by a Captain Warren. Siyolo was forced to flee into the nearby bush, leaving sixty of his dead warriors behind. On hearing this news, Thesiger broke off his own operations and diverted troops to the pursuit of Siyolo. Streatfield and the Mfengu were tasked with cutting off Siyolo's movement on the Amathole Mountains whilst Wood led his force down the Keiskamma River valley. After some initial artillery shelling of the Lotutu Bush, Thesiger sent the Mfengu on a sweep in the afternoon of 6 April. The first two sorties proved ineffective, and Captain Webster, leading his Mfengu command forward, was shot dead, probably by one of his own men, but the third and final assault of the day was a partial success when a group of Xhosa were located in a wooded area. In the night the remaining warriors once more melted away, yet the operations of the first week of April could be viewed more positively by Thesiger for it was estimated that up to 500 Xhosa had been killed for the loss of Webster, Private Collins of the 24th and 2 Mfengu dead. Collins was the first soldier of the 24th to die whilst on active service in Southern Africa; he was not to be the last.

Just when Thesiger seemed to be gaining some success he was forced to call a halt to further operations until the end of April for once more colonial troops and some of the African levies returned to their homes and farms. Again, in his report of 24 April, he wrote to the Secretary of State of his frustration, 'This lull in active operations has been most distasteful to me, feeling as I do that the only way to bring this War to an end is to constantly harass the Kaffirs [Xhosa], cutting off their supplies and preventing their obtaining fresh recruits.'[18] Although Thesiger had his strategy for victory clear in his mind, how to achieve it would continue to be a problem over the following weeks.

Before recommencing operations against Siyolo and his Ndlambe warriors in the Ntaba-ka-Ndoda region of the Lotutu Bush, Thesiger took the opportunity of a lull in the fighting to visit Colonel Palmer at Fort Beaufort and to tour the Waterkloof district. The general again reported to the Secretary of State:

I have visited the Beaufort district to see the Waterkloof country, where Colonel Palmer has lately carried out his operations, in order to judge for myself how far it was now necessary to retain the Imperial forces in that part of the colony. As I found the district quiet, and the European farmers returning to their farms, and no lack of Colonial forces there, to be called out if necessary, I had no hesitation in urging on Government the necessity of concentrating the five companies of the 90th Light Infantry to the East, where they will be of very material assistance in the coming operations against Siyolo and Sandili, and will likewise be at hand, and ready to move to Natal and Transvaal if necessary. Active operations in the district having now ceased, I have the honour to forward a brief account of the operations which Colonel Palmer, 90th Light Infantry, carried out in that difficult country. These had a successful issue and reflect credit on him and the forces under his command.[19]

Thesiger was, of course, the commander of British forces in Southern Africa and this despatch clearly indicates that the movement of five companies of the 90th Regiment can be viewed in a larger context of perhaps their future deployment against the Zulu or Pedi tribes, or even the Boers of the Transvaal. In the meantime, the 90th would provide a significant boost for the general's operations against the Xhosa in the Amathole Mountains.

Events in the Eastern Cape were also being viewed by many, in both Southern Africa and Britain, in wider political as well as military terms. As early as 4 April, Sir Michael Hicks Beach, Secretary of State for the Colonies, wrote to Frere to state:

> … measures should be taken to put a stop to the raids (which I understand are still going on) upon persons and property within the disputed territory. To allow these to continue would be a sign of weakness which could not but increase the Boers' disaffection and make Cetywayo [the Zulu king] unwilling to come to any reasonable agreement.[20]

Frere was also keen to ensure the Hicks Beach received a clear appreciation of what had so far been achieved by Thesiger. Writing from Government House in Cape Town on 30 April, Frere stated to the Secretary of State that:

> The newspapers will, I think, give you a very imperfect idea of what General Thesiger has been doing and of the degree of success which has attended his operations, and possibly he may not himself see as clearly as others, who are merely lookers-on, that he has really done all that regular troops can do in such warfare. He has broken up every stronghold in which the Kaffirs [Xhosa] had tried to rally, he has cut off their supplies of food and ammunition – and some very important chiefs have been captured – and others killed.[21]

For all Frere's words of praise for Thesiger, the general was still some way off from bringing the war to a firm conclusion, and questions were beginning to be raised, particularly by the colonial troops and settlers, as to his competence.

Thesiger had used the three-week delay to take stock and met with Colonel Wood and senior colonial officers to consider the next operations. This time was also a good opportunity for the imperial troops, as well as their officers, to recover after the exertions of the previous weeks, and Wood in particular was suffering; the glands in his groin, armpits and neck swelled, his skin began to peel and chilblain-like openings appeared on his hands. Yet, after two weeks of rest he was back in the saddle.

The transfer of five companies of the 90th from Palmer's command boosted Thesiger's numbers and he also acquired 300 mounted colonial troops, under the command of Commandant von Linsingen, which helped to swell the ranks of the FLH. In addition, more Mfengu were recruited, and on this occasion from areas that had felt the full force of Xhosa vengefulness and it was therefore hoped that these men would be more likely to fight. In all Thesiger had 4,000 men at his disposal, but the general now had to decide how best to deploy them. What was becoming all too apparent was that Thesiger showed a reluctance to accept advice, particularly from colonials. The strategy advanced by the likes of von Linsingen and others was to divide the rebel-held areas in the Pirie and Lotutu bush into military districts into which mounted troops could be stationed to continually harass the enemy, depriving them of food or shelter, until the Xhosa were forced into submission. An alternative plan was to adopt the military post approach that had been used so effectively by Colonel Palmer in the Waterkloof and Schelm Kloof to stifle the activity of Tini Maqoma and his followers. Yet, instead Thesiger displaying a hard-headiness and lack of imagination, which would also characterize his command decisions in the opening weeks of the Zulu War, and he decided to continue with the policy of 'sweeping' the bush, which had proved to be ineffective in previous operations.

The plan for the new offensive was to surround the Lotutu Bush with troops and then divide his 4,000 men into 4 columns. Thesiger proposed to converge in a tightening noose, sweeping the bush and the forested kloofs (ravines or valleys). The disputed area was only 16 square miles in extent and with the number of men at his disposal Thesiger was optimistic of success. At daylight on 30 April, Thesiger gained the eastern crest of the Tamoika ravine and ordered Major Harness of the Royal Artillery to direct his fire into the wooded areas where the main concentration of rebels was thought to be. The effectiveness of the fire resulted in this large group of warriors dispersing into smaller groups, which in turn made Thesiger's task of locating them harder. Yet, the operation, following the artillery fire, began promisingly. Redvers Buller, now in command of the FLH, was to drive down from the north, through the Gongqo and Zanyokwe valleys, whilst von Linsingen was to lead an assault from the south clearing the ground to the Lotutu plateau. This command comprised 300 colonial volunteers and a contingent of Mfengu. The aim of these two movements was to drive the Xhosas westwards towards Colonel Wood who would be waiting with the largest concentration of troops, having himself divided his own force into the last two columns.

William Molyneux, acting staff officer to von Linsingen, wrote of the difficulties of the terrain, 'What a race it was! Into holes, out again, hands and faces bleeding from thorns, knees punctured, and shirt sleeves in ribands …'.[22] The column met some initial resistance, in which seven of Siyolo's scouts were killed by Mfengu out in advance of the column. One of the Xhosas was hit by an assegai thrown from a distance of nearly 50m. Following this skirmish von Linsingen's command reached the plateau and waited there for Wood's men to be in position.

Wood's troops had the farthest distance to cover and were delayed in getting started. Major Hackett of the 90th commanded one of the infantry columns, consisting of two companies of the 90th and over a thousand Mfengu, whilst Wood himself led the other column, made up of three companies of the 90th, thirty-five colonial volunteers and two guns of the Royal Artillery commanded by Captain Stuart Smith. Both columns were to converge on the Makabalikele spur or ridge.

The progress of Wood's column was slowed by the need to drag the guns of the Royal Artillery through the thick undergrowth, which was particularly dense at the base of the Makabalikele spur. The men of the 90th had to hack their way through trees, vines and creepers and progress was only possible in single file. Suddenly Wood's advance guard, led by Captain Stevens of the 90th, came under attack:

His [Stevens] men were immediately hotly engaged, and on the Captain being shot through the face, the rebels cheering charged, to be at once repulsed. Lieutenant Saltmarshe now took Captain Stevens' place, and within five minutes he was killed. The men, however, pressed on under Colour-Sergeant Smith, and by the time Major Cherry came up and took command of the leading company, which had in ten minutes lost two officers and eight or ten men killed.[23]

Colonel Wood was full of praise for his officers and men when writing of the day's encounter to the Assistant Military Secretary, Major John Crealock:

He [Stevens] is an excellent officer, and for this reason I acceded to his request to lead the advance up the Makabalele ridge on the 30th April. As I reported that day, he and the late Lieutenant Saltmarshe offered a fine example to all. I attribute the success of the front company in checking the rebel's advance to the gallant bearing of these officers. I trust I may be excused in adding that when Captain Stevens was wounded, within six paces of a large number of Kaffirs [Xhosa], Sergeant Jeffs and Private Graham, of the 90th Light Infantry, stepped coolly forward and removed their officer under a heavy fire, and when Lieutenant Saltmarshe, who had taken his place shortly afterwards was killed, Colour-Sergeant Smith, in my presence, encouraged the men and caused them to advance.[24]

Saltmarshe's death was particularly poignant. With Stevens wounded he straight away took command and managed to push forward another 50m before he took the full discharge from a Xhosa musket to the chest at point-blank range. He died immediately and a further two men of the 90th were killed as the Xhosa rushed forward in the aftermath of the lieutenant's death. Although the advance continued under the leadership of Captain Smith, and then Major Cherry, resistance from Siyolo's men was fierce and it was only after Smith brought forward his two guns and fired canister shells into the bush at a mere 30m that any real progress could be made. Once out in the open, Wood was able to use the newly introduced system of signalling to bring forward ambulances for the wounded, before moving on once more to join forces with Buller and von Linsingen. Thesiger had tasked Crealock to develop a system of semaphore. Writing to the Secretary of State on 5 May Thesiger stated:

> The system of Flag signalling was found most valuable, it enabled me to know what was happening over a large extent of broken country and to transmit the necessary orders. Colonel Wood was able to telegraph from the position he had gained with his advance guard to the remainder of his force that had not entered the bush, 'Advance with caution,' when it would have been dangerous to have sent a Messenger, and I myself was informed of what had happened, and of the names of the Officers killed and wounded in a very short time after the occurrence, information that could only have reached me by messenger sooner than in 3 hours ...[25]

With the introduction of semaphore Thesiger showed that, contrary to some of his laboured decision-making, he was not slow to accept innovation and he would use both flags and heliography in the Zulu Campaign to some effect. He was also not as sceptical about the use of new military technology as some of his contemporaries. Indeed, it was under his Zulu command that the Gatling gun was first used in action by the British and he would later be a strong advocate for its use as an offensive weapon as well as defensive.

Wood's men captured around seventy head of cattle and many women affiliated to the Siyolo and Sandile clans who came out of the bush. It was reported that Siyolo himself had defended the Makabalikele ridge and that Tini Maqoma was also still in the Lotutu Bush. In the north Buller had had a difficult time as he moved towards the rendezvous point. His men were under almost constant fire from an unseen enemy. Just when Buller felt that he might be close to engaging with the Xhosa, a long line of women appeared and formed a human shield from behind which the warriors made their escape. By late afternoon a torrential rainstorm struck, soaking Thesiger and his men, and its arrival put an end to any further operations that day. Once reports had been received from all the columns, Thesiger was able to confirm that nearly 100 dead Xhosa had been counted and undoubtedly more would have been found in the bush if his troops could have penetrated the undergrowth. Yet, although this was the most successful of Thesiger's 'sweeps', the number of Xhosa casualties could perhaps be viewed as not proportionate for such a large-scale and complex operation.

The following morning Thesiger expected the day would end with a decisive victory. Major Degacher was ordered to move with his column westwards, again sweeping the bush before them. The general and his staff waited impatiently for the sound of gunfire to indicate that contact had been made, but all that could be heard was the sound of the men of the 90th hacking their way through the undergrowth. With growing frustration Thesiger began to fear the worst and this was finally confirmed to him when Degacher was able to signal that the bush was deserted. The apparently cornered Xhosas had stealthy slipped through the British cordon during the night. It was later learnt that Siyolo, Tini and all the other leaders, including Sandile's son Edmund, had succeeded in joining Sandile in the Pirie Bush. Thesiger's staff were met with silence for the rest of the day, as the general tried to control his anger and frustration. The following day the general's positivity had returned, and he could at least claim that the Lotutu Bush had been cleared of the Xhosa and he was now free to concentrate operations upon the last Xhosa stronghold in the Pirie Bush. Yet, Thesiger still stubbornly refused to alter his tactics. His next offensive was set for 8 May and would once again be a 'sweep'. However, Thesiger now at least realized how vital it would be to secure the high ground first and his aim was to occupy the Buffalo Range whilst at the same time surrounding the Pirie Bush to seal off an escape route back to the Lotutu Bush.

On the evening of 7 May Colonel Wood led a detachment to drag two artillery pieces to the heights near Bailie's Grave. Despite heavy rain, Wood managed to reach the set position by dawn and he was later joined by a column led by Buller. Although these movements had been a success, all element of surprise had been lost and the only thing that the British saw from the heights was a small number of the Xhosa rear guard beating a retreat into the Pirie Bush. The other columns that Thesiger had selected to drive through the Pirie were equally unsuccessful. Degacher's advance was delayed by the late arrival of his Mfengu levies, whilst von Linsingen was held up by the false news that a large concentration of warriors had been seen in the east near the Lotutu plateau. Critical time was lost whilst von Linsingen was forced to investigate. Buller's column did engage with some Xhosas, but with the exception of five warriors, the bulk of the rebels melted away into the bush. These five, armed with double-barrelled shotguns, stood their ground and killed Private Davies of the FLH and one Mfengu before all five died in a hail of Snider bullets. There was further loss of life during one of the very few encounters of the day when Sandile's warriors managed to ambush a detachment of the FLH, killing several, including its commander Captain McNaghten.

The following morning, and with Thesiger's agreement, Buller set out early to avenge the death of his FLH colleagues. He lined up his force, which included Mfengu, the FLH and two companies of the 24th for a thrust from the edge of McNaghten's Krans towards Buffalo Poort. During the sweep, fate intervened and the captain of 'B' Company, Godwin-Austen, was shot and badly injured when the Martini-Henry rifle held by a soldier walking behind him accidently discharged. The captain had to recuperate for several months and command of 'B' Company, which was to enter its place in history as the gallant defenders of the mission station at Rorke's Drift in Natal, was now given to Lieutenant Gonville Bromhead.

Buller's sweep was again unopposed and although this added to Thesiger's frustration, it did mean that the British controlled most of the Pirie Bush and could now effectively stop any movement of Xhosa in or out. However, the general realized that his 'sweeps' of the bush had not achieved the results that either he or an ever increasingly sceptical colony was expecting. Thesiger was at last ready to acknowledge that a change in tactics was now required and he reluctantly agreed to the colonial suggestions to divide the last stronghold of the Xhosa, in the eastern Amathole Mountains, into eleven military districts. In each were stationed a mounted and infantry force which were tasked with constantly pursuing and harassing any Xhosa they discovered. If the warriors then entered an adjacent or neighbouring district, then the pursuit would start afresh leaving no opportunity for the Xhosa to regroup, rest or even obtain sustenance. The British were very reliant on colonial commandants who knew the terrain and possessed a vengefulness towards the Xhosa which meant they relished the pursuit of their old enemy. On occasions operations continued into the night to seek out the Xhosa in any likely hiding place and what little food stores that remained were systematically destroyed wherever they were found. This was brutal, merciless, attritional warfare in which no prisoners were taken.

Thesiger complemented this approach by also adopting Palmer's idea of the construction of military posts or earthworks. Two such posts were built between the Buffalo Range and the Lotutu Bush; Fort Evelyn, named after Colonel Wood, was constructed on McNaghten's Krans and Fort Black was erected near the foot of Ntaba-ka-Ndoda Mountain, and was named after Major Wilsone Black of the 2/24th.

After three weeks of relentless pursuit, Thesiger now had the enemy where he wanted them, and the plight of the Xhosa was critical. Forced now to operate only in small parties and unable to forage, the warriors faced death by either a British bullet, exposure or starvation. Siyolo managed to slip through the cordons and made his escape to the Great Fish River valley, whilst Tini Maqoma also evaded capture and sought refuge in the Waterkloof. Those who were unable to flee continued to fight as best they could despite their desperately starved state. The Xhosa fought with a heroic sense of finality, perhaps realizing that no prisoners were being taken. A colonial officer wrote:

One of then got two balls through him at only a few yards distance, one through his head, from ear to ear, and the other through his chest. He fell, apparently dead, but in a moment sat up leaning on one elbow, shook his fist at us, and with a scowl rolled over backwards never to rise again.[26]

The warriors knew that the whites always stripped them of their ornaments after death and the same officer described Xhosa determination to deprive their enemies of these mementoes:

> I saw a Kaffir ... get wounded and directly he fell, he set to work to smash his ivory amulet against the stones. I have seen this done twice. They are very jealous of these amulets, and if there is any life left in them, will always smash them sooner than let them be taken.[27]

Sandile was compelled to see if the British would negotiate a surrender, and Charles Brownlee, now appointed Assistant Commissioner (also Secretary of Native affairs), informed Thesiger that the chief had made enquiries as to the terms he might be offered. In now such a strong position the general was adamant that surrender had to be unconditional. Whilst Buller and Wood maintained control of the situation in the Pirie Bush and continued to harass the surviving Xhosa, Thesiger felt confident enough in the situation that on 21 May he began a seventeen-day tour of the Transkei to discover how Colonel Glyn, still based at Ibeka, was dealing with Sarhili and any opposition the Gcaleka might still be offering.

Glyn had little to report to the general. After the Battle of Kentani, Sarhili had fled to a remote area of the Transkei and although the British tried to track the paramount, he was always able to remain one step ahead of his pursuers. Glyn was tasked by Thesiger with making sure that those warriors who had survived the crashing defeat at Kentani were not permitted to regroup or offer further resistance. By the middle of April all eight companies of the 1/24th had been transferred to the Transkei and with these troops Glyn and his second-in-command, Henry Pulleine, had led a number of unproductive 'sweeps' which served only to demonstrate that the Gcaleka was a largely spent force that was now incapable of offering any significant resistance. Thesiger toured the numerous earthwork posts that the 1/24th had constructed throughout the Transkei and, after seeing for himself how placid the area now was, decided in consultation with Glyn to cease all large-scale operations.

Whilst Thesiger was away in the Transkei the last significant act of the Ninth Frontier War occurred in the Amathole Mountains. All the significant Xhosa leaders had now either fled the area or been killed. Only Sandile, paramount of the Ngqika, remained at large in the area, but the chief knew

Chief Maqoma.

Chief Sandile.

Chief Sarhili.

A Mfengu soldier. These were allied to the British in the Ninth Frontier War.

General Thesiger's attack on the rebel chief Sandile, near King William's Town, 30 March 1878.

Colonel Glyn.

Sir Bartle Frere.

Lord Chelmsford and
his Staff, 1879. Back
row (left to right):
Major Matthew
Gosset, Lieutenant
Berkeley Milne; front
row (left to right):
Commander Fletcher
Campbell RN,
Lieutenant General
Lord Chelmsford,
Lieutenant Colonel
John North Crealock.

Lord Chelmsford in 1879.

Colonel Evelyn Wood VC.

Sir Redvers Buller VC.

King Cetshwayo.

Lord Chelmsford after his return from South Africa.

A Gatling gun with crew, as utilized at the battles of Gingindlovu and Ulundi.

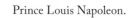

Prince Louis Napoleon.

The pursuit of the retreating Zulus at Gingindlovu.

The Zulu advance is stalled by British volley fire at the Battle of Ulundi, 4 July 1879.

Inside the square at Ulundi at the height of the battle, Wood and Chelmsford in the saddle, side by side. From an illustration by Melton Prior.

Charge of the 17th Lancers at Ulundi.

After the Battle of Ulundi, the royal kraal ablaze.

that it was only a matter of time before he was either captured or killed. He thus resolved to break out from the Buffalo River valley, where he was now virtually corralled. On 31 May, Sandile, with his forty strong bodyguard, fled the area but near isiDenge Hill, in the north-eastern plateau area of the Pirie Bush, they collided with a joint patrol of the FAMP and Mfengu. A short, but fierce firefight ensured. Seventeen warriors fell dead, including Dukwana, an elder and senior advisor to Sandile, who was a renowned marksman and who claimed two Mfengu dead and four wounded before he himself was slain. The surviving Xhosas fled the encounter, carrying a number of wounded with them. One of these was Sandile.

Sandile was carried away by his warriors. A Snider bullet had punctured Sandile's right side, smashing two ribs as it entered his body. The bullet would have shattered bone and the fragments must have caused intensive internal bleeding and damage to such organs as the liver. After days in agony, the chief died on 5 June. With no time for a burial, the surviving warriors laid Sandile's body under a bush near Fort Merriman and continued their flight. The British had no idea that the chief had even been wounded and it was only when a Ngqika warrior surrendered to a colonial patrol near Frankfort that the news of Sandile's death emerged. A party was immediately despatched to search for the corpse, and it was duly found where it had been left. Yet, identification was only possible because of the chief's withered leg for the body had been attacked by wild animals and much of Sandile's face and one of his arms had already been devoured.

The British slung the chief's body unceremoniously onto the back of a horse and it was brought back to the isiDenge camp where it was laid on a canvas sheet and displayed in a shed. It was important for the British to make sure that it became widely known that Sandile was dead, and they encouraged all to parade past the corpse, with its half-eaten face turned against the shed walls as a small gesture of respect to the chief. Mfengu warriors were permitted to dance past the body, jeering and verbally abusing their once-feared enemy. Sensation seekers were even permitted to snip off pieces of the chief's white beard as souvenirs or trophies. After two days of ritual humiliation the British finally gave Sandile a decent funeral at Schuch's farm, about 3km east of Mount Kempt. The proceedings were witnessed by about 500 Mfengu and all the imperial troops who were then in the vicinity.

Many of his contemporaries described Sandile as timid and a coward, yet he ended his days as a determined nationalist. Although an alcoholic, he managed to stop drinking when the war began. During his last years he rigorously maintained traditional customs and seldom appeared in European clothing. Charles Brownlee wrote, 'Notwithstanding his defects he was beloved by his people. They clung to him as the father of the [Ngqika] tribe.'[28]

The death of Sandile was not the only piece of good news that Thesiger was able to convey to the War Office. Writing to the Secretary of State on 12 June, he was also able to confirm that Siyolo had been killed in a chance encounter with a colonial patrol. Following Sandile's death other chiefs began to surrender. Sandile's sons, Edmund and Mathanzima, gave themselves up and received life prison sentences. Tini Maqoma was found working on a farm in the Waterkloof and captured. His death sentence was later commuted to life. These three and many other rebel leaders became prisoners on Robben Island, which would continue to house political prisoners up until 1991. Sandile's son, Gonye, was given hard labour working on a new breakwater for Cape Town harbour. Sarhili was able to avoid capture, despite a bounty of £1,000 and 500 cattle. He sought refuge in an inaccessible part of Bomvnanland territory and refused to emerge even when given a pardon in 1881. He eventually acquiesced to British rule and passed away in 1892, aged 83.

By the end of June not only was resistance at an end but the British were very keen to bring hostilities to a conclusion. The last operation in the Pirie Bush, although successful, had caused some disquiet. The colonial forces had taken to their task of hounding the last of the Xhosas with relish and reports began to emerge of the warriors being hunted down like vermin and of summary executions and other abuses. To bring a stop to further fighting the Cape government proclaimed, on 2 July, an amnesty for any Xhosa still fighting. The Ninth Frontier War had been particularly brutal. An estimated 3,680 warriors died in battle, which equated to a truly shocking 50 per cent casualty rate. This figure does not include combatants who died away from the battlefield of wounds or non-combatants who succumbed to starvation or exposure, and there seems little doubt that this figure must have run into the high hundreds, if not low thousands. Only 171 warriors were captured and again this figure illustrates the brutal nature of this war. There were 10 British and colonial officers and 48 men killed, with an additional

133 Mfengu perishing in battle. A further 10 officers, 47 men and 161 Mfengu were wounded.[29]

Although the Xhosa people had resisted stubbornly and the war had been a prolonged one, there was only ever going to be one eventual winner. Both Sarhili and Sandile knew that the Xhosa struggle with the British had really come to an end with their defeat at the conclusion of the Eighth Frontier War in 1853, yet both men had been unable to reconcile the Xhosa peoples to this truth. The younger generation, raised on the oral tradition of heroic defiance to white settlers and troops, had never known defeat and entered this final brutal conflict with an overwhelming desire to right perceived historical injustices as well as a strong sense of honour, which pervaded Xhosa society and led to unrealistic and false hopes.

In September 1878, Charles Brownlee informed the Ngqika that the colony government had decided to expel all members of the clan, even those that had not taken up arms, from the area. All Ngqika lands were to be forfeited and sold to white settlers and the Ngqika would be relocated to the western side of the former Gcaleka Reserve. Nearly 8,000 souls commenced the exodus to their new barren home. Many Ngqika managed to remain close to their ancestral lands by becoming labourers on white-owned farms whilst others moved to the Cape Peninsula as indentured labourers. Sarhili's followers, the Gcaleka, were settled close to the Ngqika in the eastern portion of the former Gcalekaland. Now disposed of their lands, their cattle and their military systems, the final tragedy of the Frontier Wars was brought to an end.

Thesiger had successfully concluded the Ninth Frontier War. Writing from Government House in Cape Town on 1 July 1878 to Cambridge, he showed his appreciation to the Duke for his appointment, 'I cannot be sufficiently grateful to Your Royal Highness for having given me the opportunity of commanding a force which by its excellent conduct has enabled me to bring a difficult war to so speedy a close.'[30] For his services in bringing the rebellion to a close Thesiger was promoted to the Most Honourable Order of the Bath to be a Knight Commander.

Yet, what of Thesiger's performance in his first independent field command? He had arrived in Southern Africa with the expectation that after the Xhosa defeat at Kentani the war was effectively over. Within days it was clear that this was not the case and he responded quickly and efficiently to ensure that imperial, colonial and Mfengu forces were brought into the field. However, he adopted Cunynghame's unsuccessful tactic of the bush 'sweep' to try to neutralize the Xhosa threat and despite repeated failures he stubbornly refused to consider alternatives. Finally, after what can be viewed an unnecessary and imprudent delay, he agreed to colonial suggestions and altered his strategy. That he at least condoned the brutal measures deployed in this last operation seems without doubt and this set a standard of how the Zulu people would be treated after the defeat of Isandlwana. Despite his gentlemanly demeanour, he displayed a ruthlessness if required.

Thesiger understood that the successful conclusion to the war rested with the performance of the imperial troops, who despite his initial misgivings had shown a resolute toughness as they marched and hacked their way across difficult terrain in sometimes appalling weather conditions. The FLH, under the tireless leadership of Buller, had also distinguished itself and both arms would do so again the following year. The general also had the grace to recognize the support of his hard-working officers and one in particular, Colonel Evelyn Wood, stood out for particular praise. Thesiger was to report to the War Office that, 'I cannot speak too highly of the good service rendered by this officer [Wood]. He has exercised his command with marked ability and great tact. I am of opinion that his indefatigable exertions and personal influence have been mainly instrumental in bringing the war to a speedy close.'[31] Thesiger would again come to praise both Buller and Wood the following year. Despite the general's inability to effectively delegate, it seems clear that once he had full trust in an individual, he would come to depend upon them.

Before the Ninth Frontier War had been officially concluded both Frere and Thesiger had turned their sights towards the east and the border of Natal where they perceived a fresh indigenous threat to British colonial rule from the Zulu nation. In his letter of 1 July to Cambridge, Thesiger had thanked the duke for sending out six further special service officers to assist the general in his efforts against the Xhosa. With that war now concluded Thesiger asked Cambridge if these officers could remain for in his eyes it was:

> ... more than probable that active steps will have to be taken to check the arrogance of Cetywayo, Chief of the Zulus. In such a case the service of all these officers will be most valuable and I trust Your Royal Highness will not object to my retaining them for a short time until I have had an opportunity of talking the situation over with Sir B. Frere.[32]

It is clear that Thesiger was already planning and plotting his next war.

Chapter 4

Plotting and Planning

The Zulu people originated from Nguni communities that took part in the great migrations of the ethnic Bantu peoples from western Africa over a period of many centuries, reaching the eastern coast of modern-day South Africa in the early sixteenth century. One group of these people detached themselves from the main Bantu migration and entered the previously unexplored coastal area on the eastern side of the Drakensberg Mountains bordering the Indian Ocean. This area measured a mere 40 by 100 miles and became settled by this group which comprised some 200 clans of the Nguni. This relatively insignificant area was attractive to these cattle-orientated Nguni peoples who thrived upon its well-watered and lush pastures. Over the next 200 years these numerous clans integrated via marriage and conquest and by the early nineteenth century the military and political power of one clan, the Zulu, came to the fore under the leadership of King Shaka.

The first significant British entry into the area that was to become Natal, which would abut the Zulu kingdom, occurred in 1822. The crew of HMS *Leven*, commanded by Captain William FitzWilliam Owen RN left Cape Town to survey the eastern coast of Southern Africa as far north as the Portuguese enclave at Delagoa Bay. Owen's voyage discovered that there was no natural harbour along this coastline and that indeed sand bars made any landings south of Delagoa Bay extremely hazardous. Yet, the arrival of the *Leven* in the area sparked the entrepreneurial imagination of two Englishmen, John Thompson, who already had a trading company at Delagoa Bay, and ex-Devonian Francis George Farewell. The latter decided to establish the Farewell Trading Company with the aim of establishing a suitable location in Natal for settlement and trade. The company's first action was to charter the merchant brig *Salisbury* owned by Captain James Saunder King. With Farewell on board, the crew failed, as Owen had before them, to find a spot to break through the dangerous sand bars. Yet, fate intervened for a violent storm drove the *Salisbury* over the bar and into Port

Natal. Here King and Farewell discovered a spacious bay, which provided shelter for shipping. Also, the surrounding countryside appeared fertile and well-watered, and the Farewell Trading Company decided that this was to be the location for the trading settlement. The *Salisbury* subsequently returned to Cape Town where Farewell drummed up sufficient interest and capital to return with two vessels and thirty settlers, led by Englishman Henry Francis Fynn, and by April 1824 the settlement of Port Natal, which would subsequently become Durban, witnessed the construction of the first buildings of the newest enterprise in Southern Africa.

Soon after landing, Fynn left most of the settlers to build shelters whilst he surveyed the hinterland. He soon discovered the local clan, named amaTuli, had only recently settled in the area in an attempt to evade constant cattle raids by the Zulu nation, led by their king, named Shaka. Fynn deduced that the whole of Natal was effectively part of Shaka's personal domain and resolved to visit the king in his royal residence of kwaBulawayo, 120 miles to the north. Farewell arrived with additional settlers and in July, having received a direct invitation from Shaka, whose warriors had been keeping a firm eye on the new settlement, both he and Fynn journeyed north. The two men must have been astonished at the sights that greeted them at kwaBulawayo. Shaka's capital, his royal kraal, was over a mile wide, spread over a gentle hillside. The central cattle pen housed nearly 6,000 cattle and was surrounded by 1,500 huts and a perimeter fence which was over 3 miles long. Shaka welcomed the two Englishmen with traditional displays of dancing, and friendships were sealed with the exchanges of gifts. The guests remained for two weeks during which time Shaka keenly learnt as much as he could from them about their language, culture and history. At the end of this time, Farewell was able to return to the coast having obtained Shaka's permission for the Farewell Trading Company to remain and trade at Port Natal. Fynn was to remain at kwaBulawayo and witnessed many of the horrors that regularly occurred at Shaka's court. The king was a mentally unstable man who was prone to sudden outbursts of cruelty and violence and Fynn was to record numerous occasions when on a whim Shaka would order random and sometimes large-scale executions of his subjects.

Just a few days after Farewell's return to Port Natal, Shaka was stabbed by a potential assassin and was severally wounded. Fynn rushed to the king's aid, washing and bandaging his injured body. Fynn's quick actions prevented Shaka's wounds from becoming infected and undoubtedly saved the king's life. Fynn's position was now assured, and he took full advantage by presenting Shaka with a deed to sign, which provided for outright title for the Farewell Trading Company to Port Natal and over 3,000 square miles of surrounding territory. It is unlikely that Shaka knew what he was putting his mark to, but Fynn was able to return to the coast with the document and on 27 August 1824 Farewell raised the Union Jack and proclaimed the area British territory.

Over the next few years, the prospects of the Port Natal settlement rose and fell depending on the health of the settlers, the level of investment Farewell could entice and even the kindness of the weather. During this period Fynn, Farewell, King and a young English emigrate, Nathaniel Isaacs, continued to build relations with Shaka. The king was obsessed with the firearms the settlers carried and Isaacs in particular spent many hours demonstrating how the muskets worked and even explained the concept of volley fire in ranks to maintain a wall of fire in battle, something that Shaka quickly grasped. Isaacs was even to lead a 5,000-strong Zulu impi (a group of warriors gathered together for war) into battle against a rival tribe and the 10 muskets carried and used by Isaacs and his men caused shock and devastation and won the day for the Zulu army.

Shaka's cruel and unstable rule was brought to a predictable end when he was stabbed to death by two of his stepbrothers, Dingane and Mhlangana, on 22 September 1828. Shaka's kingdom stretched from the Swazi border in the north to central Natal and then from there to the Drakensberg Mountains to the coast. The settlement of Port Natal, which Shaka could have obliterated at any time, remained in a vacuum. Shaka's thirst for knowledge had kept the settlers safe. This was to change with the succession of the new king, Dingane. Relations had quickly deteriorated between Dingane and Mhlangana and in a matter of just a few weeks following Shaka's assassination Dingane had his stepbrother murdered and he assumed to the throne. Like Shaka, Dingane was obsessed with gaining firearms and the settlers were able, initially, to maintain cordial relations with the new king, even supplying a limited number of muskets. Trade improved and Fynn managed to secure a regular supply of ivory. Into the 1830s Port Natal attracted more settlers and investors and the settlement continued to grow, admittedly at a slow pace. The stability that Port Natal had enjoyed was threatened with the arrival of Boer trekkers from the mid-1830s onwards as the Boers emigrated away from the Cape as part of the 'Great Trek', in search of their own independent lands.

For the settlers of Port Natal, now officially known as Durban in honour of the Cape Governor Sir Benjamin D'Urban, it was the trek led by Piet Retief with 120 families in 1837 that would have the greatest impact. Retief led his followers through the Drakensberg range into western Natal, and en route his party clashed and defeated the Matabele in battle, something even the Zulus had failed to do. On the periphery of Dingane's domain, Retief settled and then carried on with fifteen men to Durban to secure help from the settlers there to trade with Dingane and obtain the king's permission to remain. With the support of a British missionary named Gardiner, and the help of one of the original settlers of Port Natal, Thomas Holsted, acting as interpreter, Retief arrived at Dingane's royal kraal at emGungundhlovu in November 1837. Although presenting an outward show of friendship, Dingane clearly had great suspicions regarding the motives of the Boers and of the firepower they possessed. Retief was able to return to Durban with the news that Dingane had given his authority for the Boers to settle, and this was quickly conveyed to hundreds of Boers who were waiting in the passes of the Drakensberg range. The news was jubilantly received and within just a few weeks over a thousand wagons journeyed into Natal and camped in laagers (encampment encircled by wagons) along the upper Tugela River and its tributaries. Such a large migration was duly reported back to Dingane and the news seemed to confirm the king's fears that the Boers were set on invasion rather than settlement of his territory.

Retief returned with Holsted and sixty-nine Boer commandos to the royal kraal in February 1838 and after what seemed to be cordial discussions, Dingane agreed to put his mark to a document that Retief had drafted which ceded Natal from the Umzimvubu River to the Tugela and from the Drakensberg to the sea, including Durban, to the Boer leader as governor of this land. On the morning of 6 February, just at Retief and his men were due to depart, Dingane enticed the Boer party to a farewell dance. Once the Boers had settled themselves, Dingane suddenly jumping to his feet and screamed the order 'Bambani abaThakathi!', 'Kill the wizards!'. The group was seized and dragged out of the kraal to a hilltop and here each Boer was impaled and then had his head smashed. Retief was the last to die, having been forced to witness the execution of all his men. Thomas Holsted was amongst the dead, and he became the first, but by no means the last, British man to be killed at the hands of the Zulus. Dingane then sent out three impis to attack some of the laagered settlers, which with the death of the men were largely helpless against the overwhelming number of warriors. Boer victims numbered 282, including 185 children.

Dingane had clearly felt threatened and intimidated by Retief and his followers but far from extinguishing the flame of Boer expansionism, it increased the Boer ambition to secure lands in Natal as well as a desire for revenge. Whilst the Boers, under the leadership of Piet Uys and Hendrik Potgieter, hastily assembled commandos to attack Dingane's warriors, the British in Durban were in uproar at the death of Holsted and the threat that Dingane now posed. In early March John Cane led a number of Europeans out from Durban and with up to 2,000 native warriors, allied to Cane and his men, this group struck at some Zulu kraals near Kranz Kop and returned to Durban victorious with 4,000 head of cattle. Cane had been lucky for most of the Zulu warriors had been summoned to the royal kraal and he had met little resistance. Dingane naturally saw this attack as an act of war and Cane must have realized that his action would have inflamed the Zulu king. Yet, considering that an offensive approach was the best option, Cane, on 12 April 1838, once again led out a force of 17 Europeans and 800 natives towards the Tugela. This time a 10,000-strong Zulu impi, commanded by Mpande, Dingane's younger half-brother, and with Mpande's young son Cetshwayo present, descended upon Cane's command. Only 4 Europeans managed to escape, the remainder, Cane amongst them, were killed along with 500 native allies. Mpande now launched his warriors upon Durban itself and arrived on 24 April. Around half a dozen settlers were able to flee and seek refuge on the nearby Salisbury Island. For the remainder luck was on their side, for a vessel, the *Comet*, was moored off the coast and took on board these fortunate individuals. The settler families watched from the decks of the *Comet* as Mpande's warriors ransacked Durban and hunted down those natives who had not been able to flee in time.

Despite the fact that Natal and Durban clearly belonged to Dingane, and that Europeans could only reside there under the king's sufferance, the British authorities in Cape Town saw it differently. Although not willing to annex Natal, the British government viewed all Europeans, both those from Britain and the recently emigrated Boers, as British subjects under Crown law and justice. Until Dingane's assault upon both the Boer settlers and Durban the authorities had no intention of enforcing that view, but the death of Europeans at the hands of Zulu warriors had suddenly altered British policy. With pressure mounting on the new governor, Sir George Napier, for action to secure Durban once more, he finally relented and despatched eighty men of the 72nd Highlanders, under the command of Major Samuel Charters, Royal Artillery. On his arrival on 3 December 1838 Charters discovered that the Boers had been busy in the absence of British settlers and had annexed the settlement in May, reverting to its old name of Port Natal. In the absence of the Boer commando which, led by Andries Pretorius, had left to move against Dingane, Charters ignored the dubious Boer legal action and once more hoisted the Union Jack, and waited the return of Pretorius.

Pretorius and his commando achieved military success beyond their wildest dreams against Dingane. Crossing the Buffalo River, the Boers skirmished with Zulu patrols and secured for themselves a strong defensive position on the banks of the Ncome River where Pretorius ordered the formation of a wagon laager. The Boer leader gambled that Dingane would not be able to resist attacking this position and indeed on the morning of 16 December 1838 Dingane unleashed around 12,000 of his warriors against the Boers. The Battle of Blood River, as it is now named, raged for 2 hours and time and time again the Zulus hurled themselves at the Boer position, but the wagons were well secured and offered a strong barrier from behind which the Boers kept up an accurate and almost continuous fire. At the end of the fight the Boers had won a crushing victory, sustaining only 4 wounded, whilst the number of warriors killed ranged from between 3,000 and 5,000. The commando now pushed on to the royal kraal at emGungundhlovu and although Dingane had fled, Pretorius and his men had the satisfaction of burning the kraal to the ground.

Even though the Zulu army still outnumbered the Boers, the fortunes of the Europeans were certainly enhanced by the Battle of Blood River. Never again would Dingane throw his warriors at Boer laagers and his prestige and kingly power had been fatally weakened. The Boer trekkers now poured into Natal and with British troops in Durban they decided to establish the capital of 'The Free Province of New Holland' on a site 50 miles inland from Durban on Natal's central plateau, the centre of the best farming country. The new town was named Pietermaritzburg, in honour of Piet Retief and Gerrit Maritz. Although Charters still considered the Boers as subjects of the Crown, he, with his limited number of troops, could do nothing to oppose the establishment of this new republic. A sullen Dingane returned to rebuild his royal kraal whilst he continued to plot the removal of the Boers. To restore his battered military reputation Dingane ordered a successful military expedition against the Swazi, but his demand that his half-brother Mpande journey to emGungundhlovu was ignored, as Mpande feared that Dingane wished him dead. Mpande fled south across the Tugela with 17,000 of his own followers and received the political support of the Boers. The garrison of British troops withdrew from Durban in December 1839. The authorities viewed Natal as peaceful and that there seemed to be little threat to Durban from either the Boers or the Zulus. All this would quickly change.

The Boers wasted no time and with the British troops no longer in Natal the Boer flag was soon flying over Durban, much to the distress of the British residents. With the political situation now in their favour the Boers turned to the elimination of the threat from Dingane, for the Boer leadership knew the king could never be trusted. Travelling north and crossing the Tugela, a Boer commando, 350-strong and under the command once more of Pretorius, moved into Zululand on 21 January 1840 with a large contingent of Mpande's followers and Mpande himself as a hostage to guarantee the behaviour of his warriors. Whilst the Boers waited at the site of the Battle of Blood River, Mpande's warriors sought out Dingane and at the Battle of Magonggo many of Dingane's own troops deserted to Mpande's army and he was decisively beaten. Dingane fled north and sought refuge in the Lubombo Mountains. Here he was discovered by a party of Swazi and killed. The Boers quickly proclaimed Mpande King of the Zulus and their dominance over Natal now seemed complete. They had found their new home in just five years since leaving the Cape.

Yet, Boer dominance was to be the root of their eventual political retreat from the area. The British government was finally awoken to the political threat posed by the Boers' success and that in Mpande they had a king who seemed to acquiesce to the Boer demands for lands and authority. Napier was duly ordered to send troops back to Durban. The Boer parliament, the Volksraad, housed in Pietermaritzburg, resolved to oppose the British and Pretorius was once more to lead a commando, this time to Durban to confront the newly arrived troops of the 27th Foot, commanded by Captain Thomas Charlton Smith. Pretorius occupied Congella on the shores of Durban Bay, whilst Smith reacted by building an earthen fort to cover the settlement.

For nearly three weeks the two forces faced each other, neither willing to make the first offensive move. Finally, on the night of 23 May 1840, Smith led his force against Congella. Pretorius was wise to this surprise attack and positioned his men for a devastating ambush and in a brisk firefight Smith was forced to return to his fort with over thirty wounded and twenty dead. The British were now effectively besieged, low on both food and water, but Smith would not consider Pretorius' terms for surrender. Smith ordered one of the four survivors of Cane's earlier defeat to the Zulus, a man name Dick King, to escape from the fort and ride the 600 miles across country to the nearest British troops in Grahamstown. King covered the distance in just ten days, despite being pursued by some of Pretorius' men and arrived in a near state of collapse to inform the troops there of Smith's desperate plight.

The fate of the Natal republic was now sealed. The British were never going to tolerate open rebellion or allow its troops to be attacked. With Smith still holding out, the garrison at Grahamstown managed to despatch five companies, under the command of Colonel Josias Cloete, for the relief of Durban. These troops duly arrived on HMS *Southampton* and after a thirty-four-day siege Smith was relieved. Pretorius had the sense to retire back to the bush. Cloete was now ready to take the fight to the Boers. Mpande realized that his allegiance to the Boers had been misplaced and as Cloete advanced towards the Boer capital, Mpande offered the British his military support. Cloete declined the offer and when he arrived in Pietermaritzburg he found the town in turmoil, which was not calmed when he presented the Boers with his terms. These included submission to Queen Victoria, which was reluctantly accepted. With British authority now restored, Cloete departed with some of his command for Afghanistan whilst the rest remained in Durban with Smith.

The political situation remained something of an ambivalent stalemate for the next two years whilst Napier exchanged thoughts and letters with London, and it was not until December 1842 that the government decided that Natal should become a British colony. This was formally announced in May 1843 and Cloete's brother, Henry Cloete, a barrister, was appointed as High Commissioner and despatched to Natal to begin the political process. Cloete received a decidedly frosty welcome in Pietermaritzburg regarding the government's proposals and it took all the barrister's powers of persuasion to convince the Volksraad to accept their fate. On 31 August, Smith and his command were able to hoist the Union Jack in Pietermaritzburg and the

Boer republic of Natal ceased to exist. Within ten years of the Great Trek, most of the Boers who felt that they had found their new home were on the move once more. With an influx of 5,000 British settlers between 1849 and 1852, the settler society acquired a very different cast and whilst Durban prospered, Pietermaritzburg declined. Although some Boers remained on isolated farms, many journeyed north back over the Drakensberg where another Boer republic would be established in the Transvaal.

Once negotiations had been concluded with the Boers Cloete visited Mpande and it was the king's clear dislike of the Boers and willingness to work with the British that become a factor in the government's decision to make Natal a colony. Cloete and Mpande reached an agreement that the border between Natal and the independent Zululand should run along the line of the Mzinyathi and Thukela rivers, cancelling all earlier agreements with the Boers. This boundary would remain until the crisis of 1879. Critically, however, no former boundary was agreed between Zululand and the Transvaal in the north-west and this was to become the cause of later conflict. The political theatre continued with the appointment of Martin West as the first Lieutenant Governor and Theophilus Shepstone as Agent for Native Affairs to the Zulus. Finally, on 15 July 1856, Natal officially became a separate colony of the British Crown.

Mpande remained on the throne until his death in 1872 and thus became the longest reigning Zulu king. However, from the 1856 onwards his role was largely ceremonial. Although the oldest of Mpande's sons, Cetshwayo's succession was disputed by his brother Mbuyazi. To avoid conflict Mpande ceded territory to Mbuyazi and his followers on the Tugela. Each brother cultivated factions and it was Cetshwayo who eventually took direct action. He invaded Mbuyazi's lands and at the Battle of Ndondakusuka on 2 December 1856 Cetshwayo gained a crushing victory, which saw the death of his brother and the massacre of his followers. Cetshwayo now became de facto ruler and continued his father's policy of balancing relations between the Boers in the north and the British to the south-west.

Throughout this period, Shepstone, as Agent for Native Affairs, had cultivated strong links with the Zulu nation so much so that he orchestrated the 'coronation' of Cetshwayo when he was installed as king on 1 September 1873. As was customary, the new king established his own royal kraal, at Ulundi. Cetshwayo was very much aware of the encroachment of the Boers into Zululand and he used his relationship with Shepstone to urge the British to rule upon land disputes between the Boers and Zulus and a boundary commission would later find in favour of the Zulus. Cetshwayo established and maintained his own strength by following many of the military ways of Shaka and he expanded his army and attempted to source firearms. To reinforce Zulu culture, he banished European missionaries from his lands. These acts were viewed by many in Natal and beyond as aggressive measures and many missionaries and even Shepstone himself took every opportunity to warn anyone who would listen that Cetshwayo and his impis presented a tangible and immediate threat to the security of Southern Africa. Cetshwayo was portrayed by these interest groups as a bloodthirsty tyrant with a large standing army of highly disciplined warriors who could at any moment invade neighbouring Natal and the Transvaal. Whilst it is true that Cetshwayo had been ruthless in his rise to power and that the king's authority rested with his army, he never wished for war with the British and indeed did his utmost to avoid conflict.

Sir Henry Bartle Frere spent most of his political life in India and it was here that he first met Frederic Thesiger. Frere was approaching retirement when Carnarvon, Secretary of State for the Colonies, persuaded him to go to Southern Africa as high commissioner and governor of the Cape colony to pursue the Secretary of State's desire to confederate the British colonies in the sub-continent. Before his arrival Shepstone had achieved the political coup of convincing the reluctant Boers of the bankrupt Transvaal republic to join confederation. The Boers were aggrieved, and Shepstone convinced himself, and then Frere, that they might be appeased if the British took a hard stance towards Cetshwayo. Shepstone had also determined that the king was a real threat to the security of the region as the head of a massive pan-African onslaught against white dominance. Frere's experience of the recently ended Frontier War and of continued disquiet from the Pedi people of eastern Transvaal led him to choose to believe that Cetshwayo was the puppet master behind this widespread agitation. His experiences of the uprising against British rule in India in 1857, where he served in Sind Province, may also have led him to be overly sensitive to a similarly styled rebellion in Southern Africa.

Frere also possessed a hard-headed belief in his own abilities which saw him never doubting that what he thought was correct and, of course, as governor of the colony and High Commissioner the government had placed him in a position of unrivalled power. In addition, Frere had attended the

Prince of Wales on his 1875 tour of India, and helped with the organization of the tour, and after this he maintained a friendly contact with the royal family, including Victoria and the Duke of Cambridge, and perhaps this made him more willing to act independently. Captain W. Molyneux, one of Thesiger's ADCs, explained:

> He had a wonderfully quiet deliberate manner of speaking, never hesitating, and never at a loss for the right word, giving you the idea that whatever might be the subject of conversation he knew much more about it than any of his audience. He impressed us all as a cool headed diplomatist, and we recognised that he was one who was doing his best for the good of the state, and one who had the will, the determination and the power to carry out any policy that he thought would be for the best.[1]

Soon after Frere's arrival in 1877 he convinced himself that Zululand should not remain autonomous. Carnarvon, the architect of confederation and Frere's patron, resigned in 1878 and was replaced by Sir Michael Hicks Beach who failed to understand either confederation or Frere. Hicks Beach urged caution and in the final instance forbade war with Cetshwayo, yet the tone of Hicks Beach's correspondence suggests vacillation and diffidence. As early as January 1878, British troops fighting the Xhosa were openly discussing the possibility of war with the Zulus. Captain Woodgate arrived in Cape Town in June 1878 and wrote home that, 'Opinions differ as to whether there is to be a Zulu War or not, but a force is to go into the Transvaal to be in readiness', and that action against the Zulus had only been held back 'to get the Kaffir War over first'.[2] On 23 June 1878, Major Harness was confident enough to write to his sister that, 'It is said that it is determined to make Cetewayo [sic] fight or give in entirely.'[3]

In addition, there seems to have been a strong belief amongst the British in Southern Africa that Cetshwayo was the head of a movement to unsettle white dominance. Percy Barrow, who fought the Xhosa and was charged with raising a detachment of Mounted Infantry for a possible Zulu invasion, wrote in September 1878 to Sir Archibald Alison, head of army intelligence, in London that:

> The difficulties in the Cape Colony have been settled, but Natal and Transvaal have now to be dealt with and the general opinion amongst

soldiers, colonists and all is that until the Zulu power has been broken there is no possible way of permanently settling the question. We have a small campaign going on now against Sekhukune in the Transvaal. Griqualand West is also giving us trouble, but there is not the smallest doubt that Cetshwayo is at the bottom of all these disturbances …[4]

What of Thesiger's views as to any forthcoming conflict with Cetshwayo? Certainly, by June 1878 his thoughts were turning to preparation and planning for an invasion of Zululand. In early July Thesiger journeyed to Cape Town and stayed for a few days as a guest of Frere in Government House. Behind locked doors the talk was of the Zulu threat and how it might be neutralized. There is no record of what was formally discussed between the two men but there can be little doubt Frere would have used his charm, the friendship between the two men and his natural authority to convince the general of the danger Cetshwayo presented. Thesiger would also have displayed his diffidence to the political figure that Frere represented so it is hard to imagine that he would have taken much persuading that war was inevitable. Indeed, by 8 July Thesiger was writing to Shepstone that, 'The Zulus have been very kind to us to abstain from any hostile movements during the time we were so busily engaged … if they will only wait until next month I hope to have the troops somewhat better prepared than they are at present'.[5]

It is apparent the Thesiger genuinely believed that the Zulus presented a real threat to Natal and the security of the whole of Southern Africa. In a letter to Shepstone written on 21 July Thesiger clearly demonstrated that his views were now far more pugnacious than they had been just a month before:

If we are to have a fight with the Zulus, I am anxious that our arrangements should be as complete as it is possible to make them. Half measures do not answer with natives. They must be thoroughly crushed to make them believe in our superiority; and if I am called upon to conduct operations against them, I shall strive to be in a position to show them how hopelessly inferior they are to us in fighting power although numerically stronger.[6]

At the same time Thesiger wrote to Cambridge, 'Reports regarding the Zulus are very conflicting. I am quietly doing all I can to be ready for active operations against them, and Sir B. Frere is giving me every possible assistance.'[7]

Frere justified the general's military preparations by stating that they were simply defensive precautions. Throughout 1878, he began to prepare the British government for the potential of war. However, it became clear that the newly appointed Colonial Secretary, Sir Michael Hicks Beach, did not share Frere's military enthusiasm, though Frere continued to work hard to convince Hicks Beach of the threat. He magnified minor border infringements by the Zulus into major acts of aggression and generally raised the level of tension so much so that Cetshwayo himself wrote, 'I hear of troops arriving in Natal, that they are coming to attack the Zulus, and to seize me ... I do not wish to quarrel with them, but to live as I have always done at peace with them.'[8]

Frere continued to prepare the political ground for an ultimatum to Cetshwayo, not just with Hicks Beach but also officials in Natal, and in particular Sir Henry Bulwer, the lieutenant governor of Natal, with whom relations were strained. Bulwer felt, quite rightly, that Frere was trying to force an unnecessary war. Thesiger would also clash with Bulwer over manpower and the logistics of preparing for the war. Frere had even decided how Zulus would be dealt with after their defeat. His ideas were based on principles similar to those deployed in India; Zululand would not be annexed, but would be governed by indirect rule, with compliant chiefs responsible to a British agent. The border would be closed, and Zululand would be demilitarized and slot neatly into Frere's designs for confederation. Such thinking would prove to be very premature.

Throughout August to November 1878, Frere regularly communicated with Hicks Beach to paint a picture of Zulu aggression and the need for a British military response. In one letter Frere wrote:

My mistrust [of the Zulus] is not because they are semi-savages; but because they are a military nation, and Cetywayo's [sic] object is to keep up their military character. They generally believe themselves to be invincible – under similar circumstances I would not trust to any people, King or Emperor, in Christendom to abstain from aggression. I do not believe anything will induce them so to abstain unless they are thoroughly convinced of our superior power; and I do not see any chance of their being so convinced till they have tried their strength against us and learned by sad experience.[9]

At the same time Frere also frequently wrote to Sir Robert Herbert, Permanent Under-Secretary at the Colonial Office, and on 23 September 1878 Frere begged Herbert to read his 'official despatch by this mail, and to move the Cabinet by all means in [his] power to send out reinforcements'. Frere added:

> There is no lack of prophets of peace hereabouts, but I feel convinced that the Zulus are boiling over with warlike conceit and will not let us alone. If you wish for a speedy and satisfactory issue, you must give us more men of the only kind that can be immediately available to take off the edge of the attack which I feel assured cannot be long avoided.[10]

Writing to Herbert on 28 October, Frere again requested reinforcements and stated that he feared for Natal unless the Zulu threat could be tamed, '… I feel sure there will be no permanent security here, till the Zulus have learnt that they are not the greatest military power in the world'.[11]

On 10 November Frere shared his firm belief with Herbert that confederation depended on negating the Zulu threat, 'I wish H.M. Government could see plainly as I do, how everything in South Africa hangs on the Zulu question – Transvaal contentment and Transvaal finance, and all chance of Confederation depend on its being settled, to say nothing of the peace of the border'.[12]

Whilst there is no doubt that Frere acted in a contrived manner to force an ultimatum for war, there is no reason to believe that he was not firm in his belief that the military defeat of the Zulu nation was justified both in terms of security and for the political aspirations of confederation. Yet, Frere's constant requests for reinforcements to tackle the perceived Zulu threat received a body blow when Hicks Beach's letter dated 28 November reached him. With Britain heavily involved in conflict in Afghanistan the last thing the British government wanted was another war. Hicks Beach stated that he had had the 'greatest possible difficulty' in impressing upon the Cabinet Frere's request for reinforcements and that his Cabinet colleagues were 'most anxious not to have Zulu war'. Furthermore, Hicks Beach wrote, 'The Afghanistan Affair has therefore arisen at a most unfortunate time: and you will see how much the risk arising would be increased by the addition of a Zulu war. Therefore [the Cabinet] wished me to impress upon you most strongly the necessity of avoiding aggression and using all proper means to keep out of war.'[13]

Whilst Frere was attempting to manipulate the political situation, it fell to Thesiger to ensure that preparations were firmly in place for an operation against Cetshwayo. He arrived in Natal in August and immediately began to assess what he needed to do to bring his command into a ready state for an offensive. The general quickly realized that the most pressing issues were the lack of readiness of the white residents of Natal to defend their border with Zululand, the lack of wagons for the advancing army to transport stores, ammunition, etc., inadequate intelligence on, and maps of, the region and the urgent need to secure the services of a native contingent to increase Thesiger's manpower.

The last of these concerns put the general on a collision course with Sir Henry Bulwer, the lieutenant governor of Natal. Thesiger knew that he was short of mounted troops and had expected to recruit sufficient numbers from the Natal colonial community. He also wanted a force of native levies, and these men would be used for a variety of tasks, but their greatest asset would be to provide mobility to the slow-moving British columns for they could range in advance and scout the terrain and provide intelligence. On his arrival, and to his dismay, Thesiger discovered that the colony seemed detached from the possibility of a coming war and ill-prepared for its defence. Furthermore, Bulwer was determined to ward off any possible confrontation. He felt both Thesiger and Frere were set on conflict and Bulwer was very much against mobilizing either the colonists or a native levy in case such moves were misconstrued by Cetshwayo as an act of aggression. The general was forced to call upon Frere to journey to Natal to use all his skills of diplomacy, and if that failed to work, impose his authority on Bulwer.

Throughout September and into October Bulwer continued to prevaricate. Finally, he did relent and allowed the colonial volunteers to vote on whether they would be willing to serve under the British and break from tradition and fight outside the borders of Natal. The vote went in Thesiger's favour, and he acquired the services of nearly 400 mounted colonials, who would be invaluable for their knowledge of the region and their fighting qualities. It would not be until November before Bulwer conceded on Thesiger's demand to raise a native levy. Frere's timetable for invasion was now firmly in place and at this late stage Thesiger (who was by now Lord Chelmsford following the death of his father at the end of October) was forced to move quickly. Fortunately, he was aided by Lieutenant Colonel Anthony Durnford, a

Royal Engineer, who had years of experience of working with and fighting alongside the native troops.

Durnford's original plan for the native contingent was that they would be organized and officered on essentially British regimental lines and recruited largely from tribes who had been displaced by earlier Zulu aggression. Each man was to be issued with obsolete British uniforms and firearms. However, the Natal Assembly refused to agree to natives being issued with firearms in any significant quantities, fearing an armed uprising, and insufficient uniforms could be found in government stores. It was eventually agreed that just one in ten of what became known as the Natal Native Contingent (NNC) would be issued with largely old percussion rifles whilst the remainder would carry their traditional weapons. In place of a uniform each man received a blanket and a red cloth to tie around their head or arm to distinguish them from the enemy. The NNC divided into three regiments, with Durnford in command of the 1st, which consisted of three battalions each of 1,000 men. The 2nd and 3rd Regiments each contained two battalions and were, respectively, commanded by Major Shapland Graves and Commandant Rupert La Tour Lonsdale. Companies were led by white officers and the soldierly qualities of many of these men, who were often those seeking adventure or from the dregs of the colony's society, left something to be desired. Despite the various handicaps that the NNC faced, historian John Laband considered that:

> ... the NNC was indispensable to the British victory. It did much that the available British regulars could not do, and for which the settler militia was insufficient. Take the NNC away in the 2nd invasion and many more of the British infantry and lumbering British cavalry would have been tied up on lengthening lines of communication. The mounted African troops, in conjunction with similar small colonial units, were the indispensable eyes and ears of the advancing British columns.[14]

With the issue of sufficient native manpower resolved, Chelmsford's focus was upon securing sufficient wagons for his proposed invasion columns and to ensure that the necessary supplies accompanied his men forward. When he arrived in Natal in August the general soon realized that the commissariat was over-stretched, under-manned and chaotic. Led by Commissary General Edward Strickland, it had just nineteen officers and twenty-nine men available to organize supplies and transport. Indeed, logistics were to be a constant problem for the British throughout the campaign. The general appointed Colonel Wood to chair a board to examine and advise him on how to resolve the problem of insufficient transport and he urgently telegraphed London requesting a draft of captains to be sent to Natal to supplement the commissariat. Whilst the board and the commissariat decided whether to hire or purchase wagons, Chelmsford acted on his own and ordered the purchase of 200 wagons. This sudden move resulted in a significant price increase throughout the country and the army was struck hard by speculators. This was also the case with both oxen and horses. Horses which were selling for £2 per head at the start of 1878 were being traded for £40 or more by the autumn. Oxen simply could not be bought for their Southern African owners would only hire them out on a monthly basis at rates in excess of the beasts' real value. With costs soaring Chelmsford demanded that Bulwer impose martial law which would have allowed his army to commandeer all the necessary wagons and animals, but Bulwer refused.

The task confronting Chelmsford is made clear in two pieces of correspondence sent to Sir Archibald Alison from two staff officers. In the first from John North Crealock, written on 25 November, it is evident that Crealock despaired of the quality of staff in the commissariat:

The transport and commissariat is slithering on from bad to worse. The 2 senior officers Pennell [Assistant Commissary General Croker Lovell Baker Pennell] has had to throw up; the next senior man, Phillips [Assistant Commissary General George Hutchinson Phillips was senior commissariat officer, No. 5 Column], is (so say Wood, Buller and others who have worked with him) useless and there is no one to take up the reins if Strickland [Commissary General E. Strickland, head of commissariat] gives in which, which is not improbable.[15]

Cornelius Clery confirmed Crealock's view in a letter dated 6 December in which he said:

Well, I don't think you can well conceive anything so utterly inefficient as the transport department of the commissariat. This advance into Zululand has been contemplated as a moral certainty for the last six months and yet this utter neglect of transport was allowed to go on. Who is responsible for this I cannot say as I have never been at headquarters, but between ourselves the headquarters staff is very weak. This I think is partly the general's own fault as he not only does too much himself but thinks he can do without an immediate staff.[16]

Clery had perceptively commented on the general's inability to delegate and that he had far too small a staff. Clery himself was diverted from Wood's command to become Colonel Glyn's principal staff officer and in this role had direct contact with Chelmsford and his staff. The staff were Major Matthew Gosset, Lieutenant Berkely Milne RN, Commander Fletcher Campbell RN and Lieutenant Colonel John North Crealock. The latter had a reputation for haughtiness and a sharp tongue. Relations between Crealock and Bulwer were frequently hostile. In December 1878 Bulwer wrote, 'He [Chelmsford] and Major Crealock, his military secretary, are not very pleasant to deal with in official matters … To a great extent I fancy Crealock is to blame for this. He is a sort of military wasp.'[17] Chelmsford had not even considered it necessary to appoint a staff officer with responsibility for intelligence until late in the campaign, preferring to rely on reports from local agents, which would often prove to be faulty. The lack of supportive staff and his own inability to delegate would be a serious weakness. This was evident in the transport debacle.

Chelmsford, in his usual 'hands on' manner, devised a solution to the transport issue and ordered each unit to appoint an officer of transport to support the overworked commissariat. These men were tasked with coordinating and assuming responsibility for their own unit's transport requirements, assisted by a sub-conductor. By moving transport responsibilities down to this lower level those who were directly affected by the problem had to deal with it and this move by Chelmsford did alleviate the transport issues. Yet, by involving himself in the minutiae of the invasion plan Chelmsford was not only exhausting himself (Crealock was to write to Alison that, 'Our general looks sadly fagged and weary, and no wonder; he works from morning to night and he never spares himself.'[18]), he was also taking vital time away from his day when he might be better predisposed to consider his own strategy for the forthcoming conflict.

During October Chelmsford embarked on a tour of inspection of the border region to assess proposed invasion routes. From his experiences of fighting the Xhosa, he sincerely believed that he would struggle to bring a Zulu army out into the open to fight. Chelmsford even thought that if he advanced with all his forces in one large column, he would deter the Zulus from fighting, and he was concerned that one large column could easily be outflanked by the Zulus who might then threaten his lines of communication or even the weak defences of Natal. He initially proposed that his force of just over 17,000 men, which included 6 battalions of imperial infantry and 6 companies of the 99th Foot, Royal Artillery, the warriors of the NNC and the FLH, commanded by Redvers Buller, and various colonial mounted units, would advance in 5 columns, yet his logistical problems forced the general to restrict this to 3 invasion columns. The Central Column, or Number 3 Column, would advance from Rorke's Drift. Number 4 Column, commanded by Colonel Wood, would invade into northern Zululand, whilst Number 1 Column, led by Colonel Pearson, was to advance in the south. Chelmsford's aim was for all three columns to converge on the Zulu capital at Ulundi. He felt that each column would be strong enough to defeat any Zulu army it encountered and if Cetshwayo refused battle, the British would force the issue at Ulundi. Neither of the three columns, spaced as they were, could be mutually supportive of each other if they encountered opposition and each would be reliant on their superior firepower to defeat the enemy. Chelmsford placed himself with the Central Column and although this was nominally under the command of Colonel Glyn, the general's presence effectively made him the commander of this column. Chelmsford was critically short of mounted troops; there was no imperial cavalry in Africa, and he was thus reliant on the FLH and a few hundred colonial mounted units, such as the Natal Carbineers and the Buffalo Border Guard, for reconnaissance as well as pursuit of the mobile Zulu army.

Chelmsford described his plans to Frere:

The plan I have laid is not so ambitious as a rapid march upon Ulundi and the occupation of the King's kraal, but I am certain it is the only safe one under the circumstances. It would be impossible to keep a long line of road passable for a convoy of wagons and were we to advance far into the country it would be almost certain that, instead of our supplies coming to us we should have to return for our supplies. A retrograde movement would have a very bad effect on our native forces and would certainly encourage our enemies.[19]

Chelmsford realized that transport and re-supply of his advancing army would likely be problematic, so he ordered that a series of supply depots should be established along each column's line of march. Thus, in theory, the columns could be resupplied daily. The magnitude of this undertaking can be seen when it is considered that all supplies, from biscuits to ammunition, had to be brought the 150 miles from Durban by oxen, a journey of at least ten days. By the middle of November, no less than thirty-five troopships were laying outside Durban disembarking men and munitions. Transport rates between Durban and Pietermaritzburg, ordinarily quoted at from £3 to £5 per ton, had risen to £24 per ton.

The Central Column had supply depots located at Helpmekaar and Rorke's Drift, Wood's Northern Column utilized an existing Boer laager at Utrecht for its depot, and later a more advanced depot was established at Conference Hill. The Coastal Column initially used Fort Pearson on the Natal bank of the Tugela River and once Pearson had advanced the depot moved across the river to Fort Tenedos. Chelmsford ensured that Strickland was aware of his department's responsibility to provide fifteen days of supplies at these depots which, Chelmsford calculated, would allow the columns to be resupplied whilst moving 10 miles a day towards their joint target of Ulundi. Yet, with the tents for a single battalion of approximately 800 men weighing more than 9 tons and a single battalion eating at least a ton of food a day, Strickland's task was an unenviable one. With his usual hands-on approach Chelmsford in November and into December visited all the supply depots and on at least one occasion was sharp in his rebuke of Strickland, who was stationed in Pietermaritzburg, over the situation he found at Rorke's Drift. Chelmsford wrote:

I have been across the Buffalo river today to see how the depot [at Rorke's Drift] was going. I find that there is absolutely nothing there and this column cannot move until there is a month's supply in hand over and above the fifteen day's regimental supply with the column ... You must send up one of the new Assistant Commissary-Generals who are on their way out [from England] at once to Helpmekaar, or we shall have a breakdown. There is no one here like Colonel Wood to keep everyone up to the mark and Helpmekaar appears to me to have been sadly neglected ... This column will advance shortly, and it will be a sad disgrace to the Commissariat, if it is obliged to halt short of its destination for the want of supplies.[20]

Number 5 Column, under Colonel Hugh Rowlands, would remain largely static on the border of the Transvaal to guard against the three threats of Boer unrest, a possible incursion of the Pedi under Chief Sekhukhune, or even an attack by Zulus. Number 2 Column, commanded by Colonel Durnford was initially held in reserve at Middle Drift by Chelmsford but Durnford was to be called upon to support the Central Column after the invasion began. Durnford's column largely comprised native troops, with the 1st Battalion of the NNC making up the majority. Crucially, the column also included five troops of mounted Africans, the Natal Native Horse (NNH), and within these five groups some of the troops were named after the location from which they came, such as the Edendale Troop, or after their chief, the Sikhali Horse.

It would appear that by early January 1879 Chelmsford had achieved a miracle in turning around both the transport and supply issues and had even secured a sizeable force in the NNC. Although his plans for invasion had had to be modified from five invasion columns to three, through his tireless work he was able to put to Frere a plan for the invasion of Zululand. Yet, at what cost? Chelmsford's inability to delegate, and his choice of a very small staff to aid him in his work, perhaps resulted in him fitting his invasion plan into the resources he had and the supply and transport issues that he faced rather than producing a credible plan to defeat the enemy. Although forced upon him by Frere's political manoeuvrings, the timing of an offensive in January had some benefits. Despite being wet, there would be sufficient grass for oxen and horses and the Zulus would be hindered by the need to gather the harvest. Also, the rivers along the Natal's frontiers would be high thus reducing, if not nullifying, the threat of a Zulu army slipping past the British columns and invading Natal. This is an important point, for Chelmsford did consider a Zulu incursion into Natal a real possibility, but perhaps one he should have disregarded. Not only would the high rivers make a crossing by a Zulu force extremely difficult, those points where a crossing might be easily considered, such as at Rorke's Drift, could have been easily fortified and garrisoned by a relatively small number of imperial troops.

It does seem that Chelmsford had forgotten one important lesson from the Ninth Frontier War – how successful the FLH had been in provoking and defeating the Xhosa, not just in pitched battles but also in finding the elusive warriors. Ian Knight, in his book *By Orders of the Great White Queen*, argues that a better tactic might well have been to form squadrons of mounted infantry, as he had done against the Xhosa, from his available imperial infantry to strike quickly at Ulundi. Such an approach would have reduced the need for the stockpiling of supplies at various depots, as well as the requirement for the procurement of so many wagons. In addition, Chelmsford's advancing columns could only move at the pace of an oxen whereas a large force of mounted infantry would have provided him with the mobility he needed against a very active foe.

What lessons Chelmsford had taken from fighting the Xhosa were largely inappropriate when fighting the Zulu. In the Frontier War he was faced with a foe who preferred not to fight in open battle, but who waged a guerrilla-type war from mountain and bush strongholds. Chelmsford broke Xhosa resistance by establishing protected camps in enemy territory, to act as supply depots and operational bases, and sweeping out from these to contain and destroy the Xhosa warriors. Neither Chelmsford nor his officers believed that the Zulus were capable of pressing home a sustained attack across the sort of open country that characterized much of Zululand. So keen was he to induce a Zulu attack that he felt that by advancing in three columns one would be more likely to discover the Zulu army and bring it to battle. Chelmsford even instructed his artillery officers not to open fire until the Zulus were within 600yd range so as not to frighten off an attack. He believed superior firepower would compensate for the relatively small number of troops each column would deploy. In a communication to Wood in November 1878, Chelmsford wrote, 'I am induced to think that the first experience of the power of the Martini-Henrys will be such a surprise to the Zulus that they will not be formidable after the first effort.'[21]

Such was the general's level of complacency before the invasion began. This can be most clearly seen in Chelmsford's disregard of advice and the lack of importance he placed upon intelligence-gathering. In formulating his invasion plan Chelmsford was heavily influenced by his political adviser, Henry Francis Fynn Jr, son of one of the original British settlers who had once saved Shaka's life. Fynn Jr had grown up amongst the Zulus and was fluent in their language. He had succeeded his father as magistrate of M'singa, the border district that included Rorke's Drift, and in that capacity had attended Cetshwayo's coronation. His knowledge of the peoples and terrain either side of the border was unrivalled. Yet, he had never fought the Zulu.

Based heavily on Fynn's advice, Chelmsford gained an awareness of the Zulu military system and of Zulu tactics. Fynn compiled a pamphlet entitled 'The Zulu Army', and this was issued to British forces in November 1878, although some details were inaccurate. The War Office Intelligence Branch published a separate guide, *Precis of Information Concerning the Zulu Country with a Map*, although the map itself was strewn with errors. Chelmsford also issued field regulations and detailed tactical instructions to his column commanders, which was published on the eve of the war. In these Standing Orders, Chelmsford specified that all permanent camps constructed in Zulu territory should be at least partially entrenched for their own protection. In the light of the defeat at Isandlwana, this instruction came under much scrutiny, but pre-invasion, Chelmsford saw a very limited role for fortifications. He seemed unable to believe what he read or was told as to the Zulu fighting capacity, and this was clearly demonstrated by reports of conversations he had with several Boers and British settlers.

John Dunn was a Natal trader who was on friendly terms with Cetshwayo before the war commenced but would later work with the British. Writing in his book *John Dunn, Cetewayo and the Three Generals*, Dunn stated that on meeting Chelmsford the general told him that, 'The only thing I am afraid of is that I won't get Cetywayo [*sic*] to fight.'[22] This displayed one of the lessons that Chelmsford had mistakenly accepted when fighting the Xhosa; the belief that native armies would avoid a set-piece battle if they could. This was contrary to the beliefs of Bulwer who wrote to his brother after the invasion began that:

> There is a doubt the Zulus will fight in the open. I am inclined to think that they will – that they are bound to do so, for if they do not all their traditions will go for nothing. They have always been a conquering people and never in the habit of being conquered. They have always been the aggressors and not the aggrieved, the invaders and not the invaded.[23]

Frere's Secretary, Mr Stegmann, kept a diary whilst serving the High Commissioner and recorded a meeting that Chelmsford had with a delegation of Transvaal Boers in Pietermaritzburg in November 1878, which included two men, Kruger and a Mr Paul Bester, who had fought the Zulus in previous conflicts. Crealock took notes of two separate meetings in which both Boers offered their experiences of fighting the Zulus, although it appears that Chelmsford decided not to heed their advice. Stegmann's entry for 29 November states:

> I took them [the Boer leaders] to the General. Mr Kruger gave him much valuable information as to Zulu tactics and impressed upon him the absolute necessity of laagering his wagons every evening, and always at the approach of the enemy. He also urged the necessity of scouting at considerable distances, as the movements of the Zulus were very rapid ...[24]

It was not just Chelmsford who was receiving advice from the Boers. Captain Henry Hallam Parr, Frere's military secretary, who would accompany the Central Column, wrote that an old Boer who had fought at Blood River told him, '... I hope the English soldiers will beware; they are fighting now a different foe from the Cape Colony Kaffir. Ah, yes; the Zulus are different. I much fear the "Rooi-laatjes" [red jackets] have been fighting the Gaikas and Galekas so long that they will undervalue the Zulu.'[25] The general had certainly received plenty of advice, yet he failed to accept or act on much of it. His blinkered views, which considered the Zulu warriors just slightly superior to the Xhosa in martial ability, that the firepower of the Martini-Henry rifle would be decisive in any encounter with the Zulus and that his operational plan was sound, would all soon prove to be mistaken.

Whilst Chelmsford was frantically bringing together all that was required for an invasion of Zululand, Frere was working to produce the political catalyst for war. In an attempt to conclude the border dispute between the Boers and the Zulus, Sir Henry Bulwer, the Lieutenant Governor of Natal, decided to intervene and appointed a boundary commission. To Frere's annoyance the commission ruled in favour of the Zulus and he decided to withhold the result for several months whilst war preparations continued. With British troops nearing readiness, Frere summoned Zulu representatives to a meeting on 11 December 1878 on the pretext of hearing the ruling of the boundary commission. At the end of the announcement, British officials delivered a thirteen-point ultimatum to the waiting Zulus which included demands for the return of missionaries to Zululand, the appointment of a British resident within the country and, crushingly, a demand that the Zulu military system be abolished, and the army disbanded. Frere knew that the army was at the heart of Cetshwayo's authority, and he could not possibly agree to this term.

Frere set a deadline of 11 January 1879 for full compliance, or a state of war would be triggered.

Throughout this period Hicks Beach and Frere were in regular correspondence but Frere used the delay in communication to his advantage for with no telegraphic link between London and Southern Africa correspondence would endure a round journey of five to six weeks or more. In a letter dated 28 November but received by Frere on 30 December, after the ultimatum had been issued, Hicks Beach wrote that the Cabinet desired that he should impress upon Frere most strongly the need to avoid aggression and that Frere should use all proper means to keep out of a war. Hicks Beach concluded the letter by stating that he had complete confidence that Frere would do everything to avoid a conflict and that a 'policy must necessarily be one of defence and not of attack'.[26] Again, writing to Frere on 11 December, Hicks Beach demonstrated that he himself realized that he had lost control of the High Commissioner when he wrote:

I really do not know at all what you contemplate in this direction [the ultimatum]; nor do I at present see the necessity for an ultimatum, unless such necessity should arise from Zulu action ... As you will have seen from my dispatch we entirely deprecate the idea of entering on a Zulu war in order to settle the Zulu question.[27]

Hicks Beach only received official news of the ultimatum on 2 January 1879 and by then the British government was in no position to halt the war. Frere justified the invasion in a letter to Hicks Beach dated 20 January 1879 when he wrote, 'Had I hesitated to put the defence of the frontier in General's hands, or referred to you for instructions before doing so, we should almost certainly have had widespread insurrection among native tribes all over South Africa, a Boer rebellion, and a Zulu invasion of Natal ...'.[28] Whether Frere believed the Zulu threat to be that real and imminent is still open to debate. What is clear is that he had manipulated both the British government and the Natal authorities into a position in which they were unable to control either events or the High Commissioner.

Despite colourful attempts by Shepstone and Frere to portray the 40,000-strong Zulu army as a professional standing force, in reality Cetshwayo's army should be viewed more as a citizen-based one. Although every Zulu warrior would undergo military training, for most of the year these men tended the land and their herds. What the army did possess though was a strong regimental system which instilled strict discipline and won great loyalty. Separate armies, or impis, were commanded by various regimental chiefs, or inDuna. On the battlefield, the Zulu tactic was to engage closely with the enemy so a short stabbing spear, or assegai, could be used with lethal effect. Regiments would attempt to envelope the enemy in a 'horns of the buffalo' formation which was to prove successful at Isandlwana. Although the British were armed with the latest military technology, the Zulus were equipped with old flintlock muskets purchased from Dutch and Portuguese traders and were outranged by the British weapons. Unlike the slow-moving British columns, hampered as they were by the need to bring all their supplies with them, the Zulus covered huge distances in a day in forced marches. Indeed, the Boers warned Chelmsford that he should view the Zulus as cavalry due to the rapidity of their movement and speed of attack in battle.

Both Frere and Chelmsford planned and aimed for a quick decisive victory which would crush the military threat of the Zulus and remove Cetshwayo from his throne, thus allowing the British to bring Zululand and its people under British sovereignty. In addition to removing the perceived military threat, it was foreseen that the Zulu people would supply much-needed labour for the expansion of the mining industry. In Frere's words, war would bring the Zulu people to 'honest work'.[29] Yet, Chelmsford was also under no illusions as to the magnitude of the transport difficulties he would face, and it seems clear that he viewed this as a greater threat to a successful invasion than that posed by the enemy. Writing in a cautious tone to Cambridge on 8 January 1879, he stated:

> Our movements will all be made in the most deliberate manner. There is nothing to be gained by a rapid forward movement, and if I wished to make a rush I should be unable to carry it out, consequent upon the great difficulties of supply and transport ... We are now also in the most rainy season of the year, and convoys are sadly delayed by the state of the roads. I may possibly therefore be unable to finish the war with the rapidity which, under the present aspect of affairs in Europe, is evidently so desirable.[30]

He would, however, do his best to bring the war to 'a speedy close' so that he could return some of his troops to Britain.

Although Chelmsford would cross into Zululand on the day the ultimatum expired, 11 January, he had already ordered Wood to cross the Blood River on 6 January, and thus the British had pre-empted the war. Wood was just 75 miles from Ulundi, the shortest distance of the three columns, and Chelmsford was keen to protect his open left flank and also wanted Wood to begin the pacification of the mountainous country to the east of Utrecht, controlled by the abaQulusi tribe which were fiercely loyal to Cetshwayo.

Towards the end of 1878 all the troops that were to comprise the Central Column had begun to concentrate at Helpmekaar before the planned advance towards Rorke's Drift and then into Zululand itself. The 2nd Battalion of the 24th arrived to join the 1st Battalion and it would be the first time that both battalions would campaign alongside each other. Chelmsford arrived with his staff in the early days of 1879 and with the general now firmly attached to the Central Column the weather which had already been wet became worse as thunderstorms hit daily and the camp and the roads leading out turned to mud. Crealock, who had served in India, compared the rains to those of the sub-continent and wrote of two 36-hour deluges over the New Year period. Three Zulu emissaries, sent by Cetshwayo, arrived at Helpmekaar to seek out Chelmsford to request an extension to the ultimatum to allow the king more time to consider his response, but Chelmsford ignored the plea along with the six previous ones sent from Cetshwayo and furthermore banned any further Zulu messengers from entering the British camp, fearing that they might be spies. Clearly the general had decided that war was imminent.

Yet, even at this late stage, Chelmsford faced a near mutiny from his colonial mounted troops. He had decided to give command of the Natal Mounted Police (NMP) and all the Natal volunteers to Brevet Major John Russell, rather than their own commandant, Major Dartnell. In disgust the colonial troops paraded at Helpmekaar and voted unanimously that they would not enter Zululand under the command of a British officer. Chelmsford had no alternative but to compromise and Dartnell was promoted to lieutenant colonel, giving him authority over Russell. This move was soon to have unforeseen consequences once the invasion had begun. The colonials now moved towards Rorke's Drift with the rest of the Central Column.

The night before the men of the 24th left Helpmekaar, the officers of the 1st Battalion invited those of the 2nd to join them for dinner in their makeshift mess. The evening was just a few days short of the anniversary of the Battle of Chillianwala, fought during the Second Anglo-Sikh War, in which the 24th had incurred heavy losses in the course of a murderous advance across open ground towards the Sikh cannons. In speeches during this last dinner, officers William Degacher and Francis Porteous both recalled Chillianwala and toasted, 'That we may not get into such a mess and have better luck this time.'[31] Within less than three weeks these two men and many of their fellow officers were to die at the hands of the Zulu army.

Chapter 5

Disaster, Deceit and Personal Humiliation

Chelmsford had overcome the most pressing of his logistical difficulties and his strategy for the invasion had been set. Although parts of Zululand were mountainous and heavily forested, much of the kingdom was relatively open grassland. It was easy land to march or ride over, but it was cut by some sizeable rivers, numerous small streams and innumerable deep gullies and ravines called dongas. With his plan focused on the advance of three slow-moving columns, Chelmsford's forces would have to traverse at least 75 miles of this terrain to reach his ultimate target of Ulundi and, tied as the British were to their cumbersome wagons, each river or donga would present a formidable and testing obstacle. Mounted infantry could have reached the king's kraal in two or three days and if Chelmsford had not been sucked into the supply and transport issues surrounding the invasion, he might have considered this an option. However, it is clear that Chelmsford was not a risk-taker and that in his mind three independent columns, each, in his opinion, strong enough to defeat a Zulu army, were a 'safer' option.

Within both Chelmsford's thinking and that of many of his officers was the thought that the British would struggle to entice the Zulu army to battle and that even if they did so then the firepower of the Martini-Henry rifle would prove decisive. This complacency was clearly demonstrated in a letter written by Sackville Lane-Fox, who had left England for adventure and had become an officer in the NNC. Writing home after he had crossed the Tugela River, Lane-Fox stated:

There will be a howling fight as the Zulus always come out in great masses and charge and of course they will be shot down by the thousand, but after the first fight the fun will be over and the nasty work of hunting them in the bush will begin, as they will get such a lesson that they will not show their faces in the open ... The soldiers here think they will shoot a thousand of them by Sunday.[1]

Such wrong-headed attitudes were part of the Chelmsford mindset formed and even encouraged in the tents and mess rooms.

In addition, apart from the immediate border region, Chelmsford had very little intelligence on the ground over which he was to march. In December 1878 Crealock wrote to General Alison stating that the maps supplied by the Intelligence Department in the War Office were faulty and that the staff had purchased maps from Cape Town. Even after the invasion Crealock was still complaining to Alison about the lack of accurate maps when he wrote to him on 14 January:

> Thank Grover for all the maps he sent out, but though they were sent up to our camp I had to send them back to Pietermaritzburg. I had distributed to all of these troops before, and in this rain sending about good maps is (even when practicable) useless. They are destroyed in transit as everyone declares every map is useless. I suppose they are equally faulty.[2]

Even these maps placed the king's kraal 20 miles from its true position, omitted several rivers and showed others running in the wrong direction. Chelmsford was technically invading Zululand blind with inaccurate maps, and he would have to rely on local information for his intelligence.

Writing on 9 January, Crealock stated to Alison that, 'The general is very fit and as full of go and energy as ever.'[3] As the invasion date neared Chelmsford certainly seemed to be in his element and was eager to puts his months of planning into action. On the eve of his advance, he made it clear that his native troops must observe the rules of war. Anyone killing a woman or a child or a wounded man might be hanged. Anyone, white or black, setting fire to a hut without specific authority from his column commander might be flogged and indeed flogging was used upon British troops during the war, and this was to be the last time it was employed on active service before it was abolished in 1881. Nevertheless, orders were given by local commanders that every Zulu homestead and food-store in the path of the invasion force was to be destroyed. Of course, such actions caused untold misery to Zulu women and children but by laying waste to Zulu homes and stores it was intended to break the will of the Zulu people and hopefully provoke the army into attacking the invading columns. If Chelmsford's policy was not quite 'Total War', it undoubtedly caused hunger and privation amongst Zulu non-combatants.

The high moral standards, for the period, that Chelmsford demanded at the start of the campaign soon evaporated following the humiliation of Isandlwana, after which an element of revenge pervaded Chelmsford's command, which the general himself did very little to restrain. Indeed, there were to be numerous complaints of atrocities inflicted upon the Zulus, whether by the NNC or imperial troops, and Chelmsford must hold a high degree of responsibility for not stamping out such actions. He arrived with his staff at Rorke's Drift on the evening of 10 January and in the early hours of the following morning the advance guard of mounted infantry cautiously forded the swollen Buffalo River and entered Zululand; the invasion had begun.

The crossing was unopposed by the Zulus and by mid-morning Chelmsford was confident enough to leave the men of the Central Column as they continued to cross the Buffalo. He rode north to liaise with Colonel Wood whose column had already marched some way towards Ulundi. By doing so Chelmsford missed much of the confusion that surrounded the crossing. The soldiers of the 24th were ferried across on ponts whilst the men of the NNC were forced to link arms and wade into the fast-flowing river. The native troops struggled in the turbulent waters, and several were swept away by the current and drowned. Next followed the wagons and supplies and Captain Parr, Frere's military secretary, recorded that, 'Each ponderous waggon had to be brought as near to the pont as possible, then the oxen outspanned and driven round to the shallows to wade and swim across, while the waggon was passed on to the pont by hand.'[4]

After what had been an exhausting crossing the men of the Central Column erected their tents and established a camp on the Zulu shores of the Buffalo at Rorke's Drift. The men would return here each night whilst the track in the immediate vicinity was made passable. Despite Chelmsford's earlier written instructions, no attempts were made to entrench or fortify the position. A dangerous precedent had already been set and the general clearly felt that he had little to fear from a Zulu attack.

Chelmsford's immediate military concern was to attack the nearby homestead of Chief Sihayo, which was known as the 'maze' and was nestled in the folds of foothills close to the Batshe stream. Sihayo's sons had been mentioned in Frere's ultimatum as perpetrators of border incursions and Chelmsford was keen to take punitive action to demonstrate his intent. Furthermore, Sihayo was known to be a close ally of Cetshwayo and his warriors to be formidable. The chief's homestead was on the Central

Column's line of march and Chelmsford simply had to take it to also ensure that neither his supply lines nor his rear could be threatened. Chelmsford timed his advance for dawn on 12 January. The assault was led by the NNC, under Commandant Rupert La Tour Lonsdale, with support from the 2/24th. Neither Sihayo nor his eldest son Mehlokazulu were present for they and most of their warriors were at Ulundi, answering Cetshwayo's call for the army to muster. The defence of the 'maze' was left to Sihayo's youngest son Mkhumbikazulu, along with 200–300 warriors.

The NNC, with Lieutenant Harford on loan from the 99th Regiment leading the way, charged up the steep cliffs towards the homestead and came under fire from the remaining Zulus hiding in the caves and firing from behind boulders. Half a dozen NNC lost their lives, but the supporting men of the 2/24th suffered no casualties. The Zulus fought stubbornly before giving ground. Around thirty were killed, including Mkhumikazulu. A corporal of the 24th wrote of the attack, 'We were at great disadvantage owing to the rocks and bush, but we managed to rout them out in the long run after about eight hours fighting. It is very hard work travelling after these Zulus. They can run like horses.'[5]

Chelmsford was delighted with the victory and focused on the ease with which the Zulus had been defeated, rather than questioning where Sihayo and the majority of his warriors might be, again reinforcing a level of complacency which hung over the column. Chelmsford was so pleased with the result of the first engagement that he ordered two wounded Zulu prisoners to be released as soon as they were well enough so that the Zulu people would see how the British made war. Again, after Isandlwana such magnanimity was in very short supply. Chelmsford wrote to Frere after the engagement and indicated his delight at the performance of the NNC, 'I ordered Sirayo's [sic] kraal to be burnt, but none of the other huts were touched. The Native Contingent behaved very well and not a native touched a woman or child or killed a wounded man …'[6] In the same letter, Chelmsford stated, '… The soldiers are in excellent health and spirits and do not seem to feel, either physically or morally, the continuous duckings they get from the daily thunderstorms …'.[7] Over the next eight days the weather was to become Chelmsford's biggest obstacle to the continued advance. Captain Parr left a vivid description of the difficulties the column faced after taking Sihayo's kraal:

For the next week the whole energies of the column were absorbed in endeavouring to make the old waggon track, along which we were to advance, passable. Parts of the road were hard, and, if care was taken not to drive the waggons recklessly against rocks and boulders, were passable enough; but there were low-lying bits of the track on soft soil, made swampy by springs and wet weather, into which the heavy waggons sank axle-deep.[8]

Chelmsford, writing to Frere on 12 January, the day after crossing into Zululand, stated, 'The country is in a terrible state from the rain, and I don't know how we shall manage to get our waggons across the valley near Sirayo's kraals.'[9]

By 14 January, just three days into the invasion, the strain upon Chelmsford as a result of the weather and the state of the roads began to take a toll upon the general and Crealock, in a letter to Alison, wrote, 'The general is ever active and at this moment 12 miles off on the mountain top behind us routing up the commissariat. He even licked with his own hand a white bullock-driver yesterday for brutality to oxen.'[10] This was not the behaviour of a commander who was in control of either his emotions or the situation around him that he had to face.

Again, on 14 January, from the headquarters camp, Zululand, near Rorke's Drift, Chelmsford wrote:

Between this camp and Greytown alone, a distance of some seventy miles, three rivers are now impassable, and waggons have to cross by ferries, a laborious operation requiring more skilled labour than we at present have available. The road at various points requires the most constant supervision, and in some parts the heavy rain frequently dislodges huge boulders from the hill-sides overhanging the roadway, and in many places water-courses become torrents after an hour's rain. Beyond this camp towards the Izipezi Hill (my first objective point) the road will require great labour to make it passable; but strong working-parties have already been at work. The transport difficulties are augmented by the great mortality in oxen ...[11]

Writing to Wood on 27 January, Chelmsford clearly indicated that he had not only underestimated the Zulus but also the terrain and weather:

The country is far more difficult than I had been led to expect, and the labour of advancing with a long train of waggons is enormous. It took seven days' hard work, by one half of No. 3 Column, to make the ten miles of road between Rorke's Drift and Insalwana Hill practicable, and even then had it rained hard I feel sure that the convoy could not have gone on.[12]

Robert Edgerton, in his work *Like Lions They Fought*, considers that it was one of the many ironies of the war that in the week that Cetshwayo had taken to assemble his impis to meet the British threat, Chelmsford's wagons had spent the time trying to negotiate the terrain and had travelled less than 10 miles to make camp at Isandlwana. But for the mud, Edgerton argues, the battle might not have been fought at Isandlwana and the end result might have been very different.

Just days after crossing the Buffalo Chelmsford found himself having to discipline one of his column commanders. On 13 January Colonel Durnford, still on the Natal side of the river, received a letter from Bishop Hans Schreuder, of the Norwegian Missionary Society, stating that a Zulu impi had been seen massing on the Zulu side of the border and that it appeared that the warriors might be about to consider crossing over at Middle Drift and potentially threatening Natal. Durnford felt that he could not ignore such information and wrote to Chelmsford to inform him that he would be leading his column to assess the threat. Before he and his men had saddled up on the morning of 14 January, Durnford received the following tart message from Chelmsford which countermanded Durnford's own plans:

Dear Durnford,

Unless you carry out the instructions I give you, it will be my unpleasant duty to remove you from your command and to substitute another officer for the command of No. 2 Column. When a column is acting separately in an enemy's country I am quite right to give its commander every latitude, and would certainly expect him to disobey any orders he might receive from me if information which he obtained, showed that it would be injurious to the interests of the column under his command – Your neglecting to obey my instructions in this present instance has no excuse, you have simply received information in a letter from Bishop Schreuder, which may or may not be true and which you have no way of verifying. If movements ordered are to be delayed because reports hint at a chance of an invasion of Natal, it will be impossible for me to carry out my plan of campaign. I trust you will understand this plain speaking and not give me any further occasion to write in a style which is distasteful to me.[13]

Durnford was stung by this rebuke and some writers have considered that his later actions at Isandlwana might have been an attempt to redeem himself in Chelmsford's eyes. Yet, Chelmsford's words undoubtedly again reflect the pressure he was under at this time and although those who had direct dealings with the general often commented upon his gentlemanly and kindly nature, it is clear that during stressful periods this part of his character could slip. Chelmsford's actions might have been prompted by memories of subordinates not following his instructions during the Xhosa conflict which had caused him frustration. Durnford's castigation at least returned the colonel's command to the front of Chelmsford's mind and on 15 January he ordered Durnford to Rorke's Drift from where his mobile units could not only support the advance of the Central Column but also provide it with the mobility it was sorely lacking. Chelmsford's words to Durnford were not the only harsh ones he wrote. In autumn 1878 Colonel Rowlands was commanding the 80th Regiment in a holding action in the Transvaal against Chief Sekhukhune of the Pedi and was of course under the direct command of Chelmsford. Rowlands had earlier led an unsuccessful attempt to storm Sekhukhune's homestead and certainly Chelmsford viewed the Transvaal and Rowlands as an unnecessary distraction from his focus upon the Zulus. Chelmsford would write in an admonishing tone to Rowlands and also communicate with Shepstone, saying privately that he thought Rowlands 'does not possess the requisite qualifications of an independent commander of Troops in the Field ... and that the troops under Colonel Rowlands' command have lost confidence in their commander'.[14] Rowlands, a holder of the Victoria Cross, was undoubtedly a brave and proud man, and Chelmsford's management of him led him into a depression that ultimately resulted in him offering his resignation. Fortunately, Shepstone was a friend and ally whose support ensured that Rowlands would remain in his command.

Unlike the British, Cetshwayo had an effective and widespread intelligence network, not just in the border region, but also into Natal. He had received regular reports of the build-up of supplies and troops, and even the composition of the NNC. He knew that Chelmsford would invade with three columns and once the invasion had begun it would be up to the king to decide which of these columns offered the greatest threat. Whilst the king received much advice from the councillors as to the strategy he should adopt, Cetshwayo was determined to stand by the position that he was the injured party in the ultimatum and that he never wanted war and despite many advisors stating that the Zulu army should go onto the offensive into Natal, the king resisted these overtures. Chelmsford's attack upon Sihayo's homestead demonstrated that the Central Column was the greatest threat and whilst detachments were sent from the royal kraal to support the local Zulus in their efforts to resist the northern and coastal columns, the main army would be directed against Chelmsford.

It was not only the mud that Chelmsford and his staff had to fight in the first week or so of the invasion it was also a lack of intelligence not only regarding the whereabouts of the Zulu army, but also of Cetshwayo's intentions. Whilst the men of both the NNC and the 24th toiled away, under the supervision of a newly arrived detachment of Royal Engineers, to make the muddy tracks passable, Chelmsford, with a small escort, daily rode ahead of his men to reconnoitre both the next camping ground as well as search for an elusive enemy. Again, this independent roving by Chelmsford illustrated a huge degree of risk and complacency on his part. On one such reconnaissance on 16 January Chelmsford first set his eyes upon the hill of Isandlwana and he and his staff breakfasted there. Like every piece of ground that Chelmsford had covered, the area was deserted of Zulus but suddenly cattle were spotted a few miles ahead and Chelmsford rushed to investigate. He discovered that with the cattle were a large group of men, women and children, followers of the Chief Gamdana, brother of Sihayo. Gamdana soon arrived and explained to Chelmsford that he had already been in contact with the border agent Henry Francis Fynn Junior and had offered his surrender. The general was rather indignant that such negotiations had been taking place in his absence and he summoned Fynn to join him at once.

Chelmsford had constantly received intelligence reports from long before the invasion had begun. Indeed, one of the general's problems was that if anything he was swamped with information, which was often contrary. In one report he noted, 'The report from Mr Fynney [presumably Mr Fynn] is diametrically opposed to that which I have received from the border commanders during my numerous visits to that part of the country ...'.[15]

Yet, the issue was that it was the role of the commander and his staff to assess all the intelligence, but all were blinded by the overwhelming thought that the Zulus would never dare attack the British in the open and they allowed the intelligence to fit this belief. When Fynn arrived, his intelligence, which suited what Chelmsford wanted to hear, confirmed to the general his biggest fear that the Zulu army would likely evade battle and slip past his advancing column and threaten his supply lines or even Natal. Fynn informed Chelmsford that in his opinion, gathered from his own sources in the border region, the army from Ulundi would skirt behind the Hlazakazi Heights, use the cover of the Mangeni valley of Mhlazakazi Mountain and there hide in the Quidine forests until the Central Column had moved forward towards Ulundi. Then the Zulus would use the Mangeni valley to journey up the Buffalo River and so close off the column in the rear. Chelmsford considered Fynn's opinions to be true for they not only came from the lips of someone who was not a Boer but they also reinforced the general's already preconceived view. With thoughts of Zulus slipping past his advancing column, Chelmsford thus resolved to make sure the border region was clear of a Zulu army before pressing on towards Ulundi. Much would depend upon what intelligence could be gathered over the next few days and unfortunately the general was at a huge disadvantage in this area for he lacked sufficient mounted units to range ahead of the column to discover the movements of the Zulus.

Chelmsford had around 1,000 mounted men, many of them colonial volunteers, but these were split between the 3 advancing columns and that of Durnford's. The general only had a force of around 200 mounted men with which to provide flank protection to Number 3 Column as well as forward reconnaissance of the route. Although these men were able to scout up to 20 miles in advance, it was a small force to cover such a vast area. The reports that these men did provide stated that the road as far as the Isipezi (Sisipezi) Hills, 15 miles from Isandlwana, would need much repair and with this information Chelmsford decided to establish an intermediate camp at Isandlwana. From there his forces could clear the immediate area of Zulus before moving to the open ground between Isipezi and Ulundi.

With the track now made passable, the order was given for the Central Column to leave the vicinity of Rorke's Drift and march to Isandlwana Hill.

By 20 January, the troops of the column began to pitch their tents on the slopes of Isandlwana and the camp would eventually spread over a distance of ¾ mile. Even before the battle, and of course subsequently, Chelmsford's choice of Isandlwana for his camp was questioned and criticized. Captain Parr, who was to write of his exploits against both the Xhosa and the Zulu, left a vivid description of the location of the camp:

> The Isandlwana camp fronted nearly east, and was partly pitched on a neck between two small hills, the hill on the left or north being the higher and being inaccessible, and partly on the slopes below this inaccessible hill. This hill gives its name to the position, and is joined on its side remote from the neck by a range of low rocky hills [Nqutu], which curve round to the left and left front of the position. The hill on the right or south trends away in a more or less direct line, south from the position. The front of the position is open ground, but broken by sluits, watercourses, and 'dongas'. To the rear of the position the ground sinks steeply to a little stream falling into the Buffalo. Down this incline, crossing the stream, winds the waggon road to Rorke's Drift.[16]

Isandlwana meant 'something like a small hut', the name given it by the Zulus, and curiously it is shaped like a sphinx which was the badge of the 24th Regiment. This did not go unnoticed by the officers and men of the 24th as they arrived to set up camp. Although the site was criticized, Chelmsford had few options along the line of march. The camp essentials of water and firewood were readily available nearby and visibility to the front was good, extending over several miles across the plain. As long as the Nqutu Heights were patrolled and pickets posted then any enemy movements should have been easily seen. Yet, this did not stop both British officers and colonials questioning the choice of camp.

A commander of a contingent of NNC, Rupert La Tour Lonsdale, who had fought both the Asantes in West Africa as well as the Xhosa, was not impressed by the site. He commented to a fellow NNC officer, the New Zealander Hamilton-Browne, that he thought the choice for the camp was a mad one, to which Hamilton-Browne agreed. Other colonial officers were equally as vocal. Sub-Inspector F.L. Phillips of the NMP shared his concerns with Colonel Crealock that the camp only commanded a frontal view. In his view, the hill and ridges in the rear afforded excellent cover for the enemy to approach within striking distance unseen. Furthermore, Phillips counselled laagering the camp with the wagons, and looking for a less dangerous site the following day. When Crealock took these views to Chelmsford, the general responded, 'Tell the police officer my troops will do all the attacking, but, even if the enemy does venture to attack, the hill he complains about will serve to protect our rear.'[17]

Although Chelmsford had specified in his field regulations, issued before the start of the invasion, that camps should be entrenched or wagons laagered for protection, when Colonel Glyn asked about forming a wagon laager, the general dismissed the idea, remarking in a jocular way, 'why it would take a week to make one'.[18] In defence of Chelmsford he did not have many experienced wagon drivers, and it would have taken all night to unhitch the 200 teams of oxen and mules to manhandle the 1-ton, 18ft-long wagons into a huge circular barrier. Also, wagons were being used during the day to ferry supplies from Rorke's Drift. Chelmsford intended to keep moving, and when a laager had been formed it would have been time to move on to the next camp, or so he calculated. In terms of entrenching the camp, the ground was too hard and rocky to allow trenches to be dug, and there were no thorn bushes with which to form a barrier. The general must have known he was taking a risk by not fortifying the camp in some way, but he must have considered it a small one for he had received no intelligence reports to suggest that an attack was either likely or imminent. In addition, if the general had decided to turn every campsite into a fortified position, the delays he had already experienced would have been exaggerated and he, and Frere, were banking on a short, decisive campaign.

A field officer of the 2nd Battalion, of the 24th, on duty with the pickets expressed strong misgivings about the protective arrangements to the staff officer on duty, pointing out the poor defensive position of the camp and that there were no guards to the rear of it. Another officer, Lieutenant Melvill, adjutant of the 1/24th, stated at the time, 'These Zulus will charge home and with our small number we ought to be in laager, or, at any rate, prepared to stand shoulder to shoulder'.[19]

Archibald Forbes of the *Daily News*, who visited the battlefield when the British returned to bury their dead, wrote in the paper's edition of 20 June 1879:

I shall offer few comments on the Isandlwana position. Had the world been searched for a position offering the easiest facilities for being surprised, none could have been found to surpass it. The position seems to offer a premium on disaster, and ask to be attacked. In the rear laagered waggons would have discounted it defects; but the camp was more defenceless than an English village. Systematic scouting could alone have justified such a position, and this too clearly cannot have been carried out.

Forbes would become one of Chelmsford's main detractors and he always displayed a great military knowledge in his writings, which was normally based on hindsight. Yet, for most of the officers and men present in the camp at Isandlwana on the night of 20 January 1879 the site met with their approval. Water and fuel were to hand, and it was on a slight elevation overlooking a great plain. If the Zulus were to attack, they could be seen for at least 15–20 minutes before they closed on the camp. By then everyone, including Chelmsford, believed that the firepower of the Martini-Henry would have slaughtered them, just like it had the Xhosa at the Battle of Kentani, less than a year before.

Whilst the choice of Isandlwana as a camp had both advantages and disadvantages and Chelmsford's decision to neither laager nor entrench it can similarly be justified or condemned, the place would soon become notorious as the site of the most calamitous defeat endured by the British army at the hands of an indigenous foe in Victoria's long reign. It was to be Chelmsford's lack of intelligence on the intentions and whereabouts of the Zulu army that were the prime reason for the defeat. However, the geography of the site itself played a part, along with the general's inability to even consider that the Zulus would attack in the open. Chelmsford had been briefed by both Boers and advisers such as Fynn as to how the Zulu army deployed the 'horns of the buffalo' to surround their enemies and cut off any escape. Yet, by camping on the slopes of Isandlwana the British would allow the right 'horn' or flank of the Zulu army to approach unseen from behind the hill onto the rear of the camp and envelope and destroy those within in it. Such disregard for the fighting abilities, bravery, skill and tactics of the Zulu army by the British was due largely to complacency and arrogance and for that Chelmsford must shoulder the blame. A translator named Duncombe reportedly said when entering the camp, 'Do the staff think we are going to meet an army of school-girls?'[20]

With his mind fixated on the thought that the Zulu army would try to evade detection and swing around the Central Column to attack the lines of supply, Chelmsford refrained from placing picquets or patrols to the north or north-east of the camp. An old Zulu man was discovered near the camp and when questioned about the whereabouts of the Zulu army, he stated that the impi had already left Ulundi and was on its way to attack the column. When asked from which direction the old man pointed towards the north-east. Chelmsford dismissed this intelligence, and no patrols were sent out in that direction, but were once more despatched to the Mangeni valley, where no Zulus were seen. With his mindset fixed on the south-east, where, Fynn had told him, a strong Zulu force would gather, Chelmsford was determined to ensure that this area was cleared first. He outlined his strategy to Durnford, who was still en route to Rorke's Drift, in a letter of 19 January:

No. 3 Column moves tomorrow to Isalwana Hill and from there, as soon as possible to a spot about ten miles nearer to the forest. From that point I intend to operate against the two Matyanas [Matshanas, both local chiefs] if they refuse to surrender. One is in the stronghold on or near the Mhlazakazi Mountain, the other is in the [Qudeni] Forest ... I have sent you an order to cross the river at Rorke's Drift tomorrow with the force you have ... I shall want you to operate against the Matyanas but will send you fresh instructions on this subject.[21]

It would appear that even before the Isandlwana camp had been established, and the ground around reconnoitred, Chelmsford had begun to fit what intelligence he was receiving into his preconceived idea of where he expected the Zulu army to be. This was reinforced by the discovery by a patrol of NNC on 19 January, led by Hamilton-Browne, of a large herd of cattle in the Mzinyathi. Fortunately, Hamilton-Browne and his men of the NNC were wise enough to realize that this was a traditional Zulu trap to try and entice the enemy across difficult ground towards the prize of the herd, where concealed Zulu warriors would then ambush them. By not taking the bait, Hamilton-Browne had the satisfaction of watching 1,500 frustrated warriors emerge from their hiding places and head back towards a large military kraal. This encounter was naturally reported to Chelmsford and although the number of Zulus seen could have been the advance party of the main army, it was actually a group from local Chief Matshana kaMondisa's clan which would be further used to entice Chelmsford away from Isandlwana. Chelmsford had to establish where the main Zulu army was, this had to be the priority, and in this he would continue his hands-on approach.

Chelmsford's own spies confirmed that his force would be the target of the main impi. If this intelligence was correct, then Chelmsford could expect an attack from about 21 January. Thus, as the camp was being established at Isandlwana on 20 January Chelmsford set about trying to locate the enemy via a series of reconnaissance sweeps, many of which he led. The general would ride out with his staff and a small escort, and they were extremely vulnerable if a large force of mobile Zulus had been discovered or if the party had been led into a Zulu trap. This again illustrates Chelmsford's disdain for the capabilities of his enemy. Yet, they found no signs of the Zulu army.

In the early afternoon of 20 January, as his men were arriving from Rorke's Drift to establish the camp at Isandlwana, Chelmsford rode out with a small mounted escort, which included his staff along with Colonel Dartnell, Colonel Glyn and Fynn, across the plain which faces Isandlwana Hill to examine the high ground of the Malakatha at its south-eastern end. From here the party turned to follow the Ndaweni stream onto higher ground and from there they rode east, across the ridge towards the Mangeni valley and the Hlazakazi Heights. Although a few Zulu women were seen running with bundles of possessions on their heads, no warriors were discovered. On reaching the majestic setting of the heights Chelmsford could survey a landscape cut by valleys in which hills and mountains rose abruptly. It was a landscape that could hide an army unless it was properly explored. Somewhere out in the midst of this landscape was Chief Matshana's homestead where the warriors that Hamilton-Browne had encountered the previous day were surely to be found. The Hlazakazi Heights suddenly and spectacularly end at the Mangeni gorge where a thin stream of water spills dramatically over a sheer drop. It is a beautiful, if somewhat foreboding, spot and here the party halted for more than an hour. Whilst some of the men searched the countryside with their binoculars for the elusive enemy and Crealock made a watercolour sketch, Chelmsford was distant from the group, lost in thought, his mind surely set on whether Fynn's intelligence could be relied upon. He felt certain that to the east where Ulundi lay the Zulu army was already on the march. The critical question was would the enemy cross Chelmsford's left and traverse the Manageni valley high up to advance towards Isandlwana or would it, as predicted by Fynn, shift to the general's right, sweeping around the Malakatha and Hlazakazi heights and attack Rorke's Drift and his supply lines, and Chelmsford knew that he could not risk that happening.

Although no Zulus had been seen by the party, the reconnaissance had not been completely fruitless. Chelmsford had decided that the flats above the waterfall would be the spot for the next camp on the road to Ulundi and from where he would be able to isolate any enemy concentration in the Mangeni valley. By sunset, the general and his entourage had returned to Isandlwana to find the camp generally cheerful as the men busied themselves erecting the last of the tents and settling down for the night. The patrol had left Chelmsford with much to consider, and he spent the next hours formulating his plans for the following day. He decided that the heights of Hlazakazi and Malakatha would need to be thoroughly covered by his scouts not only to ascertain if any sizeable Zulu force was hiding there, but also to identify any signs of an approaching Zulu army. Chelmsford felt that his colonial mounted troops and eight of ten companies from each of the two battalions of the NNC would have the mobility and knowledge of the terrain to cover it effectively. Chelmsford appointed Major Dartnell of the NMP in overall command of this force, whilst Commandant Lonsdale and Hamilton-Browne were in charge of the men of the NNC. The combined force was to commence its operation at dawn on 21 January and return to Isandlwana by nightfall of the same day.

It would appear that Chelmsford did not consult his staff on this decision and Clery noted sourly in a letter to Colonel George Byng Harman, who was then deputy adjutant general in Ireland and clearly a friend of Clery, that:

He [Chelmsford] gave orders to the commandant of the natives to take his two battalions out at daybreak the following morning to work through some ravines about ten miles off, and he also gave orders to the commandant of the volunteers [Dartnell] to go in the same direction and cooperate. The instructions to both these commandants were given personally by the general himself, and this was absolutely necessary in this case as neither Colonel Glyn nor myself knew in the least where they were being sent to, or what they were being sent for.[22]

Dartnell departed, as instructed, early on 21 January, taking nearly two-thirds of the camp's mounted men with him, leaving less than a hundred to cover reconnaissance and picket duty around Isandlwana.

Cetshwayo had summoned his warriors to assemble for ritual purification and instruction before leaving to face the British. Confidence was high now that battle was imminent, and the king assured his warriors that one decisive victory would see an end to British aggression. Indeed, Cetshwayo was banking all on such a significant military success which would force the British to withdraw back to Natal and he hoped then, from a position of some strength, a sensible and reasonable settlement could be reached. The Zulu army totalled around 28,000 warriors as it left kwaNodwengu, the former site of King Mpande's palace near Ulundi, in the late afternoon of 17 January. It proceeded west for 6 miles as a single column, crossing the Umfolozi River and camping nearby. On the following morning, 4,000 warriors under Chief Godile kaNdela Ntuli detached from the main body and headed south to oppose the Number 1 Column, otherwise known as the Coastal Column, commanded by Colonel Pearson. The rest of the army marched a further 9 miles to the Isipezi Mountain near the Mpembeni River. Five months later the British could still see the track left by the army in the trampled down grass.

Progress of the army was deliberately slow for Cetshwayo had given firm instructions that the warriors were not to tire themselves. On Sunday, 19 January the army split into two parallel columns, with Ntshingwayo, a trusted friend of the king, leading the left and the younger Chief Mavumangwana the right. Both men would be in overall command of the main army, with Mavumangwana showing deference to the older chief. A few mounted men, under the leadership of Chief Sihayo, rode ahead. Both columns camped near Babanango Mountain having again covered around 9 miles. On 20 January the warriors now faced the danger of proceeding across open country but this they managed to do without detection, and they bivouacked on the northern side of Isipezi Mountain. In the evening of 21 January the army broke into small detached bodies to reduce the risk of being spotted and slipped into the wide floor of the Ngwebeni valley. Not only is the valley deep and sheer it is further concealed by the Nyoni Heights from Isandlwana Hill, just 6 miles to the south-west. Ntshingwayo had already received reports from his advanced scouts that the British had encamped at Isandlwana on 20 January and these men kept up a constant watch on the comings and goings at the camp. Zulu stragglers were still arriving in the Ngwebeni valley on the morning of 22 January, just a few hours before the Battle of Isandlwana, but by then Ntshingwayo had played his masterstroke and had completely deceived Chelmsford.

Ever since historians and commentators began to write about the British defeat at Isandlwana there has been debate and controversy as to whether the Zulus deliberately acted to deceive Chelmsford into splitting his command and by doing so denude the camp of half its fighting force. In recent years, the likes of John Laband, Ken Gillings and Adrian Greaves have firmly stated that the tactics of Ntshingwayo were designed to convince Chelmsford that he was facing a sizeable Zulu force away from the camp and by doing so the senior Zulu commander should be given credit for this masterstroke. It was Ntshingwayo who had ordered Matshana, the local chief of the Mangeni area, to probe the intentions of Major Dartnell's force ordered by Chelmsford to reconnoitre the Hlazakazi Hills on 21 January. By sending this force of colonial troops and NNC out Chelmsford had unwittingly started the deception that would result in disaster for his command.

Whilst Dartnell was leading his force on its fateful reconnaissance, Chelmsford too was once more engaged in leading patrols out from Isandlwana, both in the morning and again in the afternoon. After breakfast, the general, keen to confirm the surrender of Chief Gamdana, again rode to the Zulu homestead. He found it to be deserted as the NNC had passed by it only 4 hours earlier on their way to Hlazakazi Mountain and their presence had scared away both Gamdana and his remaining followers. Frustrated at not finding the chief or seeing either the enemy or any signs of Dartnell's forces, Chelmsford returned to camp by lunchtime. Here he was soon joined by an apologetic Gamdana who not only confirmed his surrender but that he had heard that Cetshwayo had sent an impi 'to eat him [Gamdana] up, for giving up his arms to the English; he had expected the impi that morning (21st) but it had not arrived'.[23] Although Gamdana was mistaken that the impi was ordered to attack him, he was correct about the date, for the impi was now close by. Chelmsford did not even record this warning from Gamdana, and it is only known from the report of Lieutenant Milne, so it can only be assumed that the general did not consider the intelligence as significant.

In a separate incident Lieutenant Browne of the 1/24th rode out with four other mounted men towards Isipezi Mountain and on their return an attempt was made by around thirty warriors and eight Zulus on horseback to cut them off. Browne ordered his men to fire, and one warrior was killed before Browne was able to return safely to camp. Naturally, Browne reported this encounter to the staff but again little seems to have been made of this, although it seems highly likely that these warriors were the advance guard of the Zulu army. In the meantime, after both lunch and the interview with Gamdana, Chelmsford once more led a patrol out, this time to the Nqutu plateau. Vedettes had already been posted on a small knoll at the edge of the plateau. From this viewpoint the troopers confirmed to the general that they had seen nothing, although with the undulations of the terrain anyone who was moving more than a mile away would have been lost to view. Chelmsford then rode on to to the final vedette which had been posted 2 miles to the east and here a gap in the range of conical koppies, or small hills, allowed an uninterrupted view of about 5 miles to the British camp. Here the troopers reported to the general that they had seen a group of mounted Zulus several times during the day. Just as the general and his staff were about to leave this final position, at around 3pm, a party of mounted Zulus were suddenly seen riding on top of a ridge about a mile away. On seeing Chelmsford and his patrols these men swiftly reined back their horses and disappeared as quickly as they had appeared. The general's only comment on seeing these Zulus was that the area must be reconnoitred the following day. It is very likely that these warriors were either from Sihayo's clan, riding ahead of the main impi, or, more likely, senior chiefs appraising the British position.

As the party was heading back towards Isandlwana they were hailed by men of Chelmsford's staff, Brevet Major Matthew Gosset and Captain Ernest Henry Buller, who had ridden out with Dartnell in the morning. The men had some important news for the general. Around 12 miles away, in the hills near the headwaters of the Mangeni valley, Dartnell had discovered Zulus in significant number and Dartnell was seeking instructions as to what action he should now take. Chelmsford did not hide his displeasure at Dartnell for by remaining where he was, observing the Zulus, he had removed all chance of obeying his earlier orders of returning to camp by nightfall. Furthermore, Dartnell did not think his force strong enough to attack the Zulus in front of him. Chelmsford had no alternative but to accept that Dartnell would have to stay out overnight, and the general arranged for blankets and food to be sent out from Isandlwana with an instruction to Dartnell to advance upon the Zulus in the morning if he felt strong enough.

For Clery, who had not been consulted by Chelmsford on the suitability of sending Dartnell out with a force of colonials and NNC, it was a vindication of his fears as to the limitations of such a command:

I had felt from the first very much averse to this movement of sending out irregulars under command of irregular officers, amounting to half the force, on a roving commission of this sort. And when word came that they were going to bivouac out, I could not help speaking strongly to Colonel Glyn on the possibility of this sort of thing dragging the rest of the force into any sort of compromising enterprise that these people may get messed up in.[24]

Glyn would not be drawn into any argument, preferring to keep his own views to himself, but there must have surely been some rising concern amongst those close to Chelmsford that the general's command was in danger of being taken over by events rather than leading them.

When Dartnell's command had left the Isandlwana camp on the morning of 21 January inevitably the NNC, on foot, had been left in the wake of the mounted colonial volunteers. Dartnell led his mounted men to the foot of Hlazakazi Mountain and turned east towards the Mangeni waterfall. The NNC reached the edge of the Malakatha and here Lonsdale divided the two battalions. He led the 2nd on a wide sweep round the western end of the mountain, whilst Hamilton-Browne was ordered to take the 1st to the summit. These various movements would result in the whole range being thoroughly scouted and Dartnell had instructed all to rendezvous at the Mangeni waterfall in the afternoon before returning to Isandlwana. All found the terrain and the oppressive heat exhausting and in particular Lonsdale's men suffered.

Once Hamilton-Browne had reached the summit, he was able to escape the heat of the valleys and gain some respite. Here he encountered several old men, women and children, but no Zulu warriors. He questioned a young girl who was herding goats and she confirmed that the main Zulu army was heading from the north-east to attack the column, and of course this intelligence would prove to be correct. Lonsdale's force had not located any Zulus at all, but Dartnell's colonials had seen 700–800 Zulus to the north and later they came across a large body of the enemy, in excess of 1,000 warriors, on the nek of Upindo Hill, east of their position. It was now about 5pm and the reconnaissance party should have been returning to Isandlwana, but Dartnell felt that he needed to confirm in more detail the report of the Zulus and ordered his men back up towards where the enemy had last been seen. Much to the colonials' surprise the number of warriors suddenly magnified and when they got within 800yd of the Zulu position an additional 1,000 warriors from Matshana's clan rose up and swept down towards them, in the horns of the buffalo formation, in an attempt to surround them. A trooper named Symons recorded the Zulu advance:

> From one end of the ridge to the other ... rose a long line of black warriors advancing at the double in short intervals of skirmishing order. It was a magnificent spectacle, and no British regiment could excel in keeping their distances in skirmishing at the double. They uttered no sound. On reaching the brow of a hill their centre halted, while the flank came on, thus forming the noted horns of the Zulu impi.[25]

Although some of the colonials hesitated at the sight before them, they were able to withdraw to a safe distance to discuss their next move with Dartnell. With input from his officers, Dartnell decided that to withdraw now in front of such a significant number of the enemy might court disaster as the warriors might pursue them as darkness fell and this could have serious consequences, particularly for the foot-bound men of the NNC. Also, after a tiring day of reconnaissance it seemed ludicrous to depart when the enemy had been located. Dartnell thus decided that his entire command must find a secure bivouac on the eastern edge of Hlazakazi Mountain, above the Mangeni gorge, and stay there for the night, 11 miles from Isandlwana. Dartnell sent Gosset and Buller back to inform the general of the contact with the enemy and of his decision to stay and await further instructions.

Dartnell's men were to spend a very uncomfortable night. Tensions were running high amongst both the colonial troops and the NNC. All were weary and hungry and the thought of a substantial force of the enemy so close by unnerved many. A shot was fired into the darkness which caused a panic and stampede by some of the NNC, and it took some time for order to be restored. Nerves were heightened by the ever-growing number of fires that could be seen coming from the Zulus camped in the heights above. When a Lieutenant Walsh of the 24th arrived through the darkness with blankets and food from Isandlwana Dartnell again considered his position. Perhaps it was the growing sense of apprehension in the camp or the awareness that the nearby Zulu presence seemed to be increasing that led Dartnell to decide to send Walsh back to Isandlwana with a note for Chelmsford requesting reinforcements to be sent in the morning. Alternatively, Dartnell might actually have considered that a fight was likely in the Mangeni gorge, but either way the request was sent. What is certain is that it was not a popular decision. Hamilton-Browne for one was furious with Dartnell and did not hesitate to tell him so. The senior NNC officer believed that it was now clear the Zulu army was close by and that a battle was likely. He urged both Lonsdale and Dartnell to break off from the contact with the Zulus above them and return through the night to Isandlwana where the position could be properly laagered, and the forces reunited so as to defend the camp. Dartnell's decision to request reinforcements had effectively ended the debate. It just remained to see how Chelmsford would react to Dartnell's plea.

Matshana had played his part, as ordered by Ntshingwayo, to perfection and had led Dartnell and his men on a merry dance across the Mangani region throughout the day of 21 January. By doing so he had allowed the main Zulu army to slip unseen from the north-east into the Ngwebeni valley. The use of fires had further spooked Dartnell and his men into believing that there was an ever-growing threat above them. Yet, even Ntshingwayo could surely not have envisaged how successfully this deception ploy would work upon the British when it would ultimately result in Chelmsford making the fatal decision to split his command still further.

Walsh arrived back in camp at 1.30am on 22 January 1879, after an uneventful ride back from Dartnell's position. Chelmsford was asleep in his tent and the note was delivered first to Clery who in accordance with military protocol took it to Glyn's tent. The colonel realized that this was of course just a gesture, and that Chelmsford would make any decision on how to react to Dartnell's request, and so Glyn directed Clery to take the note to the general. Chelmsford was shaken awake and rose from his camp bed. Clery, holding a lamp, bent over the general and struggled to understand Dartnell's scribbled note. Lieutenant Milne recorded the scene, 'At 2 am … a dispatch was received from Major Dartnell that the enemy seemed in much stronger numbers than had been supposed, and he would not attack them unless two or three companies of infantry were sent out to support his natives'.[26]

It took Chelmsford a few moments to assess the information. All seemed to fit his pre-conceived ideals for the enemy had been located by Dartnell exactly where Fynn had predicted and if he acted quicky he could stop the Zulus from slipping behind his force. By supporting Dartnell Chelmsford would remove a large proportion of the imperial troops in the camp. If a Zulu force attacked, which neither Chelmsford nor his staff believed, there would still be more than enough Martini-Henry rifles to defend the camp. Modern British rifles would stop the enemy in their tracks as they had at Kentani and as the general had witnessed twelve years before outside of Magdala, where the deadly firepower of breech-loading rifles was first demonstrated to the British. Crucially, and this fact has often been ignored by critics of Chelmsford, the general was not trying to avoid battle but was seeking it, and the enemy.

Writing to his friend Colonel Harman on 17 February 1879, Clery recorded that Chelmsford did not hesitate to act upon this new information and stated, 'Order the 2nd Battalion 24th Regiment [NB: this was far in excess of the two or three companies that Dartnell had requested], four guns and all the mounted troops to get ready to start at day-break ...'.[27] Chelmsford also stated that Colonel Durnford should be ordered up from Rorke's Drift to reinforce the Isandlwana camp. The general instructed his military secretary, Crealock, to write the order to Durnford. It appears, however, that Crealock wrote ambiguously to Durnford and did not state clearly that the commander of Number 2 Column was to reinforce and take command of the camp. The text and layout of Crealock's note was as follows:

> You are to march to the camp at once with all the force you have with you of No. 2 Column. Major Bengough's Battalion is to move to Rorke's Drift as ordered yesterday. 2-24th, artillery and mounted men with the general and Colonel Glyn move off at once to attack a force about ten miles distant.
>
> [signed] J.N.C.
>
> [P.S.] If Bengough's Battalion has crossed the river at Eland's Kraal it is to move up here.[28]

This ambiguity would have serious consequences within just a few hours.

Men were stirred from their slumbers and those who were ordered to join Chelmsford on this latest foray wiped the sleep from their eyes and hastily put on their uniforms and collected their weapons. Naturally, the whole camp was quickly abuzz with news and talk of the general's advance. Chelmsford himself was clearly focused on what he was likely to face when he reached Dartnell and was anxious to leave the camp. This impatience meant that he had to be reminded by Glyn that instruction needed to be given regarding reserve ammunition for the column, as per field regulations, for the men would only depart with seventy rounds per man. The general ordered that a wagon was to be loaded and held ready at Isandlwana to be despatched with ammunition if required. More seriously, Chelmsford neglected to issue instructions to Colonel Pulleine who in was to remain in camp as the senior officer. As the column was just about to depart Clery realized that Pulleine had been overlooked and without consulting Chelmsford wrote the following instructions:

You will be in command of the camp in the absence of Colonel Glyn. Draw in your line of defence while the force with the general is out of camp. Draw in your infantry outpost line in conformity. Keep your cavalry vedettes still well to the front. Act strictly on the defensive. Keep a wagon loaded with ammunition ready to start at once, should the general's force be in need of it. Colonel Durnford has been ordered up from Rorke's Drift to reinforce the camp.[29]

Clery sent these instructions to Pulleine via his batman and just before he rode out of the camp with Chelmsford, he personally sought out Pulleine to ensure that the colonel had received and understood the instructions. In the aftermath of the disaster Chelmsford would have cause to thank Clery for issuing the instructions to 'Act strictly on the defensive' as the general was able to use this to defect some of the criticism directed towards him for the defeat. Throughout his army career Pulleine had demonstrated an admirable ability for administration and organization but he had never commanded troops in the field and this lack of experience would soon prove to be costly.

Captain Hallam Parr rode with the advancing column as it left Isandlwana at about 3.30am and left a vivid account of the events of the day:

At 8.30 am we arrived underneath the conical hill and found near it the force which had been detached the previous day [Dartnell]. An advance was at once ordered in the direction of the Zulu force was reported to be, but the morning was spent in endeavouring to get to close quarters with an enemy who could and did avoid us at pleasure. The cavalry of the force exchanged long shots at a body of Zulus who retreated and dispersed among the hills. The Native Contingent and a detachment of the infantry cut off a small body of Zulus, and forced them to take refuge in some caves, whence they were driven with a loss of about thirty to forty killed. Shortly after noon the hills among which we were operating were clear of the enemy, and the men were ordered to get their dinners. It was a welcome order, for the infantry, having started from the camp at 4.30am., had marched for nearly four hours, and had been toiling up and down under the hot South African sun ever since.[30]

Chelmsford did not attempt to hide his annoyance for on his arrival Dartnell reported that the sizeable number of Zulus his force had confronted the day before had melted away. Thoughts of frustrating 'drives' to locate the elusive Xhosa of the year before must have returned to increase Chelmsford's angst. The actions described by Parr were part of the general's efforts to locate where the Zulus had disappeared to. It had not taken Matshana long to realize that the force now facing him was a strong one and more determined than the men he had deceived and harassed the day before. He skilfully retired in the face of the British advance and although he incurred some losses, Chelmsford's force was lured into hours of largely wasteful pursuit. The general himself had, with his staff, spent some time riding north-east in the direction that Dartnell had claimed a large body of Zulus had fled. Despite covering a wide area, Chelmsford saw no new Zulus but was able to witness his troops in action against Matshana's warriors. By 9am the general and his staff halted for a frugal breakfast and the general assessed the situation. Although he had not seen the Zulus in the large numbers he had hoped for and envisaged, Chelmsford decided that there were at least local forces that needed to be nullified and that there seemed little to be gained by his force returning to Isandlwana and so he ordered the despatch of Hamilton-Browne back to camp with the 1st Battalion of the NNC with orders for Pulleine to strike camp and march to the Mangeni valley. A rather disgruntled Hamilton-Browne, who had not eaten for over 24 hours and had had little sleep, led his tired men back towards Isandlwana.

Soon after the departure of Hamilton-Browne, at around 9.30am, a despatch rider arrived from Isandlwana with a note for Chelmsford. It was from Pulleine, written at 8.05am reporting that Zulus were advancing in force from the left front of the camp. Clery later claimed that the general received the news with indifference and when Clery asked him what should be done on the report, Chelmsford replied, 'There is nothing to be done on that.' However, the general took himself away from the group of officers and he raised his field glasses towards Isandlwana. Unable to see any signs of fighting or a large attacking force, Chelmsford sent Lieutenant Milne RN up the slopes of Magogo Hill with his powerful naval telescope to see if he could establish if anything was amiss at Isandlwana. Milne observed the camp for the best part of an hour and even with the telescope he was able to confirm little more than that the white tents still stood. As it would have been general practice to let the tents down in an engagement, so that they would not reduce the field of fire or give cover to the enemy, the general viewed the fact that the tents were standing as a sign the camp was secure and that everything was normal, and he did nothing. This was perhaps the critical moment in the day for if Pulleine's note had been more assertive or if Chelmsford had not been so convinced that the Zulu army would never attack in the open, then the general might have returned to the camp in time to offer support.

Following the departure of Chelmsford and his column Pulleine had ordered the usual placement of picquets and outposts around the camp. Roughly thirty mounted men patrolled an area about 3 miles from the front of the camp whilst sentries on foot offered a screen 1½ miles out. At about 7am mounted picquets of the Natal Carbineers first spotted large numbers of Zulus to the north of the camp and these movements were reported to Pulleine who ordered the men to 'Fall In'. It was soon after this that he sent his first note to Chelmsford informing him of the presence of Zulus near the camp. Just after 10am Durnford arrived with his column and after a brief discussion with Pulleine he as the senior officer now present assumed command of the camp, although a survivor of the battle, Lieutenant Cochrane, was to record later that Pulleine stressed to Durnford that the general's orders (in reality, written by Clery) had stated that the camp was to remain on the defensive. It is likely that Durnford was expecting to find further orders from Chelmsford when he arrived in camp, perhaps ordering Durnford's column to join him. In reality the general simply wanted Durnford closer to hand. The colonel might well have been frustrated at finding that he had simply been called upon to reinforce the camp.

As Durnford stood discussing the changing situation around the camp with Pulleine more and more conflicting reports were delivered from the picquets about the numbers and location of the bands of Zulus. What was clear to Durnford though was that the reported Zulus and the numbers now seen on the skyline appeared to have no intention of attacking the camp. It seems that Durnford became convinced that these warriors were screening a larger force which might well be heading towards Chelmsford's position and that he should attack them. Although it appears from witness statements that the two colonels were courteous and rational in their discussion, there was clearly a difference of opinion with Pulleine stating firmly that his orders were to defend the camp and that he did not think it right or appropriate to permit Durnford to remove imperial infantry from the camp. Lieutenant Melvill was seen to interject in the argument in support of Pulleine and he reminded Durnford of Chelmsford's orders to defend the camp. That Melvill felt he had to intervene suggests that he at least felt Durnford's actions were at best ill-advised and at worst irresponsible. Durnford was not to be moved on his decision to advance on the Zulus, although he did state to Pulleine that he would take his own command forward but that if he got into difficulties, he expected Pulleine to support him. What drove Durnford to take such actions is open to conjecture but perhaps he was driven by a real concern for Chelmsford's safety or even that the rebuke he had received from the general only a few days before was pushing him to redeem himself in Chelmsford's eyes. What is clear is the Crealock's ambiguous tone in his orders to Durnford magnified the confusion around a rapidly changing situation and allowed Durnford to act independently from Pulleine's instructions to defend the camp.

Durnford led most of his men out and across the plain in front of the camp at about 11.30am, whilst two troops of Zikhali Horse from Durnford's command were ordered by the colonel to ride up the northern edge of the escarpment which runs down to the plain and drive away any Zulus that were found there. After travelling about 4 miles from the camp scouts came galloping down the escarpment with startling news that the situation had radically altered, for Zulus had been found in huge numbers and Durnford and his men were in grave danger of being cut off. At first Durnford seemed angered by the note of panic in the voices of the scouts, but this disappeared when the colonel himself saw a large enemy force rise from the folds of the ground just a mile from his position.

Ntshingwayo had led the army into the sanctuary of the Ngwebeni valley during the night of 21/22 January and by the morning scouts were out watching the British camp whilst stragglers were still joining the main force. To have arrived unseen so close to the British camp was undoubtedly a masterstroke, but, like the historic debate around whether the key purpose of Matshana's actions was to screen the main Zulu army or entice Chelmsford to divide his force, a similar historical controversy surrounds Ntshingwayo's plans to attack Isandlwana on 22 January. Authors such as John Laband and Adrian Greaves firmly believe that Ntshingwayo had intended to try to divide Chelmsford's force and once this had been achieved to then attack the camp, probably late in the afternoon. Alternatively, others, such as Ian Knight, highlight that the day of the battle was the 'day of the dead moon' during which there would be an eclipse at about 2pm and that the 'dark day' was considered an unfitting and unlucky one for an engagement. Battle would be sought on the following day, the day of the new moon which was considered fortuitous. Similarly, there is debate as to whether the Zulus were aware that Chelmsford had divided his force and had left the camp in the darkness of the early hours. Whatever interpretation is correct it mattered little to the outcome of the day for the decision to attack was taken out of Ntshingwayo's hands by the discovery of the Zulu position by British scouts.

The two troops of Zikhali Horse, led by Lieutenants Raw and Roberts, who had been ordered by Durnford to sweep along the northern edge of the escarpment, rode out of the camp, passed the picquets of Lieutenant Cavaye's company of the 24th, who were in open order amongst the boulders behind the camp, onto the heights of the escarpment. Riding less than 600yd apart, both troops could see Zulu warriors falling back as they advanced. The pursuit lasted several minutes in which the troopers were drawn further away from the camp, towards the Ngwebeni valley. Seeing cattle, Raw and his men galloped towards them hoping to add them to the camp's provisions. Suddenly, both the Zulus and the livestock disappeared over the ridge which plunged down into the valley. The troopers drew back their reins at the sight before them. Trooper James Hamer wrote of what he and his comrades witnessed, '… we saw the Zulus like ants in front of us, in perfect order as quiet as mice and stretched across in a long line'.[31] With the discovery of the main Zulu army, gone now was any concern about attacking on the 'day of the dead moon'.

At the sight of Raw and his men the warriors began to rise to their feet. A volley of fire from the troopers' carbines spurred on the Zulus as they rushed to assemble into their regiments. Ntshingwayo knew that there was no restraining the warriors, yet such was the ingrained discipline within the army that the Zulu officers, in the midst of surprise and confusion, managed to regain control and the Zulu army advanced towards the British camp, largely in regimental order. Raw and his men, after firing another volley at the charging mass, galloped at full speed back to the camp to report the discovery to Pulleine, whilst other scouts raced towards Durnford to warn the colonel of the imminent attack.

It was George Shepstone who was the first to warn Pulleine of the approaching mass of warriors, when he galloped into camp at approximately 12.15pm. Adding to Pulleine's difficulties was that at the very same moment as Shepstone delivered his information Captain Gardner arrived with Chelmsford's order to strike the camp. Shepstone could see that both pieces of news had made Pulleine dither, and he felt he had to interject and said, 'I'm not an alarmist, Sir, but the Zulus are in such black masses over there, such long black lines, that you will have to give us all the assistance you can. They are now fast driving our men this way.'[32]

With Gardner supporting Shepstone's stance, Pulleine reacted and wrote a brief note to Chelmsford which read: 'Staff Officer. Heavy firing to the left of our camp. Cannot move camp at present.'[33] Gardner did not consider the wording conveyed the potential seriousness of the situation and sent a separate message of his own to Chelmsford which stated, 'Heavy firing near left of the camp. Shepstone has come in for reinforcements and reports Zulus are falling back. The whole force at camp turned out and fighting about one mile to left flank.'[34]

Both messages were received by Chelmsford at about 2pm and although it is unclear why Gardner incorrectly stated that the Zulus were falling back, which reassured the general that the camp was not under any real threat, the camp at this point was already being overrun and there was nothing Chelmsford could have then done to affect the outcome of the battle.

On hearing Shepstone's report Pulleine acted to reinforce Lieutenant Cavaye's company, which was positioned at the back of the camp below the Nyoni Heights with another company of the 1/24th, under Captain Mostyn. Shortly after Pulleine ordered the remaining companies of the 24th, along with the two 7-pounder artillery pieces and some companies of the NNC, to march forward about 600yd from the camp to a slight rocky rise facing the Nyoni Heights. Pulleine must have considered that this was where the Zulu army might attack, but even so this deployment had been forced upon him by the need to support Durnford in case his advance ran into difficulties and was compelled to withdraw back to camp. The troops now formed a long-curved firing line in open order to the east and north of the camp. By moving forward Pulleine was, if not exactly disobeying the order to defend the camp, certainly had lessened the defensive capabilities of his force by extending the troops over a considerable distance. Also, by placing them in open order he had reduced the effectiveness of any concentrated fire. This act alone demonstrated not only a contempt for the courage and fighting abilities of the Zulu warriors but also Pulleine's lack of experience in deploying troops in battle.

The sequence of events during the final stages of the Battle of Isandlwana is hard to establish with absolute certainty. Not only were there few survivors, but many things happened either simultaneously or in quick succession and often survivors, frequently traumatized by their experiences, gave confused testimonies. What seems clear is that Durnford's isolated command on the right flank of the British position was forced to retire to the camp as it was in danger of becoming outflanked by the advancing Zulu warriors and was running low on ammunition. This movement isolated Pope's G Company of the 24th, which had been sent even further forward by Pulleine to support Durnford. These infantrymen were quickly overwhelmed by the advancing Zulus and killed to a man. The remaining British firing line, seeing its right flank exposed, retreated towards the tent line so as to concentrate its position and fire. The lull in the firing whilst this movement happened allowed the Zulus, just 300–400yd away, to seize their chance and charge at the British. The suddenness of the advance sparked fear in members of a detachment of the lightly armed NNC, who promptly discarded their weapons and fled for their lives, although whether this triggered a collapse or was part of a wider general retreat is open to debate. What it clear is that before the British could reform, the Zulus were upon them, stabbing and killing with their short assegai spears. In addition, the 'horns' swung around from behind Isandlwana Hill, cutting off any possible retreat. The encirclement was complete and although the trapped men fought bravely, their slaughter was inevitable. Durnford made a last stand with his remaining troopers, but all met the same fate. Only a very few mounted men managed to successfully flee the carnage. Of the over 1,700 men who had been in the British camp, only 60 white and about 400 black troops survived. Of about 20,000 warriors engaged in the battle, losses are difficult to evaluate for there was never an accurate count, but they were numerous. The Martini-Henry rifle had claimed at least 2,000 warriors, and scores, with terrible wounds, must have dragged themselves from the battlefield to die miles away. When the news of the Zulu victory and his nation's losses reached Cetshwayo, he was heard to say, 'An assegai has been thrust into the belly of the nation … There are not enough tears to mourn for the dead.'[35]

Whilst the disaster was unfolding at Isandlwana, Chelmsford and his staff were oblivious to events. After receiving Pulleine's first note he and his staff had continued to patrol the area. The general had first ridden east over the Magogo to descend towards Isipezi (Siphezi) but still no large concentration of Zulus was seen. Chelmsford was able to watch the NNC skirmishing with some of Matshana's followers, but it had been a desultory morning's work, and all must have thought that it had achieved little of military value. Chelmsford called an end to the skirmishing and by 1pm he ordered his command to assemble above the Mangeni falls where the general intended to establish his next camp. Whilst the troops would bivouac there for the night, Chelmsford and his staff would return to Isandlwana and once the camp had been dismantled return the following day to reunite his command.

At about 2pm both Pulleine's note stating that firing had been heard to the left of the camp and Gardner's that the camp was under attack were received by Chelmsford. Clery reported that Crealock was heard to say, 'How very amusing! Actually attacking our camp! Most amusing!'[36] The general and his staff now rode towards Isandlwana in a leisurely fashion. Hamilton-Browne, who had returned with his NNC troops to begin striking camp, had begun to hear the sounds of battle, both rifles and artillery fire, as he neared Isandlwana. He sent runners back to Chelmsford reporting that the camp was under attack. By 1.30pm he had secured a vantage point to watch the last death throes of the defenders as the Zulus swarmed into the camp. Knowing that his force could do nothing to assist, he sent Captain Develing back with one last message to Chelmsford, 'For God's sake come back, the camp is surrounded and things I fear are going badly.'[37]

En route to Chelmsford Develing had encountered Lieutenant Colonel Harness with his four guns of N/5 Battery heading towards the Mangeni Hills. On hearing the report, Harness was determined to head towards Isandlwana and whilst Develing and Captain Church of the 2/24th rode on to find Chelmsford, Harness turned the guns around. This was a difficult procedure over the broken ground and Harness had not gone far when he received orders from Major Gosset, Chelmsford's ADC, to turn about and head for Mangeni as originally ordered. Harness must have been distraught but obeyed the general's order. Develing eventually reached Chelmsford and his account finally convinced the general that Isandlwana was under some sort of attack and he now spurred on his horse.

Commandant Lonsdale had left with Chelmsford just after 2pm and soon after asked the general's permission to ride ahead for he was suffering from the after-effects of a concussion he had sustained two weeks earlier and was tired and hungry. He also hoped to secure food for his men of the NNC for neither he nor they had eaten for nearly 36 hours. Lonsdale had actually ridden into the camp half asleep, and he only realized that the camp had been taken when he was attacked by a Zulu wearing the red tunic of a fallen soldier and brandishing an assegai. This quickly restored Lonsdale's senses and he saw that the camp had been lost. He quickly turned his tired horse around and fled the scene of carnage. He reached Chelmsford a few miles from the camp and when he related the news of defeat to the general and his staff, he could see the look of amazement, grief and horror on their faces. It was reported the Chelmsford was heard to say in disbelief, 'I can't understand it, I left a thousand men to guard the camp.'[38]

Awakening from his shock, Chelmsford now ordered Gosset to gallop back to Mangeni with the terrible news and to bring the men of the 2/24th to him. The general knew that he could not remain in the field with just half his force and that Isandlwana camp would have to be retaken.

Captain Parr, who had spent the day with the men of the 2/24th as they attempted to engage Matshana's warriors, recorded the moments when the troops learnt of the disaster:

At 3 p.m. we marched to the site of the new camp. We had just off-saddled, and many of us were half asleep, thinking, as is usually the case with men living in the open air, of when we should get our next meal. Suddenly (it was about half-past three) someone said, 'Hallo! There's a man in a hurry. He ought to have a horse behind every hill if he intends to keep on at that rate'. 'Who's the man?' said another, 'I can't see; have you your glasses?' said the first speaker. 'By Jove! It's Gosset, I hope nothing has gone wrong.' Interest in the rider being awakened, we watched him gallop on up the hill towards us, his horse evidently blown and weary. 'Well Gosset, what is it? You seem in a great hurry.' 'The

General's orders are that you are to saddle up and march on Isandlwana at once', said Gosset; 'the Zulus have got into our camp.' 'The Zulus have! You're not joking?' 'I wish I was. Lonsdale met the General about five miles from the camp; he had ridden up close to the camp and had the enemy in amongst the tents. The General is waiting for you with the mounted men.' 'Boots and saddles' sounded, and in a quarter of an hour the force was on its march back. While on the way we tried hard to solve satisfactorily the problem – 'The Zulus in our camp, what had become of the force left to hold it?'[39]

Parr and his comrades, though exhausted, matched determinedly back towards Isandlwana but it was not until 7.30pm that they finally reached Chelmsford and his staff, who were waiting 2 miles or so from the camp. In the darkness, the general, undoubtedly in a state of shock, spoke to the troops stating that the camp had been taken and that with 10,000 of the enemy in their rear and another 20,000 in front of them they had no alternative but to retake the camp and fight their way back to Rorke's Drift. Private P. Fitzgerald claimed that the general seemed to be near to tears, but his words were met with a cheer from his men. Captain Parr recorded:

Then with fixed bayonets, we advanced into the camp and made our way through, men and horses, stumbling and falling over tents half-upset, broken waggons, dead bodies of soldiers and of Zulus, dead oxen, dead horses, dead mules, burst sacks of grain, empty ammunition boxes, articles of camp equipment; and on the ridge, amongst the dead bodies of our comrades, formed our bivouac.[40]

The men spent a dreadful night, surrounded by the carnage of the disaster. Despite their fatigue many could not sleep whilst others collapsed immediately. Chelmsford spent the night walking amongst the men reassuring them and checking on sentries. Chelmsford tried to hurry his troops away before dawn came so that they would not be able to see clearly what lay at their feet, but many arose to find their uniforms caked with blood, entrails and brains. Some had slept in pools of blood. Other had lain only a foot away from a dead comrade. Despite the cold, the smell was oppressive. As one British soldier later wrote, '... it smelled like a sweet potato that had been cooked just when it was beginning to go bad – sweet, cloying, sickening'.[41]

Captain Parr later wrote that he and many of his comrades expected to find a repeat of the Isandlwana disaster when they reached Rorke's Drift, for the sky had been alight with flames from that direction throughout the night. Chelmsford too must have expected the worst, for if a force 1,700-strong could not defend Isandlwana how could a company of about 100 men hold Rorke's Drift? As Chelmsford's retreating column neared its destination it came across a battle-weary Zulu force moving parallel to it and heading back into Zululand. The two forces remained motionless staring at each other until one young Zulu sprang in front of a mass of squatting warriors exhorting them to attack. Suddenly he dashed down the hillside separating the forces brandishing his spear at the British. He came to within 30yd when he was shot. The other exhausted Zulus only watched his charge; they had not even risen from their squatting position. The two sides then carried on their respective ways.

Chelmsford sent forward a few of his mounted men who were able to report that the Union Jack was still flying at Rorke's Drift and it was clear that the small numbers of defenders had, somehow, been able to beat back numerous Zulu attacks throughout the late afternoon and into the following night. It was indeed an incredible tale of heroism and defiance and although Chelmsford and his men returned the cheers of the defenders as they marched to what remained of the supply depot, the general himself was again devastated for he, like many on this staff, had hoped that some survivors from Isandlwana might have found sanctuary at Rorke's Drift, but there were none. Chelmsford spent little time at Rorke's Drift. He personally interviewed some of the more notable figures who had made the defence including Lieutenants Bromhead and Chard as well as Private Henry Hook and he gave a speech to the rest of the little garrison. Gunner Howard repeated some of Chelmsford's words when he wrote home, 'The general said we were a brave little garrison, and this showed what a few men could do if they only had pluck.'[42]

Chelmsford remained at Rorke's Drift for a matter of hours before departing at about 10am with his staff for Pietermaritzburg. Colonel Glyn, who was in a complete state of shock at the loss of his regiment, was left in charge of the Rorke's Drift defences with orders to prepare for another Zulu attack. It was here that the first reports of atrocities committed against wounded Zulus by men of the NNC as well as British troops surfaced. Claims were made that Zulus found alive were 'despatched' by assegai or bayonet or even hung.

Whether Glyn was aware of such acts is open to debate, but certainly as the war progressed and such acts became more common Chelmsford knew that they had occurred and the fact that he made little effort to investigate or deter is not to his credit.

In some respects, Chelmsford had been right to place such trust in the effectiveness of the Martini-Henry rifle for its fire had certainly been devastating. Yet, even with their superior weapons, troops deployed in open order were clearly vulnerable to the determined tactics of the Zulus. Chelmsford would have to rethink how he would defeat the enemy and win the war. On the same day, the British invasion force in the south, under the command of Colonel Pearson, was attacked by 6,000 Zulus as they advanced towards the town of Eshowe, which Pearson had intended to use as a base for an advance upon Ulundi. Fortunately, scouts of the NNC discovered the concealed Zulus and prematurely sprung the trap starting the Battle of Nyezane. Pearson reacted quickly and a firing line was formed. The Zulu commander, Umatyiya, failed to keep control of his warriors who charged forward recklessly into a wall of fire which included the first use of the Gatling gun in the history of the British army. In the short engagement the Zulus lost over 500 men, the British just 14. However, this battle and the disaster at Isandlwana were to determine the nature of the war for the next three months for Pearson, upon reaching Eshowe, became besieged and Chelmsford was forced to launch a relief column. Yet, with so many men and materiel lost at Isandlwana the war would be virtually on hold until troop reinforcements arrived and provisions resupplied. For the moment Chelmsford's biggest concern was how to deflect some of the criticism he now faced for the Isandlwana disaster.

Chapter 6

Recovery and Absolution?

Frederic Dickenson was the editor on duty in the London offices of Reuters just after midnight on 10 February 1879 when he received a telegram via the island of Cape St Vincent, in code, from Cape Town. This reported the Battle of Isandlwana and contained a long list of names, not in code, which Dickenson at once realized must be those officers killed. It was clear that there had been a major disaster of British arms and Dickenson called for a relay of hanson cabs to rush the story to the London newspaper offices, sheet by sheet as it was decoded. Those newspapers that had a contract with Reuters for foreign news benefited and were able to change their front pages and run with the news of the defeat in their editions of 11 February, although it was not until the following day that editorials appeared in most of the national papers. This was not the case with some of the provincial papers which were able to report the news in afternoon editions of 11 February. The editor of the *Devon Evening Express* in Exeter wrote:

> The nation has been startled today by the sad news which has come to hand from Cape Town. The British forces have sustained a terrible reverse. Either there was a want of vigilance on the part of our forces, or the Zulus are more formidable than our military authorities have calculated. It may be that both of these circumstances contributed to the disaster which has overtaken our troops ...

For Chelmsford these words were the start of a long road, on which he would continue for the remainder of his life and would see him have to defend his conduct not just over the defeat at Isandlwana but for the whole of the Zulu War.

The general and his staff stayed briefly at Rorke's Drift but long enough for Chelmsford to write to Frere to inform him that, 'No. 3 column has maintained a terrible disaster.' He concluded the short note with an observation which clearly illustrates how much Chelmsford and his staff had underestimated the enemy. He wrote, 'The desperate bravery of the Zulus has been the subject of much astonishment.'[1] The general then rode onto to Helpmekaar, where he managed a night's sleep, before continuing to Pietermaritzburg, where he arrived on 26 January. Frere, on seeing the general, noted that he was 'looking many years older, so changed and worn by anxiety and sleeplessness'.[2] Chelmsford clearly felt that he needed to be at the political heart of the region to not only discuss with Frere the way forward but also to begin a campaign to deflect blame for the disaster away from his own conduct.

Part of that campaign began whilst at Helpmekaar when Chelmsford convened a court of inquiry into the Isandlwana disaster which was instructed to gather evidence relating solely to the loss of the camp. It was directed not to pronounce judgement or to examine the reasons behind Chelmsford's decision to lead a substantial part of his force away from the camp on the morning of the battle. The court, chaired by Lieutenant Colonel Harness RA, was composed of the three most senior officers then at Helpmekaar: Harness, Colonel Hassard RE and Lieutenant Colonel Law RA. The court assembled at Helpmakaar on 27 January, when the following officers gave evidence: Major Clery, Colonel Glyn, Captain Gardner, 14th Hussars, Captain Essex, 75th Regiment, Lieutenant Cochrane, 32nd Regiment, Lieutenant Smith-Dorrien, 95th Regiment, Captain Nourse of the NNC and Lieutenant Curling RA. The evidence taken consisted of statements made by the above officers, not one of whom appears to have been questioned and the inquiry was strictly limited to the occurrences at the camp. Harness was fiercely loyal to Chelmsford, and he clearly wished to follow his general's instructions to the letter and present stark facts without any opinions or conclusions. Also, by appointing Harness as chairman, Chelmsford removed the need for Harness himself to give evidence which might have raised the embarrassing issue of Chelmsford refusing Harness' plea to march on Isandlwana when news of the Zulu attack first reached him.

Predictably the inquiry's findings offered very little in terms of an explanation for the disaster. The survivors were mainly peripheral to the day's events and most offered rather confused accounts, which often contradicted each other. Some, like Lieutenant Curling, were clearly suffering from battlefield trauma and all this combined to present muddled findings. Yet, it achieved, for a while at least, what Chelmsford had aimed for, that being to deflect blame away from him and his staff and allowed for the focus to be directed very much on the events at Isandlwana alone. The inquiry questioned both the retreat of the NNC from the firing line, which is today open to debate, and Durnford's decision to ride out of the camp at the news of a large body of Zulus in front of it. Both offered Chelmsford ready scapegoats for no one at the time was going to defend the NNC and Durnford had conveniently died in battle. The deputy adjutant general in Southern Africa, Colonel Bellairs, forwarded the inquiry's finding to Chelmsford with the attached summary:

> From the statements made to the Court, it may be gathered that the cause of the reverse suffered at Isandhlwana was that Col. Durnford, as senior officer, overruled the orders which Lt. Col. Pulleine had received to defend the camp, and directed that the troops should be moved into open, in support of the Native Contingent which he had brought up and which was engaging the enemy. Had Lt. Col. Pulleine not been interfered with and been allowed to carry out the distinct order given him [by Clery and not Chelmsford] to defend the camp, it cannot be doubted that a different result would have been obtained ...[3]

Although the inquiry had stalled some criticism of Chelmsford, at least in Southern Africa, the British press and later such prominent individuals as Bishop Colenso and his daughter Fanny, who had been romantically linked to Durnford, questioned the findings of the inquiry, and began to ask wider questions as to the conduct of the campaign.

Crealock tried to further distance Chelmsford and his staff by attempting to shift some blame onto Colonel Glyn by hinting that Glyn was responsible for the defences of the camp and he should thus have ensured that it was entrenched or laagered. It is not clear whether Chelmsford was aware of Crealock's approach or if so whether he approved of it. Glyn was sent numerous official requests from the staff seeking his interpretation of his responsibilities regarding the defence of the camp, which Glyn ignored. Glyn was undoubtedly suffering from trauma, loss and depression, but fortunately Clery saw through Crealock's ploy and deflected much of this until Glyn was well and able enough to respond. When he did his words were damning, 'Odd the general asking me to tell him what he knows more than I do.'[4] This put an end to this line of attack and Glyn always maintained a public loyalty to Chelmsford.

With the Central Column now gone, Chelmsford's plan for a concerted advance had evaporated. He could only write to both Wood and Pearson telling them to halt their advances and that for the time being they were on their own. In the case of Pearson his position was tenuous for after the Battle of Nyezane his column had reached the old mission station at Eshowe and here Pearson and his men were besieged by Zulu forces. Until reinforcements arrived from England Chelmsford was in no position to relieve Eshowe or contemplate any further advance into Zululand. The war was effectively put on hold for nearly two months, although Wood's command continued to harass the local Zulu forces in the north of Zululand in a series of raids upon homesteads and cattle.

Chelmsford's immediate concerns were to justify himself to both Frere and the home government, to seek reinforcements and to defend himself from the criticism that was beginning to build against him. He seems to have disregarded the men of the Central Column, for its remnants languished in the cramped and unhealthy conditions at Helpmekaar and Rorke's Drift with little to do once they had fortified the depots. The rain that had been such a feature of the advance continued and the men, many of them wounded or sick, had little access to shelter or medicines. Melancholy for the loss of friends and boredom was the overwhelming emotion at this time. In lengthy letters to his father, Lieutenant Charles E. Commeline of the Royal Engineers fully described the two months of tedium awaiting reinforcements, building earthworks and roads, bringing forward stores, ammunition and equipment, and coping with transport difficulties. Amid the frustration came criticism, 'the Zulus have completely out-generalled us'. In another letter he wrote that the British had been living in 'such a fool's paradise, over-estimating our knowledge of the enemy and under estimating their strength and tactics'. As these concerns began to be reflected in the press, Commeline doubted that Chelmsford 'can remove the unfavourable impression that has been created'.[5]

Before the press began their campaign against the general in earnest and Parliament could act to censure him, Queen Victoria pre-empted any criticism by ordering a message of sympathy to be sent to her former ADC, via the Secretary of State for War, 'The Queen has graciously desired me to say she sympathises most sincerely with you in the dreadful loss which has deprived her of so many gallant officers and men and that Her Majesty places entire confidence in you and in her troops to maintain our honour and our good name.' Similarly, from the Duke of Cambridge Chelmsford received the following telegram, 'Have heard, by telegraph, of events occurred. Grieved for 24th and others who have fallen victims. Fullest confidence in regiment and am satisfied that you have done and will continue to do everything that is right.'[6]

However, the general consensus at Horse Guards was to point the finger at Chelmsford. A memorandum of 11 February, signed by three of the most senior army officers, Major General Sir Charles Ellice, Adjutant General, Major General Sir Daniel Lysons, Quartermaster General, and Major General Sir A. Horsford, Military Secretary, stated: 'The force of so-called cavalry at Lord Chelmsford's disposition was too small and not sufficiently trained to act properly as a reconnoitring screen and consequently the commander in chief was ignorant of the position and number of the Zulu forces.'[7]

An Intelligence Department memorandum of the same day was even more critical of the commander, 'He does not seem to have fortified the Camp at Isandlana. He did not keep up a proper communication with his Camp. He was led away by the Zulus who decoyed him from the Camp. In the meantime, the Zulus collected in thousands under the hills near the Camp ... Why were not scouts sent to explore?'[8]

Although Cambridge was shocked and distressed by the news, until Chelmsford's official report had been received, he was prepared to withhold judgement. The press would not be so patient.

At this time, the strain, both mental and physical, was evidently taking its toll on Chelmsford's health. Crealock, writing to Alison from Pietermaritzburg on 2 February, stated:

> He [Chelmsford] is better the last 24 hours, but still not himself and the authorities ought to realise the chance of his not being able to stand up against a long continuance of his present duties. He has pulled through so far very well, physically and mentally, but reaction comes, and a long year's hard work is telling I can see ...[9]

Yet, Chelmsford did possess considerable reserves of moral strength and tenacity. On a day-to-day basis he continued to function, and he conducted himself intelligently and with some dignity. In his own mind he clearly saw the Isandlwana defeat rested on Durnford's shoulders for he had left a sufficient force to defend the camp and although he would avoid directly blaming Durnford, he cleverly used others, such as Frere, to make the implications and accusations for him. Even so, there is no doubt that over the next weeks and months Chelmsford suffered moments of deep depression, which were often triggered by direct criticism of him. Colonel Harness wrote to his sister that, 'The papers are certainly terribly down on the general – I am glad to hear that Crealock his military secretary keeps them from him a good deal'.[10]

At a low point Chelmsford and Frere discussed the possibility of them both resigning and by 9 February the general decided to state his position in the following petition to the Secretary of State for War:

> I consider it my duty to lay before you my opinion that it is very desirable, in view of future contingencies, that an officer of the rank of Major-General should be sent out to South Africa without delay. In June 1878 I mentioned privately to His Royal Highness the Field-Marshal Commander-in-Chiefs, that the strain of prolonged anxiety, physical and mental, was even then telling to me. What I feel then, I feel still more now. His Excellency, Sir Bartle Frere, concurs in this representation and points out to me that the officer selected should be fitted to succeed him in the position of High Commissioner. In making this representation I need not assure you that it will be my earnest desire to carry on my duties for Her Majesty's service up to the fullest extent of my powers.[11]

This letter was published in the British press on 17 March 1879 and caused a sensation for it was widely seen as a request to step down by Chelmsford and thus an admission of his failings. More likely it was written when the general was feeling down and should be viewed as a request for more senior support with the difficult task that now lay before him. However, the disquiet this caused in the government and the press would begin the thinking and debate within Whitehall that would culminate a few weeks later with Chelmsford's replacement.

In the meantime, both the general and the War Office were consumed by the need for reinforcements to be sent. Chelmsford kept his request to the minimum. He asked the War Office for three infantry battalion, two cavalry regiments, a company of engineers and enough artillery to replace the losses at Isandlwana. On a more practical level Chelmsford was also in need of a dozen shoeing smiths and two veterinary surgeons. He was not, therefore, requesting a larger force, but was only asking to be reinforced to his original strength, with some additional cavalry. To have been so conservative in his demands illustrates that Chelmsford remained oblivious to the fact that mounted troops were essential to the successful re-invasion of Zululand and that the lack of such a sizeable force had been one of the main reasons for the earlier disaster. In addition, extra infantry battalions would have ensured that the both the Natal border and its unsettled and fearful residents would have had the reassurance of greater protection. The government, however, had much grander plans.

Rocked by the Isandlwana disaster, neither Disraeli's government nor the Duke of Cambridge could be considered to have acted slowly. Just two days after receiving Chelmsford's telegram informing Whitehall of the defeat, Frederick Stanley, the Secretary of State for War, cabled to Chelmsford the news that the general's requests had been met in full and then exceeded. Two regiments of cavalry were to be despatched, along with two field batteries of artillery and double the number of infantry battalions. Five were to be sent from Britain with the 57th Regiment transferred from duties in Ceylon. These numbers placed a huge strain upon the War Office establishment, which was already struggling to meet the demand for troops in Afghanistan. Between 20 February and 1 April, nineteen transport ships left London docks, Portsmouth or Southampton, heading for Southern Africa. On the same day as Stanley's telegram Cambridge wrote informing Chelmsford that reinforcements would sail from Britain within a fortnight and that they would be accompanied by three major generals: Henry Crealock, Sir Frederick Marshall and Edward Newdigate. Unfortunately for Chelmsford, the addition of these three senior officers would actually add to his woes rather than reduce them.

Although the despatch of such a significant number of reinforcements was a logistical success, for which both Cambridge and the War Office deserve credit, the quality of many of the troops was lacking, as Chelmsford was soon to discover. For example, the 91st was amongst the first to be chosen to reinforce Chelmsford. The regiment was badly understrength and could only be made fit for active service by absorbing no fewer than 374 volunteers from across 11 different regiments. Many were young recruits who were only partly trained in musketry, some of whom had hardly ever fired their

Martini-Henry rifles. Surprisingly, after some initial scares these troops would rise to the challenges that they had to face.

The men of the 60th Rifles arrived in Durban on 27 March 1879, having landed from England two weeks before. They were paraded in front of Chelmsford. In his lecture to these troops the general clearly demonstrated that any complacency that he had felt about the fighting abilities of the Zulus had rapidly disappeared after Isandlwana. Captain Edward Hutton was present to hear Chelmsford and in 1928, Hutton, by now a lieutenant general, wrote in the *Army Quarterly* of April of that year about Chelmsford's words to him and his men:

On the afternoon of our arrival [27 March] Lord Chelmsford told us to forget the drill to which we had been accustomed, and to adhere strictly to solid formations such as the square and echelon movements; the enemy was to be treated as cavalry. The impression left on our minds [by Chelmsford's speech] was that the Zulus were very formidable foes, and we soon found out that this unfortunate sentiment prevailed on all sides, and that hesitation and vacillation were the natural result. Our men, especially the young soldiers, were not slow to share the general feeling of uneasiness which the disasters at Isandlwana and elsewhere had caused.[12]

With the fear of God now placed in his troops and his own mind as to the dangers presented by the Zulus, Chelmsford focused on the most pressing issue he faced, the relief of Eshowe. As early as 10 February Chelmsford had travelled to the Lower Drift of the Tugela River to inspect the two strong positions still held there by the British. Each were garrisoned by detachments of the Buffs, the 99th Regiment and the Naval Brigade. Fort Pearson, built on a knoll on the Natal side of the border, overlooked the Tugela, whereas Fort Tenedos had been built on the Zulu bank by Pearson's men as they had advanced towards Eshowe. Although Tenedos was a simple earthwork surrounded by a ditch, it was considered sufficient to resist even the most determined attack, whilst Fort Pearson was thought to be impregnable. Life for the garrisons was made difficult by the continued bad weather, the concerns for their comrades besieged in Eshowe and the regular sightings of Zulu scouts on the surrounding hills which created a sense of threat and foreboding amongst the troops. On top of this, the lack of intelligence and numerous rumours as to the wellbeing of those in Eshowe and of the Zulu's intentions reduced morale still further and resulted in several moments when the garrison troops were stood to arms with the expectation of an enemy attack that never materialized.

Whilst visiting the garrisons Chelmsford took the opportunity to speak to the troops and touched upon the reasons behind the Isandlwana defeat. To be repeated many times by him, the general attributed the disaster, by implication, to Durnford's decision to leave the camp. He stated he had a:

> ... firm conviction that the troops there present would have been more than sufficient to have repulsed the attack of the 18,000 or 20,000 Zulus reported to have been engaged in the attack, if only they had been kept together, and had not lost their formation, when at a distance from the camp, where they could not renew their ammunition when exhausted ...[13]

These words were recorded by the correspondent of *The Standard*, Charles Norris-Newman, who claimed that the general felt that this reason alone explained the sad loss at Isandlwana. Furthermore, Norris-Newman noted the general's new respect for the Zulus when he told the assembled troops never to underrate or despise the enemy, but to check their attack by close, accurate and steady firing and on no account were they to break their ranks, but to maintain their ground and formation, fighting it out, if need be, back-to-back with the bayonet. It seems that Chelmsford was learning by his own mistakes.

Chelmsford quickly realized the force at the forts was insufficient to mount an advance towards Eshowe and that Pearson would have to fight his way back to the Tugela. On 11 February two 'runners' arrived from the Lower Tugela with a despatch from the general, which required Colonel Pearson to retire with half his force to the Tugela, leaving the remainder to garrison the fort. Pearson, after consulting with his senior officers, decided that it was not practicable to follow the general's orders, for Pearson's intelligence was that the surrounding countryside was occupied by Zulus in force. Pearson's decision seems, in retrospect, a defeatist one. He had already decisively beaten the Zulus in the open at Nyezane, where the scouts of the NNC had discovered the waiting Zulus which had triggered the battle. The firepower of the Martini-Henry rifle and the naval Gatling guns had decimated the Zulu attack. Pearson's men were armed with the latest military technology and the fact that he and his officers felt unable to respond positively to Chelmsford's order clearly shows how much the perceived Zulu threat had unsettled the British. Chelmsford must have been frustrated to have received Pearson's negative response which now tied the general into a strategy in which the relief of Eshowe became his top priority. Over the next weeks Chelmsford focused on building up his forces and improving his intelligence network.

The general was faced with multiple challenges, some of which would haunt him over the following months. Transport continued to present major difficulties. Not only had the British already procured the vast majority of wagons and oxen teams in Natal, the defeat at Isandlwana had deprived him of the use of numerous wagons and had seen the death of the oxen left in the camp. Over 3,000 oxen had also died from disease, overwork and misuse. Prices for both livestock and wagons continued to increase, and this also hindered the Natal economy which itself became crippled by the logistical demands of the British. In addition to this the continued bad weather had turned the already poor tracks into muddy quagmires. These factors would force Chelmsford to adopt a different approach when he advanced to relieve Eshowe.

Yet, it was not all bad news for the general for he received a boost of significant numbers of mounted troops, which would prove to be vital as he marched towards Eshowe. After the defeat at Isandlwana, the Frontier Light Horse began to recruit again and managed to create a new 138-strong unit named the Natal Light Horse. Some 200 men were recruited from the Cape Colony and over 100 men joined from the Transvaal. Also, many of the mounted men who served under Durnford, and who had survived the fate of their commander, had returned to their clans to recruit afresh and in total 560 natives now returned to join the 850 additional colonial volunteers. Chelmsford, though, still considered that the support he had received in Natal, and in particular from Sir Henry Bulwer, the governor, to be lacking.

The two men had disagreed for months over Natal's contribution to the war effort and the general was no doubt aggrieved by Bulwer's reluctance to support the imposition of martial law, which would have made the procurement of supplies, manpower and transport far easier. The two men reached loggerheads over Chelmsford's desire to arm a considerable force of Natal natives who would then, he envisaged, raid into Zululand to tie down large numbers of Zulu warriors whilst the British advanced on Ulundi. There was no way that Bulwer could countenance the arming of natives on a large scale, although he did concede and made available several thousand men to enter Zululand with the British to act as labourers, and he did permit that the NNC regiments be allowed to replace their losses in the ranks.

Although Chelmsford was able to maintain a civil relationship when face-to-face with Bulwer, both men expelled a great deal of needless energy in opposing each other's stance in a series of pointed letters. Chelmsford felt that Bulwer was being deliberately obstructive in the general's efforts to build up supplies and transport and even as the reinforcements began to arrive his ability to act decisively was seriously hampered. After the crushing defeat of Isandlwana, with his reputation already under severe scrutiny, the image of Chelmsford as being slow to act began to be established. In retrospect this is somewhat unjustified for particularly in the area of transport much was out of his control, yet he never considered a change of tactic in the second invasion of Zululand, where, once more, the British advance would be tied to the pace of the oxen they employed.

Despite the frustrations he was experiencing, Chelmsford was able to secure his biggest success by recruiting the services of John Dunn, one-time friend and advisor to Cetshwayo and former resident in Zululand, where the king had granted him lands in the Lower Tugela region; the very lands over which Chelmsford would have to lead the relieving force towards Eshowe. Dunn had been very reluctant to take sides in the conflict, but he knew that despite the Isandlwana defeat British reinforcements and superior firepower would inevitably be victorious. Thus, when he received a personal approach from Chelmsford himself Dunn felt he had little choice but to side with the British against his old friend Cetshwayo. The general had a specific role in mind for Dunn as Chief of Intelligence and when the relief column finally moved towards Eshowe Dunn was at its head along with nearly 250 of his own armed native retainers. Yet, even before the advance Dunn was collecting and receiving intelligence from a network of spies within Zululand, specifically from a man named Magumbi, who as the advanced party neared submitted a report that gave very specific information about where the enemy was placed and in what numbers, which would prove to be highly accurate.

By early March Chelmsford had built up a strong enough force to attempt Pearson's relief. He had 400 men from HMS *Shah* and 200 from

HMS *Boadicea* with 2 Gatling guns. In addition to the Buffs and 99th left at the Lower Drift, Chelmsford had the newly arrived 57th, 91st Highlanders and 60th Rifles. The NNC had been reorganized by Chelmsford; he had dropped the battalion system and established independent units mostly under the command of their original officers. The men were also more widely and better armed, many with Snider rifles. These men and the mounted troops, under the overall command of Major Barrow, made up the balance of the relieving column. The total strength was 3,390 white and 2,280 native troops.

It was Chelmsford's original intention that the column would be commanded by Major General Henry Crealock, but as Crealock did not reach Natal in time, Chelmsford took personal command on 23 March. It is perhaps bewildering, and this is no doubt indicative of Chelmsford's mental state at the time, that he had even considered Crealock to lead the relief force. This was Chelmsford's first opportunity to try to restore some of his battered reputation as a field commander and he was clearly reluctant to seize this chance. Chelmsford had finally been spurred into action by a message received from Pearson on 16 March, which informed him that his supplies would run out by 4 April. With this new information Chelmsford was convinced that he must start for Eshowe no later than 28 March. There was no alternative but for Chelmsford to head towards the Lower Tugela to assume command of the relief column. Yet, before this could happen the general was furious to learn of another British reversal when on the morning of 12 March, a British supply train, which had been forced to encamp at Intombi Drift due to bad weather, was surprised in a dawn attack. Captain Moriarty and over sixty men of the 80th Regiment were killed in a rush attack. The British position had not been entrenched and nor had the wagons been sufficiently laagered to offer much protection and although the appalling weather on the night of 11 March had probably made such precautions impossible, the placing of just two sentries was clearly remiss. Chelmsford was determined that his force would not suffer a similar fate and with his new respect for the fighting abilities of the Zulus caution would be the general's watchword as he advanced towards Eshowe.

On the 25th Chelmsford sent a despatch to Colonel Stanley, the Secretary of State for War, outlining his plans:

The Column will not advance by the road which Colonel Pearson's column took but by one which runs nearly parallel to it, but nearer the coast. The advantage of this line is that the road runs through an easy open country for three quarters of the distance, whereas by the other line the road runs through bush country nearly the whole way. The force will advance without tents, and with only a blanket and waterproof sheet for each man. Notwithstanding, however, this reduction of weight, the convoy carrying a month's provision for the garrison and 10 days' supplies (without groceries) for the relieving column, will consist of 44 carts and about 100 wagons …[14]

Even with Chelmsford's best efforts to reduce the weight of supplies to be carried on the advance he would still be leading a substantial, and slow, wagon train, which would be over 3 miles in length. Naturally, he feared that the Zulus would attack this vulnerable column whilst on the move, but this would go against the tactics deployed by the Zulus to attack in the open. Furthermore, Chelmsford had received intelligence via Dunn's scouts that he could expect a concerted attack from a large Zulu force around 10 miles from Eshowe.

Shortly before leading the relief column across the Tugela Chelmsford issued a memorandum of standing instructions to all his officers, which clearly demonstrated that he had learnt the lessons from Isandlwana. They included companies to be held in close order, ammunition to be readily available, as were entrenching tools, and a specific directive was given for the force to form a square laager each night, surrounded by a shelter trench, with European and native troops placed up to a mile outside of the laager to provide advance warning of an attack. In addition, the general now had a substantial force of mounted troops and with these men he could ensure that scouts were deployed well in front of the advancing column, as well as on its flanks. Chelmsford was not leaving anything to chance in his latest foray into Zulu territory.

The relief force had assembled at the Lower Drift by 27 March and two days later, at 6am, the long-awaited advance began. The men and wagons were laboriously ferried across the Tugela on ponts before moving off in earnest. The column initially followed Pearson's original path before veering off to the right at the St Andrew's mission station and from there the troops followed the coastal track. The incessant rain had made the ground soft and wet, and the wagon wheels soon turned the track to a muddy quagmire, yet despite this the column was able to cover 10 miles on its first day. Chelmsford had appointed Captain William Molyneux of the 22nd Regiment as 'laager master' on the expedition and he recorded that the first night's laager was not a success for the wagon drivers had no real experience of creating a laager, and after a few unsuccessful attempts '… a laager was made anyhow, and it would only hold one third of our oxen. So much for our first laager on our first trek.'[15] Fortunately, with more practice, and a few choice words of advice from Dunn, the wagon drivers became more adept as the advance progressed. The troops must have cursed Chelmsford's decision not to bring tents for that night, as on subsequent ones, the rain was incessant and although some men managed to gain limited shelter underneath the wagons, many simply tried to sleep in the mud, with only a blanket and grey coat for protection.

The march was delayed the following day by a persistent morning mist, and it was not until 8am that the column began its slow advance once more. Barrow personally led his mounted troops, and it was on this day that they first saw groups of the enemy which seemed to be congregating to the north-west. By evening the column had covered 7 miles and encamped on the southern bank of the Amatikulu River, the last major natural barrier before Eshowe. The following day Barrow led his mounted men and Dunn took his scouts across the raised river. The troops were forced to wade across, with boots and rifles above their heads, the water up to their shoulders. Each wagon had to be double-yoked and it took 8 hours for the whole force to make the river crossing. A laager was constructed a mile and a half from the Amatikulu and the exhausted men settled down for yet another wet night.

By midday on 1 April, Chelmsford and his men neared the vicinity of Nyezane. Barrow's scouts had reported the growing presence of larger groups of Zulus, and Pearson, using a heliograph, had been able to inform Chelmsford that a large Zulu army, in the region of 12,000 warriors, was, according to his own intelligence, being assembled to block the British advance on Eshowe. With the terrain and vegetation offering cover to the Zulus for a surprise strike, Chelmsford took no chances and decided that to advance further might risk an attack whilst on the line of march. Molyneaux and Dunn rode ahead and selected a position on the summit of a slight knoll to construct the British camp. The site was known as Gingindlovu to the Zulus, meaning the place of elephants. The British troops soon demonstrated their sense of humour by christening the site 'Gin gin I love you'. Molyneaux marked out the corners of the laager and by the time the first wagons began to arrive he was ready to guide them into place. The laager was finished by 5pm just before the rain once again descended. Dunn later swam across the Nyezane River, under cover of darkness, to report to Chelmsford the presence of a large enemy force. Dunn informed Chelmsford that in all probability the British would be attacked at dawn.

The British position was certainly a strong defensive one, thanks in part to Molyneaux's skilled control of the wagon drivers, but also Chelmsford's determination to ensure that the laager was as solid as it could possibly be to resist the charge of the Zulu impi. The wagon laager was formed over 117m², giving sufficient room inside to accommodate 2,000 oxen, 300 horses and over 2,000 native troops. The 3,400 imperial troops were positioned in the enclosing shelter trench, which was 144m² and roughly 13m from the laagered wagons. The corners, the weakest point, were reinforced by placing the 9-pounder guns, the Gatling guns and rocket tubes at each. Although the British had worked tirelessly throughout the afternoon to prepare their strong defences, darkness and heavy rain, which was to soak the British throughout the night, meant it was not possible to cut back the high grasses and bush that encroached to within 100yd of the defences.

As the sun rose through the early morning mist, the Zulu force, commanded by a trusted alley of the king, Somopho kaZikhale, viewed the British position on the open plain as one that was ripe to be enveloped by traditional tactics. The shelter trenches concealed to Somopho the true strength of the British position. Chelmsford's advance had placed Cetshwayo in a dilemma for he had viewed the northern column, commanded by Colonel Wood, as the biggest threat, but with the attempt to relieve Eshowe Cetshwayo had to divide his forces. Whilst the majority of the warriors who had assembled at Ulundi were sent north to attack Wood a proportion would travel south to counter Chelmsford's advance. This force was augmented by 4,500 men from local clans and an additional 3,000 warriors under the command of Prince Dabulamanzi, the king's half-brother, who had commanded the Zulus in the vicinity of Eshowe. In total Somopho had around 11,000 warriors to oppose Chelmsford's force of roughly 5,500.

At almost 6am, the Zulus on the far side of the Nyezane River, to the west of the British position, came into general view. Chelmsford had deployed men of the 60th Rifles, the 91st and NNC as picquets and it was these men that first saw and encountered the advancing Zulus. So rapid was the advance that one man of the 91st, Private Marshall, who had gone to the river to obtain water was overwhelmed and killed. The picquets managed to fire off several shots at the charging mass of warriors before they raced back to the sanctuary of the laager. The troops in the shelter trenches were roused from their early morning lethargy by the sound of firing and riflemen assumed positions on top of wagons, from where they could direct fire over the heads of the British firing lines.

The Zulus crossed the Nyezane in columns at two drifts, separated by a distance of a mile or so. As they advanced up the slope towards the British position, the Zulus deployed in the 'chest and horns' formation; one column veered off to the left to form the left 'horn', the other fanned out to create the 'chest'. Suddenly, from around a knoll on the British left, known as Misi Hill, appeared the right 'horn'. The British position had been enveloped in little over 15 minutes.

At a distance of 800m the petty officer of HMS *Boadicea*, in charge of one of the Gatling guns, begged Lord Chelmsford's permission to test the range of the weapon. Chelmsford nodded his ascent for a short burst, and at the turn of two handles, the gunfire was directed at the charging Zulus. Although a clear lane was cut through the body of warriors, the fire did not slow the Zulu advance in the slightest. Within a few seconds the attackers had reached the 400m distance markers which had been diligently set out the night before. Yet, Chelmsford gave orders for the men to hold their fire until the Zulus were within 300m, the Martini-Henry's most effective killing range.

With cries of 'they are encircled!', the Zulus tried to close in on the British position. The first Zulu assault was upon the north side of the position, manned by soldiers of the 3/60th Rifles. Regaled with gruesome stories of the slaughter at Isandlwana, the young inexperienced soldiers were now confronted by hordes of fearless warriors. Captain Edward Hutton was not surprised that the first volley seemed so ineffectual for it 'could hardly be expected to have done much execution, since there were but a number of darting figures at irregular intervals and distances …'.[16] Many troops simply froze or fired wildly. Officers, including Hutton, reacted quickly; some troops received a swift rap across the back from a parade-ground stick, others the venom of their officer's tongue. As Hutton wrote, 'a smart rap with my stick soon helped a man recover his self-possession'.[17] John Dunn noted that the young soldiers were failing to adjust their rifle sights as the Zulus closed in on the British, with the result that many bullets would have sailed over the enemy's heads.

Taking cover in the long, wet grass, the Zulus returned an ineffectual fire on the British square. Some of the warriors were armed with Martini-Henrys, plundered from the battlefield of Isandlwana, but, fortunately for the British, their fire was mostly high. Apparently, the Zulus also had difficulty in adjusting the range sights. Although the Zulu fire claimed some notable victims, including Lieutenant George Johnson of the 99th and Colonel F.V. Northey of the 3/60th, the final British butcher's bill of thirteen killed and forty-eight wounded was, considering the intensity of the battle, remarkably light. Chelmsford's decision to prepare shelter trenches undoubtedly saved the lives of many riflemen. Norris-Newman of *The Standard* told of Chelmsford's close call with a Zulu bullet and of the general's energy throughout the battle:

> ... poor Johnson of the 99th, Instructor of Musketry, fell dead, being shot right through the breast within a yard or two of his commanding officer and myself. The General and his staff [NB: Crealock sustained a slight flesh wound whilst standing next to Chelmsford] were omnipresent; Lord Chelmsford on foot, with his red nightcap on, encouraging the men, directing their fire, and instructing them to fire low and steady ...[18]

As the Zulu advance ground to a halt, the warriors comprising the 'chest' began to edge to their right, past the corner of the square, and attempted to attack the men of the 99th on the left face. The left 'horn' had pushed forward to a point where they were able to make a determined attack upon the front right corner. It was here that one of the Gatling guns was placed and the 1,200 rounds it fired was sufficient to beat back the attackers, although it was claimed one Zulu warrior managed to get close enough to the Gatling to actually touch it before being cut down. The Zulus moved further against the 99th. Their threat seemed so intense that even the special correspondent Norris-Newman grabbed a Martini-Henry and claimed at least one Zulu victim. Again, as with the charge on the front face, the attack on the left stalled. At this point the right 'horn' appeared from Misi Hill and deployed to attack the rear face of the laager, defended by men of the 91st.

Although as inexperienced as their colleagues in the 60th, the men of the 91st equipped themselves well in their first engagement. Their sights were adjusted down as the warriors approached and no Zulu got within 30yd of the shelter trenches. The Martini-Henry fire of the 91st was ably supported by fire from two 9-pounders and, at the other end of the line, a Gatling and rocket tubes. The sustained fire made the Zulu attack recoil from the rear face and roll round to attack the right face, desperate to find any place to break into the defences and engage the British in hand-to-hand combat. The defence of the right face was left to the seasoned veterans of the 57th who met the Zulu charge with steady, well-directed volley fire. The battle had now been raging for an hour and, although stalled, the Zulus showed no sign of retreating, but clung on to the cover afforded by the long grass and continued their sniping at the British.

A rocket was sent skimming over the grass, its flaming tail seeming to cause some panic amongst the Zulus and Chelmsford considered it was time to unleash Major Barrow's Mounted Infantry, who filed out of the square and launched themselves upon the warriors of the right 'horn'. Yet, the general's order had been premature for the warriors soon regained their composure and threatened to surround the mounted men. Chelmsford quickly realized the danger and ordered Barrow to return to the laager. Barrow and two of his men were wounded. Although the British fire had halted the attack, the Zulus showed no signs of abandoning their positions so Chelmsford once more turned to Barrow's men to ride out and descend upon the Zulu right flank. Armed with their swords, the troopers charged out. A few warriors made a determined stand and sold their lives, but the majority of their comrades fell back rapidly. Barrow later claimed that about fifty warriors fell to his men's swords.

Barrow's men were followed by the riders of the Natal Carbineers, who used their weapons to cut down warriors without mercy. Chelmsford then ordered the NNC out to deal with any Zulus attempting to hide, yet these men, who could not be controlled by their officers, killed every Zulu they could find, including the wounded. More than 500 Zulu bodies lay around the laager, including one Zulu wearing an officer's sword belt taken from Isandlwana, and many more bodies could be seen along the line of retreat. The Zulus lost more than 1,200 killed during the actual assault against the British position. The ruthless pursuit and killing of fleeing and wounded Zulus would give rise to many uncomfortable questions about Chelmsford's conduct during the campaign, as would the claim by a British soldier, James Foxwell, that he had witnessed wounded Zulus being thrown alive into burial pits after the battle. It is clear that after the disaster at Isandlwana any sensibilities British troops might have had towards their foe had evaporated and it seems that many officers, including Chelmsford, were happy to look the other way when such acts of brutality were committed.

On 20 March Chelmsford had written to Wood to outline his planned advance to Eshowe and asked the commander of Number 4 Column to demonstrate so as to draw off some of the strength from the impi reportedly congregating to attack Chelmsford. Although Wood had firm intelligence that his command could expect another impi to attack his position at Kambula, he decided to support Chelmsford's plea with a daring raid upon Mbilini's stronghold on top of the mountain plateau of Hlobane. Chef Mbilini's warriors had been using the Hlobane position for sanctuary and from which to launch raids in the area. Wood's planned two-pronged assault began on the morning of 28 March and quickly ran into difficulties with the British, led by Redvers Buller, meeting stiff resistance from the defenders. In addition, the second assault, led by Colonel Russell, was unable to assail the mountain and Wood himself, at the base of the mountain, was pinned down under sniper fire and played no meaningful part in the resultant debacle. Once on the mountain top, Buller saw to his horror that the large impi which had been despatched by Cetshwayo was rapidly approaching and that all hope of escape was evaporating. Buller led the remains of his command down what became known as 'Devil's Pass' and although he managed to escape, and win the Victoria Cross in the process, British casualties were high at ten officers and eighty troopers killed. These figures included notable colonial officers, such as Colonel Frederick Weatherley and the Boer leader Piet Uys, whose death resulted in the overnight desertion of the only remaining Boer units fighting for the British. In addition, several hundred Zulus opposed to Cetshwayo, and who fought for the British, were also killed.

One of the many consequences of the British defeat was that Buller refused to work alongside Colonel Russell and Wood recommended to Chelmsford that although Russell did not lack personal bravery, he was not fit for front-line service. Chelmsford already had a low opinion of Russell and did not hesitate to accept Wood's suggestion that Russell should be moved to command a remount depot. Thus, Chelmsford demonstrated that he could be ruthless in his handling of subordinates when it suited him, yet he would later fail to show such determination and resolve when confronting the poor performance of officers sent from London.

The following day Wood was given an opportunity to restore his reputation at the Battle of Kambula. At about midday, he and Buller stood facing the approaching Zulu army behind the barricades of Kambula. After the defeat at Rorke's Drift, Cetshwayo had forbidden his warriors to attack the British if they were behind prepared positions and indeed it seemed that the large Zulu army would bypass the British and raid into the Transvaal. Wood ordered Buller, and his mounted troops, to ride out to within a few hundred yards of the Zulu army and fire volleys into them. The provocation had the desired effect and the Zulus charged forward in an uncoordinated manner which never saw the left and right horns of the buffalo attacking at the same time. The British fought off numerous attacks over a space of 4–5 hours and although some warriors got within the adjacent cattle kraal and had to be turned back by sword and bayonet, the battle, under the steadfast command of Wood, was rarely in doubt. As the exhausted Zulus retired their retreat became something of a rout and massacre as they were pursued by Buller and his mounted troops. The Zulu dead may have been as high as 2,000, with perhaps two-thirds killed in the vicious British pursuit, whilst the British lost 28. This complete victory, combined with Chelmsford's success at Gingindlovu and the relief of Eshowe, meant that the outcome of the war was now not in doubt, but both Wood and Chelmsford would later have to answer some uncomfortable questions about the killing of wounded Zulus after each of their respective victories.

Pearson and his men had been able to witness Chelmsford's victory and send the general not only congratulations via an improvised heliograph, but also news of Wood's empathetic victory at Kambula. Chelmsford must surely have been jubilant. He replied to Pearson with instructions, 'Ekowe will be evacuated after relief and an entrenched post put somewhere else near here (Inyezane). 3 regt. will leave here for you tomorrow, you will bring all you can and destroy the rest.'[19]

Chelmsford had realized that following the Isandlwana defeat the initial invasion plans were in disarray and that, therefore, there was no strategic value in maintaining a presence at Eshowe. It was clear to the general that it made more sense to return across the Tugela and start the campaign afresh, once all the reinforcements had arrived. This decision was not universally liked amongst those who had been besieged and had lost friends and colleagues during the ordeal, but Chelmsford was adamant that Eshowe was to be abandoned and on 3 April, leaving a garrison in the laager at

Gingindlovu, Chelmsford pushed on to Eshowe with a convoy of fifty-eight carts with stores. The advance was unopposed, but the difficulties of the country were such that it was nearly midnight before the rear-guard had covered the 15 miles and entered Eshowe.

Chelmsford was keen to leave the fort the following morning and Pearson and his men loaded any materials of military value on to the wagons that had remained at Eshowe. Chelmsford though was set on one final gesture and mounted a raid early on the morning of 4 April to destroy Ezulweni, or 'The Heavens', the principal homestead of Prince Dabulamanzi, about 8 miles from Eshowe. As Molyneux was to record, the general was determined 'to show the King's brother that he too had a long arm to strike with'.[20] Although the force largely comprised Barrow's mounted troops, Chelmsford and his staff accompanied the foray. Following their defeat of just two days earlier, the Zulus were in no mood to close when the Volunteers and Native Horse put the huts to the torch, but they kept up an angry, but harmless, fire from the crest of an overlooking hill.

By the time Chelmsford and the force returned to Eshowe Pearson had already begun the march back to the Tugela. This took several days and was unopposed by the Zulus. One feature, though, was the nervous nature of many of the troops and this was displayed on the morning of 6 April when pickets fired at what they believed to be a Zulu, and this started a panic which resulted in some of Dunn's scouts being shot. Chelmsford was furious and firm disciplinary action was taken against the perpetrators. Such events, however, were to be repeated during the Second Invasion. Chelmsford and Pearson crossed back into Natal on 7 April and the returning troops were greeted as heroes not only by their comrades in Forts Pearson and Tenedos but also the wider populace of Natal. Chelmsford was delighted with the results of his foray to Eshowe and by fulsomely praising Pearson he was able to use this as an opportunity to again deflect some criticism of the earlier disasters. Pearson was credited with:

> ... so tenaciously holding on to Ekowe after the bad news of the Isandlwana affair had reached him. The occupation of the post, and of that one held by Colonel Evelyn Wood during a time of considerable anxiety had no doubt had a very powerful moral effect throughout South Africa, and diminished the effect of what would otherwise have been considered a complete collapse of our invasion of Zululand.[21]

Of course, in truth Chelmsford knew that with just two fortified posts within Zululand, both close to the border, his invasion plans were in tatters as soon as the Zulu impi stormed into Isandlwana. He now rode on to Pietermaritzburg to begin marshalling the reinforcements for the Second Invasion. However, his task would soon be overshadowed by growing calls for Chelmsford to be replaced. In the meantime, the general did order limited border raids to keep the pressure upon Cetshwayo. On 9 April, Major Dartnell led a force of 2,000 men from Rorke's Drift into Zululand which destroyed a total of 12 previously undamaged homesteads within a 10-mile radius of the border. No opposition was met for the people had time enough to flee, taking their cattle with them. Dartnell's men left the homestead dwellings burning and crops destroyed. At the Middle Drift Major A.C. Twentyman, the commander of the Greytown garrison, led a force across the border in early April and once again homesteads were burnt as the Zulus fled with their cattle. These incursions did, however, heighten the argument between Chelmsford and Bulwer as to the use of colonial forces and who had authority over such troops, which would only be finally resolved on 19 May when the imperial government decreed that command of all troops in Southern Africa lay with Chelmsford.

Back in Pietermaritzburg, Chelmsford's staff attempted to keep from him the growing press criticism of the general's performance as well as the clamours for his replacement. The news of the relief of Eshowe was received in London on 22 April and the press coverage was, universally, one of relief that Pearson and his men were now safe, and that Chelmsford had achieved a notable victory at Gingindlovu. However, within a matter of days critical editorials began to appear in both the London and provincial press. For example, the editor of the *Daily News* wrote on 24 April that:

> … it can hardly be contended that the proceedings of the war have given us much to be proud of. Up to the present our invasion has simply resulted in a series of defences, which have unfortunately not always been successful, and in which we have almost invariably been taken by surprise. It is perhaps not unreasonable to ask when the invasion [Second] is to begin, and how it is to be conducted … this can scarcely be considered a satisfactory result to have arrived at after some three months of continuous warfare with a barbarian foe.

Similarly, the editor of the *Devon Evening Express* of Exeter wrote on 2 May:

> The relief of Col. Pearson at Ekowe has been the only redeeming feature in the war, so far as our forces are concerned. And even the advance to Ekowe has been followed by an equally hasty retreat. So far as the divisions under Lord Chelmsford and Colonel Pearson are concerned, we are no further advanced than the day before the Isandula disaster. The invasion has to be recommenced.

Weeks before news of the relief of Eshowe had reached London, Disraeli's government was under immense pressure to replace Chelmsford. It was not just the British press that was calling for the general to be sacked. On 12 March, in one of his regular meetings with the queen, the prime minister informed her that most of the Cabinet had called for Chelmsford's recall and two days later in the House the Liberal MP Edward Jenkins demanded Chelmsford's sacking on the bases that when 'any General suffers such a defeat as … Isandula, there is a *prima facie* case of incompetency against him'.[22] It was only the vigorous defence of Chelmsford by many of his aristocratic allies, such as Sir Stafford Northcote, the Chancellor of the Exchequer, that forced Jenkins to withdraw his motion. Others, such as Lord Salisbury, were clamouring for Frere's recall and although he was defended by Hicks Beach, it did not stop motions of no confidence in Frere being debated in both Houses and despite these being defeated along party lines, it was becoming apparent to Disraeli that he would have to act. On 12 April Disraeli had told the Prince of Wales, a supporter of both Frere and Chelmsford, that he feared that there was a 'want of energy' in Southern Africa which he considered deplorable and that a general of genius might rectify the situation. The prime minster clearly considered that Major General Sir Garnet Wolseley, hero of the Asante War, was the man of the hour, and Disraeli had already contrived that Wolseley should return to London from Cyprus, where he was acting as High Commissioner, to sit on a Board of General Officers which was reporting on the short-service system. Disraeli's ploy to remove Chelmsford was made easier by the erosion of support for the general at Horse Guards, particularly from the Duke of Cambridge who had been dismayed by Chelmsford's response to his request for answers to specific questions and events surrounding the Isandlwana defeat. Cambridge considered Chelmsford's words were at best half-truths.

The duke also had little confidence in the general's plans for the Second Invasion and was horrified by the growing and seemingly out of control expenditure on transport and stores. In this he was receiving regular reports from the newly arrived General Clifford, who wrote of disharmony amongst the general's staff, that Crealock 'controlled' access to Chelmsford and heavily influenced him, and that he considered Chelmsford to be 'mad'.[23] In addition, Hicks Beach had been dissatisfied with Frere for failing to consider overtures of peace made by Cetshwayo in late March. With support diminishing, Disraeli decided to act, although he still had to overcome the queen whose support for Frere and Chelmsford remained as strong as ever. Again, the prime minister was fortunate in that Victoria departed for Balmoral on 21 May and although she would be furious with her prime minister for acting against her wishes, her wrath was from a distance and Disraeli was able to weather her anger.

On returning from Cyprus Wolseley first saw Major General Sir Charles Ellice, Adjutant General, who gave Wolseley to understand that it was entirely the Horse Guards influences that had saved Chelmsford from being recalled. Wolseley then met with Colonel F.A. Stanley, Secretary of State for War, who told him in strictest confidence that it had been settled and that Wolseley was to go to Natal with full civil and military powers and that both Frere and Chelmsford were to be recalled. Wolseley was then summoned to Downing Street for a private audience with the prime minister who was keen to discuss the military situation in Southern Africa. Disraeli told Wolseley that he was not satisfied with the way affairs had been conducted in Southern Africa and referred in strong terms to the mismanagement of military operations. He said, 'partly mismanagement and partly ill-luck, for ill-luck always attends upon mismanagement'.[24] After a series of Cabinet meetings and numerous letters to pacify the queen, to the disquiet of Cambridge, whose distrust of the progressive Wolseley would never abate, Disraeli was finally able to confirm Wolseley's appointment. He left London on 29 May for Southern Africa with the overwhelming support of the press and even the Liberal opposition. Wolseley's main concern was that he would reach Natal too late and that the war would be over.

With Pearson's force now safely back in Natal, Chelmsford could focus on his plans for the Second Invasion, which included consideration for the route or routes to be taken as well as how to best accommodate the plethora of major generals. Again, transport difficulties became the dominant problem facing Chelmsford and here he was perhaps blinded by the logistical demands he was up against. Chelmsford, despite having the services of Generals Crealock, Marshall and Newdigate, continued to be very much 'hands on' in focusing on the transport problems perhaps at the expense of seriously considering the strategy that should now be deployed. Whilst Chelmsford may have learnt some serious lessons from Isandlwana and had gained a strong respect, if not fear, for the fighting abilities of the Zulu warriors, he failed to grasp the need for mobility. Now reinforced with two regiments of cavalry, which included the 17th Lancers, as well as substantially more colonial mounted units, Chelmsford could utilize this force to ensure that an advance upon Ulundi would be fully supported with reconnaissance so that no large Zulu force could ever surprise the British again. Chelmsford should have considered using his mounted units to cover a rapid march of infantry to form staging posts along a single route, knowing that he need not fear a surprise attack, even on the line of march. Yet, there would be no rapid advance with minimal baggage as with the relief of Eshowe, but once more the invasion would be of slow-moving columns, the movement of which would be hampered by both the terrain and the pace of the oxen.

Chelmsford considered that he could, to some extent, alter his first invasion plans, although the objective remained Ulundi, for neither England nor the Zulu nation would be convinced the war was over until the royal kraal had been burnt and Cetshwayo captured. There would now no longer be numerous columns, which in theory could offer mutual support to each other, but rather just two which, much to the Duke of Cambridge's surprise and annoyance, would act independently. The main thrust came from the newly created Second Division, which would strike into northern Zululand, supported by Evelyn Wood's column. Known as 'Wood's Flying Column', this would retain a separate identity, although still work to support the main thrust. Wood had been given the local rank of brigadier general and his promotion and the maintenance of a separate command seems little more than an acknowledgement by Chelmsford of Wood's previous loyalty towards him as well as a recognition of Wood's overwhelming victory at Kambula which had provided the British, and thus Chelmsford, with some welcome news and placed Cetshwayo very much on the defensive.

A further column, which would later receive much criticism for its lethargic advance, known as the First Division, would advance along the coastal strip, earlier favoured by both Pearson and Chelmsford. This column was to be commanded by Major General Henry Crealock, brother of Chelmsford's military secretary, and its main role was to secure the right flank of the Second Division as well as diverting some Zulu forces away from the main thrust. Although Chelmsford would accompany the Second Division, command would rest with Major General Newdigate. Chelmsford struggled to find roles for the remaining major generals, but Frederick Marshall was appointed commander of the Cavalry Brigade, which was attached to the Second Division, whilst the Hon. Hugh Clifford VC was given the remit of guarding the garrisons and lines of communication in Natal. Within this role Clifford was ordered to improve both the transport system, which was haemorrhaging money, and relations between the army and Bulwer's colonial administration. In these last two areas Clifford would act independently of Chelmsford, although the general's constant inability to delegate saw him clash with Clifford on more than one occasion.

With the decision made that the Second Invasion would comprise two independent columns Chelmsford calculated that each battalion would consume over a ton of foodstuffs per day and possibly 1½ tons of firewood. It would also require ninety tents, weighing over 4 tons when dry or 5½ tons wet, 2 tons of ammunition in the regimental reserve and another 9 tons of light camping equipment. Overall, Chelmsford had to move some 1,500 tons of equipment, ammunition and rations. Compounding the delays was the labour of building small forts along the line of communications and cutting wood, which was a scarce commodity. When united with Wood's column there were 7,000 fighting men in the Second Division which required 900 wagons drawn by 15,000 oxen, hence the claim of a soldier in the 21st 'that a British army is a terribly cumbrous machine, and quite incapable of rapid movement'.[25]

The choice of routes for the Second Invasion was left solely in the hands of Chelmsford and in making his decision he demonstrated how the defeat at Isandlwana had affected his mindset. The most obvious, and direct, route was to follow that which he had taken in January; Helpmekaar to Rorke's Drift and cross into Zululand there. Yet, this would have meant that Chelmsford's troops, many of them raw recruits, would have had to march pass the unburied bodies of the fallen at Isandlwana. Whether Chelmsford decided against this route based on the sensibilities of his men or of his own mind is open to debate. Instead, Chelmsford moved north to the town of Dundee and established a supply base here, with another camp at Landman's Drift where the track crossed the Mzinyathi. This route meant crossing another river, the Ntome, and with the country considered difficult for oxen to traverse, it was felt that the Second Division would have to divert further north. Fortunately, however, scouts from Buller's FLH were able to report that an acceptable route had been found across the Ntome at Koppie Alleen, which took a southerly track, skirting Isandlwana before reaching the Babanango Heights. From there an existing track crossed over the Mhonjaneni ridge and then dropped down to the Umfolozi valley and then on to Ulundi. Even so, this route involved a detour of about 100 miles and added a month's delay, but no one could persuade Chelmsford to take the direct route via Isandlwana.

Although London had flooded Southern Africa with reinforcements, it had not sent food for the 9,000 imperial troops or forage for the 3,000 to 4,000 horses and mules, so once again Chelmsford had to focus, in his mind at least, on the mundane issues of planning the Second Invasion. Days, became weeks, which turned into months and still no advance was made. It was not long before morale amongst the men suffered and for this Chelmsford and his staff must shoulder much of the blame, for with his inability to delegate came a reluctance to communicate and this led to frustration, as can be seen in a letter written by Herbert Stewart to Archibald Alison from Ladysmith on 8 May 1879:

The commander-in-chief came to Durban for a few days after the relief of Eshowe and then left for the northern frontier. I speak only from rumour, but rumour has it that our headquarter staff is not a homogenous body; however, we have few opportunities of judging personally. Of one thing I think I may be pretty certain and that is that secrecy as to their whereabouts is one of their guiding principles. For the last 10 days nobody near us, including General Marshall, has had an idea where they were to be found, and on one of our staff enquiring for information as to their probable whereabouts he was informed by the assistant military secretary that that was a matter which was always kept a secret. This method of campaigning has at any rate the advantage of novelty, but that being admitted it seems to me it can claim no other consideration.[26]

As a conservative and a member of the Indian School, Chelmsford seems to have been wary of Staff College graduates, unlike Wolseley, and he appointed his staff on the basis of personal acquaintance. Even after the arrival of reinforcements, this select group remained at the core of decision-making and included no one who was trained in staff duties and no chief of staff. It was not until May that Chelmsford even recognized the necessity of appointing a proper intelligence department, and this fact alone must be considered at best remiss and at worse verging on unforgiveable, especially after the debacle of Isandlwana. Chelmsford finally appointed a Natal civil servant, the Hon. William Drummond, as its head. The organizational effort to prepare for the new invasion was enormous, and the burden, under Chelmsford's limited command structure, fell on a small and insufficient group of untrained officers. It is, therefore, perhaps not surprising that those officers, such as Herbert Stewart and indeed even Major General Marshall, considered themselves out on a limb when it came to understanding Chelmsford plans and thoughts. Stewart concluded his letter to Alison with the damning comment, 'I think I may safely say that neither General Marshall nor Colonel Lowe or any other cavalry soldier, has ever has an opportunity of expressing his opinion'.[27]

Even Clery, who had earlier been supportive of Chelmsford, was losing patience. This is clearly seen in an undated letter he sent to Alison, probably in early May 1879:

> In formal letters I have tried to account to you in some way for the disasters out here. I do not know that I find reason to change my opinions in any way – in one only, perhaps, and that was rather a matter of hope than of opinion, and it was hoping against hope that the general was rather unfortunate than incapable. I really begin to be convinced now that the right man is not in the right place. At this moment I regret to say that I don't believe the general has any plan, or knows what he is going to do. I do not say this lightly, but unfortunately from conviction.[28]

Such words from Clery were damning and it was clear that Chelmsford was unpopular amongst officers of a lower rank. Lieutenant Curling, one of the few survivors of Isandlwana, wrote to his mother on 28 April at his dismay that he would be serving directly under Chelmsford, 'I am sorry to say our column is still to be commanded by the General [Lord Chelmsford]. I think these disasters have quite upset his judgement or rather that of his staff and

one does not feel half so comfortable under his command as a man like
Col. Wood ...'[29]

In addition, the press, now in Southern Africa in large numbers, began
to report the delay in the advance of the Second Invasion with some
frustration. Frederick Mackenzie, reporting for *The Standard*, wrote from
Pietermaritzburg on 12 May:

> It is impossible for me to inform you with any certainty of what is going
> to be done, as the Commander in Chief is continually changing his
> plans, to the utter confusion of the Commissariat and of the General
> Commanding at the base. Orders given one day are countermanded the
> next; irresolution, vacillation and confusion are rampant at headquarters.

The troops themselves were kept busy escorting supply convoys through
Natal to the Zulu border, where more troops guarded the growing supply
dumps. A newly arrived officer of the 58th Regiment described what the
period was like:

> Camp life here is dreary and monotonous. The number of men in the
> convoy, say, 1,000, may look very large on paper, but when you have
> this number distributed among 100 or 200 waggons they do not look so
> imposing. Every waggon on the road must have its guard, as none can
> say when an attack is likely to be made ... The civilians here wonder
> how in such a climate, with seventy rounds of ammunition, belts, water
> bottle, haversack filled, rifle and bayonet, an English soldier can march
> twenty miles a day under the roasting sun. After a march we have to
> laager the convoy. On drawing all the waggons together ... these are
> entrenched ... we act always on the assumption that the Zulus may be
> upon us at any moment.[30]

Chelmsford's General Orders required every soldier to sleep with his boots
and ammunition belt on, his rifle at his side, with all the men stood to,
ready to fight every morning an hour and a half before daylight, and this did
nothing to improve morale.

Troops became exhausted by the constant state of vigil and predawn
assemblies. The days passed with the physical strain of loading and unloading
wagons as stores were collected, mixed with long periods of boredom. Both

morale and discipline plummeted, and floggings increased, with Chelmsford having no qualms over the use of the whip to maintain order. With many of the reinforcements raw recruits, nerves were frequently on edge and false night-time alarms from imaginary Zulus became commonplace, which added to the troops' tiredness and ill-humour.

Finally, after nearly two months of planning and stockpiling the Second Invasion seemed imminent. As a diversion Chelmsford ordered the border forces to once more raid into Zululand, and again Major Twentyman was at the heart of the action. He led a substantial force of around 1,000 natives with 37 Natal volunteers across the border and into the Thukela valley. The incursion was strongly opposed by local Zulu forces, and it was only when Twentyman fired three rockets into the mass of warriors that they dispersed, and he was then able to lead his force on to destroy numerous homesteads. Once Twentyman had retired back to Natal small parties of Zulus crossed the river at various points and destroyed several homesteads on the Natal side, just as Bulwer had feared and predicted. Although these retaliatory raids inflicted minimal damage, they did cause an 'invasion' panic in the border district. In June, whilst the Border Guard was dispersed collecting taxes, Zulu warriors raided across the Middle Drift with impunity and Chelmsford was forced to order the deployment of imperial troops who were tied down strictly on the defensive. Thus, these raids had a contrary effect to that which Chelmsford had desired in that they restricted the use of British troops rather than diverting large numbers of the enemy. Bulwer must have considered that his opposition to the border raids had been fully justified.

Chelmsford ordered two further incursions into Zululand before the commencement of the Second Invasion. On 15 May, Major Black of the 24th, now a newly promoted lieutenant colonel, led a patrol to Isandlwana which was fired upon and opposed by Zulu warriors. This was a reconnaissance for a larger force composed of mainly troops of the 17th Lancers and commanded by General Marshall, who had been given responsibility over Chelmsford's newly arrived cavalry forces. They returned to the battlefield to retrieve forty wagons which Black had identified as serviceable. In addition, Chelmsford was facing increasing criticism that no attempt had been made to bury the fallen at Isandlwana. Marshall's troops hastily buried some of what were now skeletons in shallow scraped graves, but it would not be until March 1880 that all the bodies were properly interred. Both Archibald Forbes and Melton Prior of the *Daily News* and the *Daily Telegraph* respectively accompanied the force, and both wrote poignant articles on the melancholy sights of the aftermath of the defeat, which again reflected poorly upon Chelmsford and in particular his delay in burying the slain.

With the additional forty wagons and troops now in place the Second Invasion could finally begin in earnest. With a new depot built at Koppie Alleen and stores in situ, the Second Division finally crossed into Zululand on 31 May to join the advance of Wood's Flying Column from the north. Troops were instructed to construct wagon laagers every night, which, of course slowed the advance from the beginning. Yet, with the mounted units at his disposal Chelmsford should have had no fear that the long, slow-moving column would suffer a surprise attack for the horsemen could scout and screen far in advance. These troops left in their wake a line of destruction with Zulu homesteads and crops burnt and flattened as Chelmsford effectively waged war against the civilian population.

When Chelmsford returned from Eshowe, he was met with the news that he would now face an additional responsibility, for amongst the reinforcements coming from England was Prince Louis Napoleon. The young man was the son of Napoleon III, who, along with his family, had had to flee France for England after France's disastrous defeat in the Franco-Prussian War of 1870. Louis had trained at the Woolwich Artillery School, although as a French national he was not permitted to enlist in the British army. With news of Isandlwana Louis longed for adventure in Southern Africa and his widowed mother, Empress Eugenie, lobbied both the Duke of Cambridge and Disraeli for an unofficial placement. With both men reluctant, it took the intervention of Queen Victoria for Louis to secure his position on the *Danube*, which docked in Durban on 1 April. Chelmsford arrived there on 9 April and Louis quickly sought him out and presented him with a letter from Cambridge which outlined that Louis was looking to see as much of the new campaign as possible. Chelmsford must have despaired for Louis was an added headache he certainly did not need. With Cambridge vague as to what Louis was expected to do, Chelmsford decided to place the prince, who was able to charm all that he met, on his staff.

On 8 May Chelmsford appointed Colonel Richard Harrison as acting quartermaster general with a staff that included Lieutenant Carey and Prince Louis. One of Harrison's responsibilities was to provide reliable sketches and maps of the terrain over which the Second Division was to advance and during the next three weeks both Carey and Louis were frequently employed on reconnaissance and fact-gathering operations. Louis, who seemed intent on seeking out glory and danger, soon demonstrated a rashness that unnerved many including Redvers Buller, who voiced his concerns to Chelmsford about Louis' behaviour in the field. The prince had ridden off, far in front of Buller and his men, in pursuit of some Zulus that he had spotted in the far distance and Buller stated that he would not allow Louis to accompany him on a reconnaissance again. Chelmsford had more to consider than the foolishness of a somewhat immature young man, and without directly confronting Louis, he ordered Harrison to confine him to safer duties around the camps. As Chelmsford himself put it, 'The Prince Imperial went on a reconnaissance and very nearly came to grief. I shall not let him out of my sight again if I can help it.'[31] For someone who struggled to delegate this was perhaps one instance when Chelmsford should have become directly involved and impressed upon the prince that such reckless behaviour would not be tolerated again.

On 1 June, perhaps almost inevitably, the prince was killed in a surprise attack of around sixty warriors as he and his comrades had offsaddled to rest for lunch. The party had left on a sketching mission and had done so without the escort of Dragoons which should have accompanied them. Whilst the majority of the party, including Carey, fled at the first sign of the Zulu attack, Louis had been unable to mount his horse in time and met a brave death with his face to the enemy. When the news of yet another disaster reached Chelmsford, he was crushed. He had not asked for the extra burden of responsibility Louis' presence had imposed and he had not even been aware that Louis had left the camp that day. Yet, somehow, Chelmsford still retained the faculty for rational thought and whilst others around him were panicking he refused to let out a party of inexperienced troops into the night in enemy territory to search for the prince, who everyone now assumed, rightly, to be dead. Although this was the correct, and possibly brave, decision, it was damned by Paul Deleage, the French correspondent of the Paris-based *Le Figaro*. That night Major Grenfell saw Chelmsford 'in his tent with his head on the table in a state of absolute despair'.[32] Clery wrote to his wife from the camp that night, 'Poor Lord Chelmsford is awfully cut up about it as he will be blamed for letting him go with so small an escort'.[33]

Indeed, the death of the prince would result in further criticism of Chelmsford, particularly in the British press. Next morning an expedition went in search of the prince's body. Chelmsford could not bring himself to go in person, and he sent Captain Molyneux, one of his ADCs, to represent him. Although some sympathy can be directed towards Chelmsford, for he had certainly not asked for Louis to be 'dumped' upon him, he must be criticized for not realizing how vital it would be, particularly for his own reputation, that the prince remained safe. Especially after Louis had displayed such recklessness, Chelmsford should surely have either sent the prince away from front-line duties or ensured that he never left his own side. Chelmsford resorted to the same tactic he had employed after Isandlwana and called for an inquiry into the events surrounding the prince's fateful reconnaissance. Once more Chelmsford had a ready scapegoat, this time in form of Lieutenant Carey, who was nominally in charge of the operation and had fled the scene without establishing the fate of the prince. Although the subsequent inquiry and court martial found Carey guilty of cowardice, the verdict would later be overturned on a technicality. More importantly the inquiry exonerated Chelmsford of any responsibility. Despite being overturned, the court martial had effectively destroyed Carey's reputation, and whilst he remained in the army until his death from peritonitis in 1883, he was ostracized to the end. The Empress Eugenie never considered that Chelmsford held any responsibility for her son's death, and she presented Lady Chelmsford with an emerald and diamond bracelet with an inscription that acknowledged the kindness Chelmsford had shown her son.

One further consequence of Louis' death was that Chelmsford became even more tentative in his advance towards Ulundi, much to the frustration of his men, the government and the many special newspaper correspondents who seemed to take great delight in highlighting the sedate progress made. Some of the troops in Wood's Flying Column bemoaned the slowness of the advance, attributing it to the 'vacillation which has characterised the Commander-in-Chief's actions ever since the fatal day of Isandala'.[34] Lieutenant Curling wrote home to describe the snail's pace of the advance, whilst on 16 June the correspondent of *The Times* reported:

We are wandering towards Ulundi much as the Children of Israel wandered towards Canaan, without plans, or even definite notions for the future. It would seem not impossible to form some plan of campaign – something, at any rate, more definite than the hand-to-hand-mouth manner in which we are now proceeding. Deep science and tactical skill are not necessary with savages; a simple method and plain common-sense suffice, if backed by energy, decision and determination.[35]

Even local pressman of the Natal dailies resorted to biblical similes to describe the way the general dawdled on the march to Ulundi. One correspondent stated, 'The British army may be likened to the children of Israel wandering aimlessly in the wilderness.'[36]

The editor of the *Devon Evening Express* of Exeter wrote rather exasperatedly on 10 June, '... Lord Chelmsford has done nothing with the 10,000 fresh troops sent out to him ... We have received no military intelligence, indeed, by the last few mails nothing but of sickness among the troops, difficulties of transport and commissariat, plans of attack arranged, only to be abandoned, and general confusion and helplessness.'

Archibald Forbes of the *Daily News* was to later write in *Nineteenth Century* magazine in February 1880 of the 'Perverse pedestrianism' of the advance and even Lord Chelmsford's brother in England, Lord Chief Justice Thesiger, felt constrained to send him a cable which read, 'For God's sake do something. Wolseley supersedes you.'[37]

The slowness of the advance was compounded by the need to build 'forts', in reality glorified supply depots, en route. Wagons constantly travelled back and forth from Landman's Drift bringing up fresh supplies, first to Fort Newdigate and then on to the newly constructed Fort Marshall, which was built near Isipezi Hill on the direct route to Ulundi. Fort Newdigate had been the site of a night-time panic on 5 June by sentries from the 58th Regiment which resulted in the wounding of five soldiers and had earned the fort the jibe 'Fort Funk'. Such nervousness amongst the troops, especially at night, would continue to the end of the conflict, such was the fear of the enemy.

A few days before he had received his brother's telegram informing him that he was to be replaced by Wolseley Chelmsford had received a letter from Colonel Stanley which had hinted at his removal, but with definite news that Wolseley was now en route Chelmsford must have felt humiliated. After all the hardships and setbacks Chelmsford had endured he was now just 40 miles from his goal of Ulundi, with 10,000 troops, supplies for a month and, at last, sufficient transport. The indignity he now felt manifested itself in both anger and a determination to see the job done and at last the advance was spurred on by Chelmsford. For the next ten days the Second Division pushed on doggedly along the trail to Ulundi. Now 4–5 miles were being covered in a day, twice what had been achieved before. However, it was felt by many that it was Evelyn Wood who was at the heart of the renewed vigour. Wood's energy and determination were becoming legendary, and Wolseley delighted in writing to a friend in England with a riddle that was passing around the British troops: 'Why is it that the men of Lord Chelmsford's column cannot be regarded as Christians? Answer: Because they make an idol of Wood and do not believe in the Lord!'[38]

By 25 June the British had reached Jackal Ridge and for once Chelmsford seemed relaxed as progress had been good and the natural strength of the camp allowed him to dispense with the need to entrench around the laager. The men's morale was further boosted when Chelmsford ordered an issue of grog and an extra half pound of meat for their dinner. Three days later the British were bivouacked on the heights of Mhonjaneni, with the Mahlabahini plain and Ulundi itself visible now just 16 miles away. Surely even the most pessimistic of the accompanying press must have believed that the end was in sight.

Whilst Chelmsford remained with the Second Division, Major General Henry Crealock led the First Division. He arrived at Fort Pearson on 18 April and his only orders from Chelmsford were to advance and burn the military kraal at emaNgwene and the great kraal at Undi. However, before this could happen Crealock had to establish advanced supply bases. This was to prove difficult for Chelmsford was monopolizing wagons and oxen for the Second Division and Crealock was left to pick up what crumbs were left. The First Division had over 9,000 troops to move and supply and had to cover terrain in which malaria was endemic and no quinine was available. Over 800 troops became seriously ill, including Colonel Pearson. Not only was the column slow in building up supplies, but it had to bridge the Tugela and march along tracks which had already been badly damaged by Pearson and Chelmsford in their earlier advances. The hopes that supplies could be delivered along the coastal route by the Royal Navy were dashed when HMS *Tenedos* was badly damaged trying to negotiate the dangerous surf that raked the coastline.

Crealock seemed to have the same cautious nature as Chelmsford, but unlike his commander, Crealock had a love of comfort and there were mutterings amongst his men about the twenty-seven precious wagons he utilized to move his own personal baggage. The lack of drive Crealock installed into the advance may be partly explained by the fact that he was suffering terribly from haemorrhoids which made riding a horse tortuous, but whatever the reason for the slow march the column acquired the nickname amongst the press of 'Crealocks Crawlers', and it became the laughing stock of the army. Wolseley considered Crealock a terrible snob who was afraid to advance and spoke to his officers and troops as if they were 'dogs'. Wolseley wrote, 'He [Crealock] has no dash and judging from his past history is very careful of his own hide and not likely to expose his valuable person to any dangers.'[39]

Major (later General Sir) Bindon Blood would later write in defence of Chelmsford but was very critical of Crealock, with whom he served as commander of the Royal Engineers with the First Division. He was clearly mortified by the division's lack of purpose and drive:

> When the 1st Division was formed, it was 9,215 strong, of all ranks, and when Lord Chelmsford told me at Durban of my appointment to it he said, 'You will get to Ulundi long before any of us – yours is far the easiest route.' As things turned out, the division sat at the mouth of the Tugela for about three months, then advanced some thirty miles, halted there while the action at Ulundi was fought, went back thence – and was broken up.[40]

It is hard to conceive of a greater waste of resources, both men and materials, than the First Division. To say that it was irrelevant to the outcome of the Second Invasion is not an exaggeration and as the commander of forces in Southern Africa Chelmsford must take the blame for not only its very existence but also its wastefulness. It was not just an unnecessary side show but it paralysed Chelmsford's strategy, for the 9,000 troops could surely have been better utilized along the line of march of the Second Division, allowing for greater mobility as the main force, with mounted units to the fore, descended upon Ulundi. It seems that Cetshwayo had a better grasp of the tactical threat presented by Crealock's column than Chelmsford did, for when it became clear to the Zulu king that Crealock was never going to combine his forces with that of the Second Division the king essentially ignored the threat from the First Division. Thus, Crealock and Chelmsford failed even in their basic aim of dividing the Zulu army.

It seems evident that Chelmsford gave little thought not only to the progress and whereabouts of Crealock's command but also its very purpose. As he neared Ulundi Chelmsford had had no contact with Crealock for weeks. As the commander-in-chief he must be considered to have been at fault in his handling of the First Division and of neglecting his duty towards it. At the very least, when Crealock was being heavily criticized by both the press and others in the army, Chelmsford should have imposed a firmer hold on Crealock and ensured the pace of his advance was increased. As it was, Chelmsford seems to have viewed the First Division as very much an independent command which was in competition with the Second for transport and resources and this was not the approach of a commander who had a firm grasp of the campaign. As Wolseley was to write in a damning fashion of the First Division in his diary for 7 July:

As far as this war is concerned, this first Divn. might as well have been marching along the Woking and Aldershot road. If he had been eager for the fray he [Crealock] might have brought the enemy to an engagement near the Inyezane or Emlalazi rivers and so had the credit of finishing this war before Chelmsford did so but Crealock is more of the Autumn Manoeuvre General than the fighting leader in the field.[41]

Throughout the month of May and into June, Cetshwayo sought peace terms with Chelmsford. Envoys were despatched which were finally able to speak with Chelmsford on 4 June just as the advance had recommenced following the Prince Imperial's death. The envoys wanted to know what Cetshwayo would have to do to stop the war and Chelmsford outlined several demands which included the surrender of specific regiments, the return of rifles and artillery pieces captured at Isandlwana and a tribute of royal oxen to be paid. These measures would stop the war, but Chelmsford still intended to march to Ulundi where peace terms would be discussed in person. In truth, whilst Cetshwayo was sincere in his desire to end hostilities, Chelmsford sought a final victory. The Zulus had been under arms for six months and had suffered severely both in battle and due to the scorched earth tactics of the British which meant Zulu food stocks were low, and unless some form of settlement was reached before the spring rains when planting began, they faced famine. Yet, for the British, and Chelmsford, a victory in a formal battle was needed to protect political, military and personal reputations. Thus, as the advance towards Ulundi progressed the chance of a peace settlement became more and more unlikely.

By 29 June Chelmsford was within touching distance of Ulundi. The day before Wolseley had arrived in Durban, and on 1 July he sent a message to Chelmsford ordering him to retire upon the First Division and stating his firm objection to the two divisions acting independently. Wolseley also demanded daily updates from Chelmsford on his progress. The message was not received by Chelmsford until 3 July, the eve of the Battle of Ulundi, and Chelmsford and his staff simply ignored it. By 30 June Chelmsford was leading his force into the valley of the Umfolozi, with the majority of the troops carrying neither kit nor tents and just ten days' rations. Finally, Chelmsford had recognized the need to resort to similar measures to those he had employed on the march to Eshowe, thus increasing the mobility of his force. The next morning Zulu envoys brought the Prince Imperial's captured sword to Chelmsford and the commander reiterated his demands to be sent to Cetshwayo, but because of a misunderstanding amongst the envoys the details of Chelmsford's latest offer never reached the king. The final battle was now inevitable.

By 2 July both the Flying Column and the Second Division had reached the banks of the Umfolozi River, and a strong wagon laager was constructed on high ground around half a mile from the drift. On this day Cetshwayo made one last attempt to secure an end to the war by sending the royal herd of white oxen as a peace offering, but before they could cross the river warriors of the uMcijo regiment halted their progress for they believed there would be no surrender whilst there were Zulus still ready to fight. This act demonstrates that Cetshwayo himself had lost some authority amongst his people, although their loyalty was such that warriors still massed to defend him and Ulundi from the British. The following morning Buller led the FLH across the Umfolozi to locate a favourable site for Chelmsford to position his troops to face the Zulu impi, for the general was determined that on this final occasion he would stand up to and defeat the Zulu warriors out in the open. Although Buller's reconnaissance was ultimately successful and identified a rise close to kwaNodwengu which Buller thought would be ideal to place the British troops, it almost ended in disaster when some of the force was encircled in a Zulu trap. Three troops were killed and many including Lord William Beresford, who would win the Victoria Cross for saving an injured colleague, had narrow escapes.

That evening Chelmsford declared his intention to attack early the following morning and instructed that Colonel Bellairs would remain behind to defend the laager with five companies of the 1/24th; the 24th was not going to be allowed to redeem some of its honour and gain revenge for Isandlwana. The officers of the regiment were furious with Chelmsford's decision with many of them taking it as a slight upon the regiment, yet the new recruits had demonstrated a nervousness verging on panic when in laager a few nights before and Chelmsford felt that he could not risk that they might not be steadfast in battle.

At first light on 4 July the troopers of the FLH once again crossed the Umfolozi and fanned out to offer a protective screen to the infantry as they followed behind. Chelmsford's troops met no resistance from the enemy as they rose from the river and reached open ground and undoubtedly the Zulus missed an opportunity to attack the force before it had assembled into a large hollow square formation. Chelmsford now took personal command and wheeled the rectangle half-right, to face the Ulundi kraal, halted it, faced the men outwards and ordered the ranks to be dressed and the ammunition boxes to be placed to hand and opened. The square moved slowly across the Mahlabahini plain towards the rise that Buller had identified the day before. Here Chelmsford halted his command and when the men of the Flying Column, who were on two sides of the square, began to construct an entrenchment Chelmsford ordered them to stop for he was adamant that in this final battle he would beat the Zulus in the open and that the only walls around his position would be walls of troops. Chelmsford refused Wood's request for his men to entrench saying, 'No, they [the Zulus] will be satisfied if we beat them fairly in the open. We have been called ant-bears long enough.'[42] This of course referred to the fact that the British had preferred to fight behind entrenched or fortified positions whenever possible with the Zulus suggesting that the British sought any cover, including anthills. Curiously, for generations the Zulus knew the battle not as Ulundi but as Ocwecweni, 'the battle of the sheet-iron fort'. The sun glittering on the rows of bayonets, four deep around the square, had given the impression, from a distance, that it was protected by a screen of corrugated iron.

By 8am the British were safely in position with the FLH a mile or so in front of the square. Suddenly, one Zulu regiment rose from the grass in front of the mounted men, then another, and another, until Cetshwayo's last great impi, 20,000 warriors strong, was united as one and begin to move towards Chelmsford's square. The mounted troops were pushed back to the sanctuary of the British position, firing their carbines into the great mass of Zulus as they retired. The Zulus formed a semi-circle as they advanced on the British and Buller sent twenty men of the FLH forward once more to goad the Zulus to attack, just as at Kambula. This move had the desired effect and as the warriors rushed forward the last of the mounted troops galloped to safety, just as rockets shot from the square into the charging mass, quickly followed by the first artillery shells from the twelve guns present. With the Zulu now at full charge, the battalions opened with volley fire and the two Gatling guns rattled out their deadly fire.

The initial British rifle fire was high, but the men soon adjusted their sights, and the Martini-Henry rifles began to claim victims. Fortunately for the British in their massed ranks, what Zulu rifle fire there was once again mostly went high and over the soldiers' heads. Chelmsford, mounted and in full uniform, with Wood and his staff by his side had little to do once the battle had commenced. Chelmsford trotted around behind the lines, dodging the wounded and the bandsmen struggling with heavy ammunition boxes. Once or twice he ordered a company to fire faster, shouting to make himself heard over the din, much to the disdain of special correspondent Melton Prior who later wrote:

I ran down to where the 21st and 58th Regiments were heavily engaged with some Zulus, said to be 6,000 strong and 3 deep, who were charging, and it was then that I heard Lord Chelmsford say to the troops, 'Men, fire faster; can't you fire faster?' Now it is not my business to question the wisdom of this remark, but I cannot help contrasting it with Lord Wolseley's well-known order, 'Fire slow, fire slow!'[43]

At one point Chelmsford pulled a Gatling gun out of the line to send it to a hard-pressed corner. Morshead, one of the gunners, was hit in the thigh, his blood pouring over the frame that held the barrels. Chelmsford waved the litter-bearers aside and sank down behind the gun to help load the drum. Although Prior might not have been overly impressed by Chelmsford's conduct, others, such as Sergeant O'Callaghan of the 58th, thought Chelmsford had 'proved himself an able general, and a cool, brave, and determined leader'.[44]

As in previous battles, the Zulu warriors skirmished magnificently and used every patch of dead ground to close on the British and several regiments got within 130yd of the right of the square but here they were checked by rifle volley fire, and no Zulu got within 30yd of the British position. By the time the final Zulu reserves had flung themselves unsuccessfully against the left corner of the square, only to be repelled by artillery fire, the battle had lasted a mere 30 minutes and now the warriors began to retire. At this moment Chelmsford resorted to the tactic he had employed so decisively at Gingindlovu and unleashed the cavalry and mounted troops. As the 17th Lancers left the square Chelmsford shouted at their commander, 'Go at them, Lowe!' The Lancers charged across open country and fell upon the Zulus, showing no mercy as they speared and hacked at the fleeing and wounded warriors. The mounted irregulars then joined the slaughter shooting the Zulus with impunity. Several Zulus lay in the grass hoping to evade both lancer and sword but once the immediate area around the square was secured, the NNC was unleashed and readily butchered any Zulus wounded or trying to hide. The indiscriminate killing continued for another 2 hours, with only two Zulu prisoners being taken over the whole day.

As soon as the last groups of Zulus had been forced back over the hills Chelmsford ordered the destruction by shellfire of King Cetshwayo's royal kraal. The mounted troops were now recalled to the square having killed any warriors they could find. Chelmsford addressed his gathered men and thanked them for their efforts, good conduct and steadfastness in facing the Zulu attack. The entire force then turned and with Ulundi well ablaze, marched back towards the Umfolozi River with the band playing 'Rule Britannia' and the 'Royal Alliance March'. Chelmsford's decision to leave Ulundi and not seek out the whereabouts of Cetshwayo received much criticism at the time, particularly from the press and Wolseley. Yet, his force had insufficient provisions to remain at Ulundi for more than ten days and Chelmsford saw little to be gained politically by remaining at the site of the Zulu capital now that it had been destroyed. Furthermore, the last thing Chelmsford wanted was to be bogged down in potentially weeks of fruitless searching for the fugitive king. He had other battles to fight now.

Chelmsford had gained his own personal victory and in doing so hoped he had nullified much of the criticism directed towards him after Isandlwana. However, the British success was not viewed in glowing terms by some elements of the British press. For example, the editor of *The Graphic*, in commenting on the British victory at Ulundi, wrote on 26 July:

… although our boy recruits deserve the highest praise for the steadiness with which they repelled the Zulu onset, there cannot be much of that overrated article called 'glory' in a contest where, as it is shown by the relative slaughter on either side, the combatants are so unequally matched in those qualities and appliances which in modern warfare are the chief conditions of success.

Similarly, the *Illustrated London News* did not hesitate to use the final battle of the conflict to express its indignation at the war as a whole in its editorial of 26 July, 'There is really nothing satisfactory to show for it [the war]. Neither the interest nor the honour of England called for the war, and it has been attended by a succession of misfortunes … still, the affair is one which the British public would fain forget, and which it will be glad to set closed'.

In addition to this lack of enthusiasm from much of the British press towards the final victory the accusations of British atrocities towards Zulu warriors led to growing criticism in both the press and Parliament. Although Chelmsford had been in command at both Ulundi and Gingindlovu at which the actions of British, colonial and native troops had seen the wholesale slaughter of large numbers of fleeing or wounded Zulus, he was undoubtedly fortunate in that most of the outrage at such acts was directed towards Colonel Evelyn Wood and Major Redvers Buller for the latter's pursuit of the retreating Zulus after the Battle of Kambula. This initially stemmed from a letter by a Private Snook of the 13th Regiment who had written to his uncle in Tiverton. Snook claimed that over 500 Zulus had been slain after the retreat of the Zulus. Snook's uncle sent the letter to a local Devon newspaper which was seen by a member of the Aborigines' Protection Society and the story quickly became a national story, with the issued raised in Parliament by Mr O'Donnell MP. Under mounting pressure, the War Office was forced to initiate an inquiry into the claims. This was to be one of the first acts by Wolseley, who instructed Wood to provide his side of events. It appears that in his letter Snook incorrectly stated the date when the apparent atrocities had occurred, and Wood was able to focus on this and provide an alibi for where his troops were on that date. Wood's account was published in the British press on 1 September and was viewed as an official denial by both Wood and Wolseley of Snook's allegations.

Whether there was any truth in Snook's claims, and they remain controversial to this day, it is clear that Wood, Buller and Chelmsford, especially after the defeat at Isandlwana, pursued a policy of 'Total War' against the Zulu nation, in which Zulu civilians, property and crops were targeted in what historians would today call a 'scorched earth' approach. It is also beyond doubt that wounded Zulus and warriors offering no resistance were killed in the pursuits following Kambula, Gingindlovu and Ulundi. Whether Wood or Chelmsford could have stopped, or indeed wanted to stop, such slaughter is open to debate. What is evident is that Chelmsford as commander-in-chief could have taken a firmer stance against such apparent atrocities but that in the atmosphere of revengefulness and fear which followed Isandlwana he chose not to. All this added to the weight of argument from some sections of both the press and Parliament, and the wider public, which maintained the war was unjust and cruel and this was particularly seen in the words of the Liberal leader, William Gladstone, who used such material to denounce the Disraeli government.

On the evening of 5 July, having marched his force back to the Mhonjaneni Heights, Chelmsford wrote to Colonel Stanley, Minster for War, informing him of the victory at Ulundi and offering his resignation from his command on the grounds that he had 'done a considerable amount of work' over the past months, and he finished his letter with the hope that his request would be 'favourably received'.[45] Of course it would be for Chelmsford had become an embarrassment for the government and his continued presence in Southern Africa with Wolseley now in place made Chelmsford superfluous. Whilst Wolseley would remain sympathetic to the situation Chelmsford now found himself in, privately he too was keen for Chelmsford to return to England. Chelmsford followed Wolseley's instruction to lead the Second Division towards the coast to unite with Wolseley who was now with Crealock's column.

Wolseley had acted in his usual direct manner and had ended the advance of the First Division leaving most of the troops to garrison the line of forts that had been built en route. He then pushed on with just 1,600 troops to rendezvous with Chelmsford at the mission station at St Paul's. In his diary for 12 July, Wolseley wrote:

Chelmsford wants to go home to relieve himself from the 'false position' in which he finds himself, and to leave at once pending reply to an application he had addressed direct to Secty. of State for War. I replied through Chief of Staff that I had no objection whatever to his retiring and wished to know whether he would resign or go home on leave.

I can understand his being very much put out by my arrival, but his contumacious disobedience of my orders to correspond only through my Chief of the Staff does not recommend him to me as a soldier.[46]

Chelmsford and Wolseley finally met on 15 July and again Wolseley recorded his feelings in his diary for that day:

I cannot say that my meeting with Chelmsford was a pleasant one. He has persistently ignored my military authority over him, although I have told him I have a Commission giving me command of the Troops in South Africa. However, I try to make every allowance for him for his feelings must be unpleasant finding a superior officer sent to supersede him. I put up with dear old Wood: both he and Buller say Chelmsford is not fit to be a Corporal. That he is in every way a very different man today from what he was before his action on the 4th instant. I found him in good spirits, and I think glad to think he was going home: I never saw him [Wood] looking better.[47]

Chelmsford had placed great faith in both the abilities and loyalty of Wood and Buller, and whilst it appears that the two subordinates at least maintained an outward show of respect towards Chelmsford, when these two men returned to England, they were critical of many aspects of Chelmsford's generalship.

By 20 July Wolseley had had enough of Chelmsford's presence, as he clearly illustrated in his diary entry, as well as showing his almost legendary distain for those at Horse Guards:

My line is to get Chelmsford out of the country as soon as possible: he has now no power, and although I have the poorest opinion of his ability as a general or a public servant, I have a feeling for the position in which he finds himself at present and don't want to rake up old complaints against him. Why kick a dead horse? In war he can never be again employed although I have no doubt Horse Gds. will cover him with Honours and give him Aldershot or some equally good place.[48]

On the evening of 24 July Wolseley, much to his disquiet, had to attend a dinner held in Durban for Chelmsford. Once again, his diary entry is both pithy and enlightening on his views towards Chelmsford:

Dinner given by the Mayor and Corporation to Chelmsford who is the hero of the hour: having had his successful fight at Ulundi, all is now forgotten and forgiven, whilst it is remembered that he is Bartle Frere's associate in bringing the war about, a war which will be the making of Natal. Frere's policy is so believed in by the South African Colonists, that anyone who is or was associated with him in carrying it out is high in favour. Evelyn Wood's speech was a very, very good one from every point of view and Chelmsford's was very good also: he had a difficult speech to make, and he made it well. He was a little far-fetched however when he referred to the devotion of his subordinates to him, one and all of whom proclaim him as a useless General. He especially referred to Wood and Buller as his right and left arm and of the loyal assistance he had received from them. This was rather to him [them?] as both declare that nothing would ever induce them to serve under him again and both say he is not fit to be a 'Corporal'. However, he is a gentleman and a very nice fellow, but the Lord forbid that he should ever again have command of troops in the field.[49]

By 25 July Chelmsford was preparing to leave for England, via Cape Town, and Wolseley was able to have one last meeting with Wood and Buller, both of whom expressed their frustration that Chelmsford had insisted that they all travel back together. Chelmsford had earlier informed Wolseley that Wood and Buller were exhausted from all their campaigning and were unable to continue, although certainly Wood felt able to remain in Southern Africa. The two men told Wolseley they believed that Chelmsford was using their presence to deflect possible criticism away from him and that they felt resentful that the general had claimed that they were too weary to remain in Southern Africa. This resentment would be later seen in criticism of Chelmsford by both Wood and Buller once back in England.

Chelmsford had one last act in Southern Africa. On the evening of 26 July, he, with Wood and Buller in tow, attended an official reception in Cape Town at which he had to give yet one more speech. Chelmsford used this as an opportunity to both justify and defend his actions, especially during the Second Invasion. The speech is reproduced in full in Gerald French's book *Lord Chelmsford and the Zulu War*, and it is an extraordinary diatribe against his critics and a somewhat pathetic defence of his actions, and its tone and words would have to be repeated again and again once he reached England.

Yet, it is a defiant speech which is summed up in this line, 'The soundness of my plan of campaign is of course fairly open to criticism; but I have no hesitation in saying that had I the work to do over again, I should make no change in my arrangements.'[50] These few words illustrate perhaps how Chelmsford's mindset had led not only to the initial defeat of Isandlwana, but had also resulted in the ponderous advance of the Second Invasion. It can only be imagined what Wood and Buller made of the speech.

Chelmsford's victory at Ulundi at least allowed him to return to England with some of his reputation restored. Wolseley now had the responsibility of establishing a post-war settlement. The war had cost the British 93 officers and 1,337 men killed or died from disease, along with a similar number of colonial and native Natal auxiliaries. Exact figures for Zulu casualties are difficult to establish but at least 10,000 warriors died in action and, conservatively, around the same number died of their wounds.[51]

Wolseley quickly set about formulating his plans for the political settlement of Zululand as well breaking up Chelmsford's large army. He wrote, 'I shall thus get rid of useless Generals and reduce expenditure.'[52] Whilst he maintained a correspondence with Cetshwayo, who had fled Ulundi to avoid capture, Wolseley also began to entice various Zulu chiefs to agree a political settlement. He was adamant that Cetshwayo needed to be removed from the region or he would remain a rallying point for further dissatisfaction. Thus, when Cetshwayo was finally captured by a British patrol on 28 August he was despatched to Cape Town prison where he was to remain for the next three years.

In discussion with Bulwer, Wolseley resolved to divide Zululand into thirteen independent chiefdoms. Wolseley confirmed his thinking by stating, 'Such breaking up of the cohesion of the country will, I firmly believe, preclude for the future all, or almost all, possibility of any reunion of its inhabitants under one rule.'[53] Wolseley relied upon the advice of John Dunn, the former confidant of Cetshwayo. Dunn was rewarded for his support with his own chiefdom. Wolseley wrote:

He [Dunn] is a power in Zululand and I intend making as much use of him as possible. My idea is to increase his powers by making him paramount Chief over the District of Zululand lying along the Thukela and Buffalo Rivers frontiers of Natal. I shall thus secure the civilizing influence of a white man over the district of Zululand nearest to us, and he and his people will be a buffer between us and the barbarous districts of Zululand beyond.[54]

The Zulu people were informed of Wolseley's decision on 1 September when he summoned chiefs and dignitaries to Ulundi. Militarily defeated by the British, Wolseley now ensured the demise of the Zulu political system. All thirteen newly appointed chiefs had either fought alongside the British in the recent war or had deserted Cetshwayo and it seems clear that their appointments were deliberately chosen to create political rivalry and disunity. Wolseley's imposed settlement also ensured that there would be no restoration of the Zulu military system and it allowed for Zulus to leave their territory to seek employment in the mines of the Transvaal and Orange Free State, which further undermined the cohesion of Zulu society.

Anarchy was the almost immediate result of Wolseley's judgement for within just a few weeks Zulu fought Zulu as the new kingdoms frequently cut across old tribal lands. It is thought that more Zulus died in the years following the Anglo-Zulu War in a period of chaotic civil unrest than did in the war itself. In addition, Wolseley appointed a boundary commission which confirmed that the northern limit of Zululand would be moved southwards, with the Pongola River as the new natural boundary and the 1878 boundary commission was ignored with the Boers of the Transvaal gaining Zululand in the west. Although Wolseley's settlement had served to satisfy the immediate needs of the British government to remove their military and political responsibility for Zululand, the resulting chaos caused thousands of deaths and the collapse of the economic and political system. From his Cape Town prison, Cetshwayo received regular updates on the upheavals in his former kingdom and in 1882 he successfully petitioned the British government to visit London so as to state the case for his restoration to power. Here he charmed the queen, the government and the British public and in 1883 he was allowed to return to his homeland.

Within weeks of Cetshwayo's return to Ulundi he and his followers were at war with two of the northern tribal leaders and his forces were routed at the Second Battle of Ulundi on 21 July 1883. Cetshwayo was forced to flee and sought sanctuary in the west of his former kingdom. He died near Eshowe on 8 February 1884, either of poisoning or a heart attack. His son, King Dinuzulu, desperately tried to restore royal authority and was successful in defeating his father's northern rivals at the Battle of Tshasheni on 5 June 1884. However, there was a heavy price for this victory, for it was secured with the support of the Boers who then claimed a protectorate over Zululand. The British, nervous of Boer intentions and not wishing to see the Boers secure access to the coast again, intervened and Dinuzulu was exiled to the island of St Helena in 1888, after he had led armed resistance against the British. Turmoil continued up until 1906 when a veteran of the 1879 conflict, Mehlokazulu kaSihayo, led a rebellion against harsh taxes imposed by the authorities. This final uprising against the political and economic servitude imposed upon the Zulu nation by the British finally took place at the Battle of Momo Gorge on 10 June 1906 and here 1,000 warriors charged towards the British who were armed with the latest technology, including the Maxim machine gun. The outcome was inevitable with over half of the Zulus left dead on the battlefield. The last military defiance of the Zulu nation was at an end.

Chapter 7

Reputation Saved?

The queen was in her residence Osborne House on the Isle of Wight when she received the news of Chelmsford's victory at Ulundi. She had remained his staunchest supporter and was still aggrieved that her prime minister had gone against her wishes and replaced him with Wolseley. Victoria at once wrote a note of congratulations to Chelmsford and she would continue to offer her former ADC her royal patronage. Indeed, the queen would remain in the minority in supporting Chelmsford for on his return to England he would be forced to fight yet again, this time to save his reputation in light of the defeat at Isandlwana and the slow advance of the Second Invasion. This was to be a battle that he would fight for the remainder of his life.

Chelmsford arrived in Plymouth at the end of August and was immediately invited to Balmoral for his royal patron was eager to see him and hear his account of the war. Naturally, Chelmsford was keen to make a favourable impression on Victoria and aimed to ensure that she remained a firm supporter. Chelmsford arrived at Balmoral on 2 September and by the afternoon he had a private audience with the queen, who found him very thin and tired looking. At this meeting Chelmsford knelt to receive from his monarch the Knight Grand Cross of the Order of the Bath (GCB) as a recognition of the successful conclusion of the war. In the evening Chelmsford dined with Victoria and sat next to her throughout. The monarch recorded in her journal that, 'He [Chelmsford] talked most agreeably and gave very interesting accounts of the war – people, – country. The conviction I came to, was, that he was not so much to blame after all (though at one time I had thought him incapable) for Isandlwana, the slow progress, and retiring from Ulundi.' The following afternoon after lunch Chelmsford had another private audience with the queen at which he presented her with a black and white Zulu shield, measuring 4ft 6in by 2ft 4in, as well as a map of Zululand which Chelmsford used to illustrate the difficulties of campaigning over such terrain. Once again, Chelmsford used the meeting to place his views and 'spin' on the events surrounding Isandlwana and his decision to retire after the victory at Ulundi. The visit was such a success that Chelmsford was invited to stay another day and on 5 September, in his final meeting with the queen, Chelmsford was able to firmly state his defence of the many claims of delay and incompetence that he had now had to face.

It is worth quoting in full from Victoria's journal written on the night of this fateful meeting to show how Chelmsford was economical with the truth in recounting his side of events:

> Chelmsford brought me a map and showed the distances, on which he had written and pointed out the impossibilities of proceeding in directions people thought he could, owing to the broken ground. With regard to Isandlwana, Lord Chelmsford said, no doubt poor Col: Durnford had disobeyed orders, in leaving the Camp as he did; and poor Col: Pulleine had also done wrong, though for some time he refused to come, only going to the assistance of Col: Durnford, when the Zulus had almost already got there Lord Chelmsford knew nothing, Col: Durnford never having sent any message to say he was in danger, and the person Lord Chelmsford sent, to see what was going on (whose name he prefers not giving) seem not to have done what he ought, but too much thereby complicating matters still more. – I could not attempt to repeat all Lord Chelmsford said, for I could not explain it, but this much is clear to me, viz: that it was not his fault, but that of others that this surprise at Isandlwana, took place. He said, 'I cannot attack dead men,' but I hope he will be able to prove how unjust people have been towards him.
>
> I told Lord Chelmsford, he had been blamed by many, and even by the Gov^t, for commencing the war, without sufficient cause. He replied that he believed it to have been quite inevitable; that if we had not made war, when we did, we should have been attacked and possibly overpowered. He never believed the Zulus were so strong, and thought they had a force of 20,000 men, whereas it was 60,000, but it had been impossible to obtain correct information on this point. The Opposition and Press had done much harm by pronouncing judgement on what they neither knew or understood thoroughly. Ld Chelmsford showed me on the map, how impossible it had been for him to go the shorter way, as people had expected of him, on account of the broken ground, and of the enormous transport, 700 large, long waggons, drawn each

by 16 oxen, having to be dragged along, one line. They tried to keep 4 abreast but went very slowly.

Lord Chelmsford expressed his gratitude for my support, and gratification at his visit. It evidently did him good, but he suspects, that Lord Beaconsfield is the one, who insisted on his recall. I never thought this, till lately but Lord Beaconsfield was greatly disappointed and irritated with the war, and he has really been rather unjust about poor Lord Chelmsford, which I do not think right.

Chelmsford could rightly consider that his visit to Balmoral had been both a personal and propaganda success. He had charmed Victoria and, in her eyes at least, Chelmsford had vindicated his conduct in Southern Africa. Yet, regarding Isandlwana he had at best been economical with the truth, implying that he had given instruction to Durnford to take command on his arrival at Isandlwana and that he was unaware of the danger facing the camp, despite the fact that he had received numerous messages from Pulleine and others. The queen's Private Secretary, Major General Sir Henry Ponsonby, was less easily taken in by Chelmsford's performance, for he wrote to his wife on 7 September, 'Everyone must like him [Chelmsford] for he is quiet and easy to get on with and so free from swagger or bitterness against any one ... But all these things do not make a General. I don't feel satisfied. There is always someone who has not served him properly.'[1]

The queen's own loyalty towards Chelmsford was modified somewhat when both Redvers Buller and Evelyn Wood journeyed to Scotland and stayed at Balmoral from 9 September. The queen pinned a Victoria Cross on Buller's chest and knighted Wood. The two joined Victoria for dinner that evening and both men remained at Balmoral for a couple of days. Victoria, ever willing to be flattered, fell into an immediate friendship with Wood, which would last for the remainder of her life. In a private audience with the queen on 10 September, Wood declared that 'Lord Chelmsford is the kindest and most loveable of men, but he is *not* hard enough to be a soldier.' Pressed more by his monarch, Wood stated although Chelmsford was a 'brave as a lion, he was nervous about responsibility'.[2] After a subsequent meeting with both Wood and Buller, at which both men pointed out errors in the map Chelmsford had presented to the queen, Victoria recorded in her journal that the two men had informed her that Chelmsford had made an error in dividing his forces and that it was at their urging that Chelmsford had reached Ulundi. Buller was even more frank in conversation with Ponsonby when he stated Chelmsford became lost in detail which had made him hesitant in his advance and Buller concluded by stating, 'I hope I may often meet Chelmsford again as a friend, but I trust I may never serve under him again as a General.'[3]

Yet, despite now having some doubts over Chelmsford's conduct, Victoria maintained her royal patronage and affection for Chelmsford which would secure for him several prestigious positions as the years passed. She pressed Disraeli to accord Chelmsford the honour of an official invitation to the prime minister's country residence, Hughenden Manor, but Disraeli categorically refused his monarch. However, he did, begrudgingly, have a brief and frosty interview with Chelmsford at Downing Street.

The Duke of Cambridge, whilst publicly supporting Chelmsford, was privately well aware of the general's failings during the campaign. On 11 August, Sir Charles Ellice, the adjutant general, had delivered his confidential report on the Isandlwana disaster in which he outlined six reasons for the defeat. Of these, five, according to Ellice, could be attributed to Chelmsford and the main conclusion was that Chelmsford had under-estimated the offensive fighting power of the Zulu army and had failed to place sufficient importance on intelligence gathering. Whilst this report remained confidential Chelmsford could at least largely maintain his military reputation in his own lifetime, although he had to battle to do so. As the weeks and months passed after his return from Southern Africa Chelmsford resorted more and more to the use of the implication that Durnford was in command at Isandlwana and thus the blame should rest firmly on his shoulders for not remaining on the defensive. Chelmsford was aided in this deception by his former military secretary, John Crealock, who had obtained from Colonel Black his own order book which Black had retrieved from the battlefield when he returned there in May 1879 to bury the dead. The book contained Chelmsford's original order written in the early hours of 22 January 1879 to Durnford which had instructed the colonel to take his column to Isandlwana to support the camp, but which made no mention of Durnford assuming command. Crealock kept this find a secret between only himself and Chelmsford, so the general was certainly disingenuous when he later claimed Durnford was in command at Isandlwana.

The press would maintain its questioning and criticism of Chelmsford's conduct throughout much of 1879 and into the following year, and indeed questions would again be raised on Chelmsford's death. It is clear that press scrutiny blocked Chelmsford's future career. The only employment offered to Lord Chelmsford on his return home was the command of the Western District in 1880. Yet, he declined this citing his desire for an Indian command and on account of his limited private income. On 1 January 1881, Chelmsford sent a letter to the Duke of Cambridge, accompanied by a record of his service, in a bid to further his hope for an Indian command. It is notable that whilst he made mention of his Indian experience several times, he did not mention his Southern African command once. Chelmsford surely realized that he needed to distance himself as much as possible from the controversy surrounding Isandlwana. For Chelmsford his service in India was undoubtedly when he had been at his happiest and he still maintained a high reputation there for the service he had given. So, Cambridge, despite his misgivings and his annoyance that Chelmsford had declined the Western District, still wanted to offer Chelmsford a new command. However, Stanley fearing the public reaction, stated that he would have to take the matter to the Cabinet and here the matter ended. By 1884 even Cambridge had conceded that the continued controversies surrounding the Zulu War meant that Chelmsford could never be offered another command. Chelmsford even became a figure of parody in the music halls of Britain and the following lines appeared in the song 'By Jingo':

> Lord Chelmsford is the man,
> To skedaddle if he can,
> And leave our men to be
> Slaughtered by the Zooloos.[4]

In 1880 Chelmsford was once more on the defensive. In February, Archibald Forbes, the Special Correspondent of the *Daily News*, who had written so movingly of the scenes that confronted him when he visited the battlefield of Isandlwana with Colonel Black's burial party, published an article entitled 'Lord Chelmsford and the Zulu War' in the magazine *Nineteenth Century*. Forbes had been particularly vocal over the slow advance of the Second Invasion and was always willing to express his frustration with Chelmsford's command. The article largely focused on the events of Isandlwana, and Forbes was very critical of the choice of the camp as well as the fact that no attempt had been made to entrench. Forbes was also damming of Chelmsford's strategy of separate columns in the First Invasion.

Rather unwisely, Chelmsford decided to respond to Forbes' criticism in a personal memorandum. Fortunately, his words, which ran to several pages, were not widely published, but were circulated amongst his friends and some senior officers and a copy even reached the queen. It is a rambling long-winded defence which if it had received wider coverage may well have been seen as the act of a desperate man by Chelmsford's critics. Again, he was fortunate in that the Forbes' attack stimulated Colonel Harness to respond. In an article published in the April 1880 edition of *Fraser's Magazine*, cleverly entitled 'The Zulu Campaign from a Military Point of View', Harness not only defended Chelmsford's choice of camp and the decision not to entrench, but also justified his own role in the subsequent inquiry and its validity. Forbes' attack angered many in the military and Captain N. Walford RA, an instructor at Sandhurst who had no connection with either Chelmsford or the Zulu War, published a work named *Mr Archibald Forbes and the Zulu War*, which was less of a defence of Chelmsford, but more written in moral outrage at Forbes' accusations.

The attack by Forbes again brought the controversy surrounding Isandlwana to the fore and this was seen as an opportunity by Lord Strathnairn to attack Chelmsford and the government. On 19 August 1880 Strathnairn framed a debate in the Lords around the failings of the short service system and cleverly used this to widen it to an examination of Chelmsford's command during the Zulu War. Chelmsford fell into the trap and made a number of controversial comments which included a reassertion that Durnford was in command at Isandlwana and he had acted against Chelmsford's orders to defend the camp as well as other statements that were contrary to his official despatch of 27 January 1879. Lord Strathnairn used these discrepancies to frame an indictment against Chelmsford which was debated in the Lords on the following evening.

Strathnairn began the debate by highlighting that in his official despatch of 1879, Lord Chelmsford had stated:

So long as the soldiers kept their faces to the Zulus, the enemy could not drive them back, and they fell in heaps before the deadly fire poured into them, but when the Zulus got round the left flank of these brave men they appeared to have lost their presence of mind, and to have retired hastily through the tents, when immediately the whole Zulu force surrounded them, and they were overpowered by numbers and the camp was lost.

The plain English of that statement, continued Strathnairn, was that they misbehaved before the enemy, but in his speech in the House, on the evening of 19 August, the noble and gallant lord said, 'What could they do more than they did, and that was to die like gallant soldiers?' Strathnairn remarked, 'I must now leave the noble and gallant lord to reconcile these two opposite statements. Such inconsistent statements were not calculated to promote devotion or discipline among soldiers.'[5]

Chelmsford was visibly upset by Strathnairn's attacks and was forced to take a few moments to compose himself before he vigorously defended his earlier words and reaffirmed that the troops at Isandlwana had fought gallantly. Chelmsford received support from both Lords Ellenborough and Denman, the latter remarking that Chelmsford's interesting explanation ought to satisfy any reasonable man. With the ranks pulling around him, the debate ended without a vote of censure. Yet, Chelmsford's comments in the Lords resulted in Edward Durnford, brother of Colonel Durnford, publishing a detailed refutation of the general's claims. Edward cooperated with Frances Colenso to produce a work entitled *History of the Zulu War and its Origins* in which the authors wrote of the 'undisguised attempts that have been made to throw the blame on the dead'.[6] They maintained that those who had died were not responsible for the choice of the campsite, the inadequate scouting, the subdivision of the force or the refusal to respond to messages of concern from Pulleine and others. For Chelmsford these were damming words, but he at least now had the sense not to enter into a debate. Although the controversies of the war would never go away, they lessened as the years passed and in his own circle at least Chelmsford was able to maintain a strong personal reputation.

Despite the hostility Chelmsford had experienced at the hands of the press and in the House of Lords he fortunately still retained Victoria's support. He had been promoted to lieutenant general in 1882 and he remained on half-pay until 1884 and with retirement from the army looking likely, the queen stepped in and appointed him Lieutenant of the Tower of London and his eldest son was made a Page of Honour. In 1888 he was made a full general and he held a number of honorary colonelcies, including the 4th Middlesex Rifle Corps, the Sherwood Foresters (the former Derbyshire Regiment in which he had served in India) and in 1900 he received that of the prestigious 2nd Life Guards. The queen also made him Gold Stick, or her personal attendant at royal occasions. He retained this position under King Edward VII. Finally, in 1902, he was gazetted a Knight, Grand Cross of the Victorian Order (GCVO). He served in an organizational role at Victoria's funeral and had a similar position at the Duke of Cambridge's funeral in 1904.

Away from royal patronage Chelmsford busied himself in various positions. In 1893 he became the first in a long line of high-ranking army officers to serve as governor of the Anglican Church Lad's Brigade, a more militaristic and middle-class body than the Boy's Brigade. He was chair for twenty years of the Royal Victoria Patriotic Asylum in Wandsworth, which had originally been established as an orphanage for children of troops killed in the Crimean War and continued to house and school orphans. He was also, for twenty-five years, a churchwarden at St Jude's Church, Collingham Place, Kensington, London. Chelmsford was also chair of the Committee of the Royal Military Exhibition at Chelsea Hospital in aid of the establishment and maintenance of Church of England Soldier's Institutes. Chelmsford continued to enter into debates on military matters. For example, after his experiences in the Zulu War he became a firm advocate of the use of the machine gun but argued that such weapons should be removed from the Royal Navy or artillery and should be used as an offensive infantry weapon. He stated that, 'So utilized, they [machine guns] might, I feel sure, be used most effectively not only in defence, but in covering the last stage of an infantry attack.'[7] In such thinking Chelmsford was years ahead of his time.

At 9.30am on 9 April 1905 Lord Chelmsford was declared dead. He was 75 years old. He had suffered a stroke the previous evening whilst playing billiards at the United Services Club and he had been so poorly that he could not be moved to a hospital. On 13 April 1905 his funeral, with full military honours, was held at his parish church of St Jude's, Collingham Place. The coffin was carried on a gun carriage, draped in the Union Jack, with men of the 2nd Life Guards and Irish Guards as a guard of honour, with a little knot of girls in red cloaks from the Royal Victoria Patriotic Asylum, Wandsworth walking behind. He was buried in Brompton Cemetery. The Duke of Connaught and King Edward VII were present, which reflected Chelmsford's royal support to the end. Of the military General Sir Archibald Alison and Lord Methuen attended and Lord Roberts should have been a pallbearer but was unwell on the day. It is perhaps telling that neither Wood, Buller or Wolseley were in attendance. Even the attendees at Chelmsford's funeral reflected that he was and always would be a product of his background.

Conclusion

'A Very Regrettable Incident'

T he Anglo-Zulu War had been engineered by Frere and Chelmsford with the aim of encouraging political and economic confederation within Southern Africa, whilst at the same time removing the perceived military threat from the Zulu nation. It resulted in years of anarchy, civil war and economic hardship within the region and crucially failed in its primary aim of confederation. The Boers of the Transvaal, resentful of their own loss of sovereignty, were able to witness the military strength of the British being humbled by the Zulus. This fuelled their own ambitions for independence which manifested itself in conflict in 1880–1, which saw the defeat of the British. Cetshwayo, in a letter composed after the war to Sir Hercules Robinson, wrote, 'I did you no wrong, I have done you no wrong, therefore you must have some other objects in view in invading my land.'[1] Indeed, the British did have 'other objects' but due to the bravery of Cetshwayo and his warriors their primary political objectives were not achieved.

Yet, together with the final victory over the Xhosa people, Britain, and its commander in Southern Africa, Lord Chelmsford, had within a remarkably short period of time achieved the military conquest of the last two great ethnic groups in Southern Africa, who had offered the main resistance to the British dominance of the region. However, despite the dislocation of their country, the Zulus remained a military focused and disciplined people and this has stayed with them. It has been the Xhosa-speaking people who have provided the political leadership in South Africa, and they have done so because of the constitutional and economic advantages they managed to retain, despite the military dominance of the British, and later the white South Africans.

The British army's performance in the Anglo-Zulu War has been the subject of criticism and debate since the events of 22 January 1879 and this continues today. Of course, much focus has been upon Lord Chelmsford and it is perhaps fitting that the thoughts of Major Clery, Colonel Glyn's staff officer, are given credence for he was with Chelmsford in the weeks leading up to Isandlwana and in the days after. In a series of letters to Sir Archibald Alison who was in the Intelligence Department in Horse Guards throughout the Zulu conflict, Clery gave his views as to why the disaster at Isandlwana had occurred and his points provide a contemporary relevance that offer a blunt assessment as to why Chelmsford was outwitted by the Zulu commanders. Writing to Alison from Helpmekaar on 18 March 1879, Clery states:

> ... I think the general and his staff wholly underrated the enemy. Possibly their experience of the kaffirs in the Colony was the cause of this. They did not appear to believe in the possibility of a real attack by the Zulus. It was so much doubted that the Zulus would really come on, that orders were issued to the artillery that they were on no account to open fire at a distance greater than 600 yards, for fear of frightening the enemy and deterring them from coming on or inducing them to run away. So that the real truth is that the general and his staff did not anticipate that the enemy would venture to attack him, but if they should do so the only thing to be apprehended was that the fire of our people would frighten them so much that they would never come near enough to suffer any serious loss. So that as to taking any precautions for defence against an attack, such as entrenching, etc., such a thing was never dreamt of. I think in all this business the general has had a great deal of bad luck. His own energy and activity are inexhaustible, and he had terrible difficulties to contend with in the commissariat and transport services here. I think, however, he wanted what he certainly had not – a man of ability and solidarity at his elbow, for his staff is I think very weak. ... This I think is such a mistake, for the time I have seen him spend in doing that work I used to think would be so much better employed in thinking over really important matters. Wolseley was and is so different. His idea is that he cannot get too many or too good men about him ...[2]

Again, writing to Alison on 13 April, Clery offered a further assessment of the defeat:

> There were two things to my mind that greatly contributed to what has proved to be faulty in all Lord Chelmsford's plans, and these were the misleading experience he had of kaffir warfare in the Piri Bush; secondly the smallness of the force that he knew the government would

consent to giving him for any kafir [Zulu] war, for until the Isandlwana affair nobody at home would admit that one kafir was a whit better than another. Therefore, it was that in the first place Lord Chelmsford or his staff would not admit that they were going to contend with anything more than a superior (perhaps?) class of kaffir, who had only to be hunted; also that no reverse of any kind was to be anticipated that would make it necessary to look after base depots, etc. I mention all this to show you that what was left undone was not the result of negligence so much as design. The idea was never entertained of being apprehensive that the enemy would come on and attack, but on the contrary, that he would not come on and attack, and that we should have to hunt him up.[3]

Thus, it was clear in Clery's mind at least, that the reasons for the disaster of Isandlwana rested solely with Chelmsford and his staff for underestimating the fighting abilities of the Zulus and within this Chelmsford's inability to delegate and surround himself with a sufficiently large and talented staff. Of course, Clery had his own motives for writing as he did, for he remained protective of Glyn and had a dislike of Crealock, but his words are perceptive and ring true even today. Chelmsford should receive some credit for rallying himself to lead British forces at Gingindlovu and Ulundi and in both these engagements the tactics he deployed showed that he had learnt from his earlier errors and had a fresh respect for the enemy. In contrast, in his advance during the Second Invasion he displayed a hesitancy that was directly caused by the disaster of Isandlwana and the death of Prince Louis. On his return to England, he largely avoided the controversy that surrounded the events of 22 January 1879 and was able, with the considerable help of Victoria's patronage, to maintain some personal prestige and pride and there is no doubt he threw himself into a number of worthwhile causes. Yet, even in death, the defeat at Isandlwana would not leave Chelmsford for these words appeared in his obituary in *The Times* of 10 April:

In the conduct of the campaign against the Zulus, some questioned Lord Chelmsford's dispositions in the early stages of the war. It was a case, as it has invariably been with us, of underestimating the enemy, with the result to which with have become so painfully accustomed. The disaster at Isandlwana was, of course, a very regrettable incident ...

Notes

Chapter 1

1. G. French, *Lord Chelmsford and the Zulu War* (Bodley Head, 1939), p. 1.
2. For a detailed breakdown of the composition of the Victorian officer corps and the role of purchase see Gwyn Harries-Jenkins, 'The Development of Professionalism in the Victorian Army', in *Armed Forces and Society*, Vol. 1, No. 4, August 1975.
3. French, *Lord Chelmsford and the Zulu War*, p. 4.
4. Ibid., p. 5.
5. S. Corvi and I. Beckett (eds), *Victoria's Generals* (Pen & Sword, 2009), p. 95.
6. A. Clayton, *The British Officer* (Longman, 2006), p. 86.
7. D. Morris, *The Washing of the Spears – The Rise and Fall of the Zulu Nation* (New York, Simon & Schuster, 1965), p. 258.
8. French, *Lord Chelmsford and the Zulu War*, p. 7.
9. P. Smith, *Victoria's Victories – Seven Classic Battles of the British Army 1849–1884* (Tunbridge Wells, Spellmount Ltd, 1987), p. 128.

Chapter 2

1. T. Hunt, *Ten Cities that Made an Empire* (Penguin, 2015), p. 149.
2. Ibid., p. 155.
3. G. Theal (ed.), *Records of the Cape Colony* (London, 1897–1905), Vol. 1, p. 17.
4. Ibid., Vol. 1, p. 26.
5. Hunt, *Ten Cities that Made an Empire*, p. 169.
6. Theal (ed.), *Records of the Cape Colony*, Vol. 1, pp. 267–8.
7. J. Laband, *The Land Wars: The Dispossession of the Khoisan and AmaXhosa in the Cape Colony* (Cape Town, Penguin, 2020), p. 105.
8. Ibid., p. 109.
9. Ibid., p. 182.
10. J. Percy-Groves, *The War of the Axe: Or, Adventures in South Africa* (Blackie & Son Ltd, 1888), pp. 144–5.
11. R. Ross, *The Borders of Race in Colonial South Africa, The Kat River Settlement, 1829–1856* (Cambridge University Press, 2014), p. 204.
12. T. Stapleton, *Maqoma – The Legend of a Great Xhosa Warrior* (Cape Town, 2016), p. 207.
13. K. Smith, *Harry Smith's Last Throw – The Eighth Frontier War 1850–53* (Barnsley, Frontline Books, 2012), p. 118.
14. Laband, *Land Wars*, p. 258.

Chapter 3

1. K. Smith, *The Wedding Feast War* (Barnsley, Frontline Books, 2012), p. 115.
2. Laband, *Land Wars*, p. 273.

3. P. Gon, *The Road to Isandlwana* (Johannesburg, A.D. Donker Publisher, 1979), p. 136.
4. Smith, *Wedding Feast War*, p. 212.
5. General Sir A.T. Cunynghame, *My Command in South Africa 1874–8* (Macmillan, 1879), p. 310.
6. Gon, *Road to Isandlwana*, p. 145.
7. Ibid., p. 146.
8. French, *Lord Chelmsford and the Zulu War*, pp. 7–12.
9. Ibid., p. 9.
10. Ibid., p. 13.
11. Morris. *Washing of the Spears*, p. 262.
12. Smith, *Wedding Feast War*, p. 217.
13. A. Delavoye, *Records of the 90th Regiment (Perthshire Light Infantry)* (Richardson & Co., 1880), p. 225.
14. Laband, *Land Wars*, p. 282.
15. E. Wood, *From Midshipman to Field Marshal: 2 Vols* (Methuen, 1906), Vol. 1, p. 309.
16. Thesiger to Secretary of State for War, 25 March 1878, TNA, WO 32/7688.
17. Thesiger to Secretary of State for War, 10 April 1878, TNA, WO 32/7688.
18. Thesiger to Secretary of State for War, 24 April 1878, TNA, WO 32/7690.
19. Delavoye, *Records of the 90th Regiment*, p. 226.
20. B. Worsfold, *Sir Bartle Frere – A Footnote to the History of the British Empire* (Thornton Butterworth Ltd, 1923), p. 71.
21. Ibid., p. 72.
22. Smith, *Wedding Feast War*, p. 229.
23. Delavoye, *Records of the 90th Regiment*, p. 228.
24. Ibid., pp. 230–1.
25. Thesiger to Secretary of State, 5 May 1878, TNA, WO 32/7692.
26. N. Mostert, *Frontiers – The Epic of South Africa's Creation and the Tragedy of the Xhosa People* (Pimlico, 1993), p. 1251.
27. Ibid.
28. Ibid., p. 1252.
29. Smith, *Wedding Feast War*, p. 240.
30. French, *Lord Chelmsford and the Zulu War*, p. 27.
31. C. Williams, *The Life of Lieut.-General Sir Henry Evelyn Wood* (Sampson Low, Marston & Company, 1892), p. 70.
32. French, *Lord Chelmsford and the Zulu War*, p. 26.

Chapter 4

1. S. Clarke, *Invasion of Zululand 1879 – Anglo-Zulu War experiences of Arthur Harness: John Jervis, 4th Viscount St Vincent; and Sir Henry Bulwer* (Johannesburg, The Brenthurst Press, 1979), p. 19.
2. F. Emery, *The Red Soldier, Letters from the Zulu War, 1879* (Bergvlei, Jonathan Ball, 1983), p. 39.
3. Clarke, *Invasion of Zululand 1879*, p. 35.
4. Ibid., p. 45.
5. S. David, *Zulu – The Heroism and Tragedy of the Zulu War of 1879* (Viking, 2004), pp. 39–40.

6. French, *Lord Chelmsford and the Zulu War*, p. 33.
7. Ibid., p. 32.
8. R. Cope, *Ploughshare of War: The Origins of the Anglo-Zulu War of 1879* (Pietermaritzburg, University of Natal, 1999), p. 222.
9. Worsfold, *Sir Bartle Frere*, p. 82.
10. Ibid., p. 93.
11. Ibid., p. 99.
12. Ibid., p. 112.
13. Hicks Beach Papers, Gloucestershire Archives, D2455/PCC/22.
14. S. Miller (ed.), *Soldiers and Settlers in Africa, 1850–1918* (Leiden, Brill, 2009), p. 60.
15. Clarke, *Invasion of Zululand 1879*, p. 63.
16. Ibid., p. 61.
17. Ibid., p. 26.
18. Ibid., p. 66.
19. R. Coupland, *Zulu Battle Piece – Isandlwana* (Tom Donovan, 1991), p. 48.
20. R. Lock and P. Quantrill, *Zulu Victory – The Epic of Isandlwana and the Cover-Up* (Greenhill Books, 2002), p. 96.
21. KwaZulu Natal Archives, Durban, Wood MSS, II/2/2, Chelmsford to Wood, 23 November 1878.
22. D. Moodie (ed.), *John Dunn Cetywayo and the Three Generals 1861–1879* (repr., Barnsley, Pen & Sword, 2014), p. 93.
23. Clarke, *Invasion of Zululand 1879*, p. 215.
24. Worsfold, *Sir Bartle Frere*, p. 199.
25. Captain H.H. Parr, *A Sketch of the Kafir and Zulu Wars – Guadana to Isandhlwana* (Kegan Paul & Co., 1880), p. 162.
26. Worsfold, *Sir Bartle Frere*, p. 134.
27. Ibid., p. 151.
28. Ibid., p. 162.
29. David, *Zulu*, p. 30.
30. Ibid., p. 80.
31. Gon, *Road to Isandlwana*, p. 206.

Chapter 5

1. S. Wade, *Empire and Espionage – Spies in the Zulu War* (Barnsley, Pen & Sword, 2010), p. 10.
2. S. Clarke, *Zululand at War 1879 – The Conduct of the Anglo-Zulu War* (Houghton, The Brenthurst Press, 1984), p. 74.
3. Ibid.
4. Parr, *A Sketch of the Kafir and Zulu Wars*, p. 180.
5. E. Spiers, *The Victorian Soldier in Africa* (Manchester University Press, 2004), p. 38.
6. Coupland, *Zulu Battle Piece*, p. 61.
7. I. Knight, *Zulu Rising – The Epic Story of Isandlwana and Rorke's Drift* (Macmillan, 2010), p. 216.
8. Parr, *A Sketch of the Kafir and Zulu Wars*, p. 185.
9. J. Laband (ed.), *Lord Chelmsford's Zululand Campaign, 1878–1879* (Stroud, Army Records Society and Alan Sutton Publishing, 1994), p. 61.
10. Clarke, *Zululand at War 1879*, p. 74.

11. F. Colenso, *History of the Zulu War and its Origins* (Chapman & Hall, 1880), p. 264.
12. Ibid., p. 273.
13. French, *Lord Chelmsford and the Zulu War*, p. 61.
14. W. Alister Williams, *Commandant of the Transvaal – The Life and Career of General Sir Hugh Rowlands, VC, KCB* (Wrexham, Bridge Books, 2001), p. 131.
15. Wade, *Empire and Espionage*, p. 80.
16. Parr, *A Sketch of the Kafir and Zulu Wars*, p. 187.
17. W.H. Clement, *The Glamour and Tragedy of the Zulu War* (John Lane, The Bodley Head, 1936), p. 129.
18. Clarke, *Zululand at War 1879*, p. 121.
19. A. Greaves, *Rorke's Drift* (Cassell, 2002), p. 85.
20. R. Edgerton, *Like Lions They Fought – The Last Zulu War* (Bergvlei, The Free Press, 1988), p. 81.
21. David, *Zulu*, p. 92.
22. Clarke, *Zululand at War 1879*, p. 131.
23. *Report of Proceedings of 21st, 22nd, 23rd and 24th January 1879*, from Lt. Milne, R.N, Lugg files, Campbell Collections, University of KwaZulu-Natal, Durban.
24. David, *Zulu*, p. 100.
25. Lock and Quantrill, *Zulu Victory*, p. 138.
26. Ibid., p. 148.
27. Clarke, *Zululand at War 1879*, p. 76.
28. Ibid.
29. Ibid., p. 82.
30. Parr, *A Sketch of the Kafir and Zulu Wars*, pp. 192–3.
31. Knight, *Zulu Rising*, p. 344.
32. David, *Zulu*, p. 128.
33. Ibid., p. 129.
34. Ibid.
35. Morris, *Washing of the Spears*, p. 387
36. Clarke, *Zululand at War 1879*, p. 77.
37. Knight, *Zulu Rising*, p. 392.
38. Ibid., p. 448.
39. Parr, *A Sketch of the Kafir and Zulu Wars*, pp. 193–5.
40. Ibid., p. 197.
41. Edgerton, *Like Lions They Fought*, p. 94.
42. K. Stossel, *A Handful of Heroes – Rorke's Drift – Facts, Myths and Legends* (Barnsley, Pen & Sword, 2015), p. 36.

Chapter 6
1. Laband (ed.), *Lord Chelmsford's Zululand Campaign*, p. 78.
2. Coupland, *Zulu Battle Piece*, p. 113.
3. Greaves, *Rorke's Drift*, p. 164.
4. Ibid., p. 165.
5. Spiers, *Victorian Soldier in Africa*, p. 49.
6. Greaves, *Rorke's Drift*, p. 178.
7. David, *Zulu*, p. 220.
8. Ibid.
9. Clarke, *Zululand at War 1879*, p. 93.

10. Ibid., p. 26.
11. Clement, *The Glamour and Tragedy of the Zulu War*, pp. 107–8.
12. I. Knight, *With his Face to the Foe – The Life and Death of Louis Napoleon, The Prince Imperial – Zululand 1879* (Staplehurst, Spellmount, 2001), p. 135.
13. C. Norris-Newman, *In Zululand with the British Throughout the War of 1879* (repr. Greenhill Books, 1988), p. 107.
14. Laband (ed.), *Lord Chelmsford's Zululand Campaign*, pp. 130–1.
15. I. Castle and I. Knight, *Fearful Hard Times – The Siege and Relief of Eshowe, 1879* (Greenhill Books, 1994), p. 183.
16. Emery, *The Red Soldier*, p. 200.
17. Emery, *The Red Soldier*, p. 201.
18. Norris-Newman, *In Zululand*, p. 138.
19. Castle and Knight, *Fearful Hard Times*, p. 216.
20. Ibid., p. 225.
21. Ibid., p. 230.
22. David, *Zulu*, p. 224.
23. Ibid., p. 288.
24. A. Preston (ed.), *The South African Journal of Sir Garnet Wolseley, 1879–1880* (Cape Town, A.A. Balkema, 1973), p. 27.
25. E. Spiers, *The Scottish Soldier and Empire, 1854–1902* (Edinburgh, 2006), p. 43.
26. Clarke, *Zululand at War 1879*, p. 177.
27. Ibid., p. 179.
28. Ibid.
29. A. Greaves and B. Best (eds), *The Curling Letters of the Zulu War –'There was Awful Slaughter'* (Barnsley, Pen & Sword, 2001), p. 126.
30. Edgerton, *Like Lions They Fought*, p. 141.
31. Knight, *With his Face to the Foe*, p. 178.
32. Ibid., p. 211.
33. Ibid., p. 214.
34. Spiers, *Victorian Soldier*, p. 51.
35. Colenso, *History*, p. 440.
36. Clement, *The Glamour and Tragedy of the Zulu War*, p. 109.
37. Ibid.
38. J. Lehmann, *Sir Garnet: A Life of Field Marshal Lord Wolseley* (1964), p. 255.
39. Preston (ed.), *South African Journal of Sir Garnet Wolseley*, p. 47.
40. Edgerton, *Like Lions They Fought*, p. 144.
41. Preston (ed.), *South African Journal of Sir Garnet Wolseley*, p. 52.
42. I. Knight, *'By Orders of the Great White Queen' – Campaigning in Zululand through the Eyes of the British Soldier, 1879* (Greenhill Books, 1992), p. 249.
43. M. Prior, *Campaigns of a War Correspondent* (Edward Arnold, 1912), p. 119.
44. Spiers, *Victorian Soldier*, p. 53.
45. David, *Zulu*, p. 353.
46. Preston (ed.), *South African Journal of Sir Garnet Wolseley*, p. 55.
47. Ibid., p. 56.
48. Ibid., p. 61.
49. Ibid., p. 63.
50. French, *Lord Chelmsford and the Zulu War*, p. 237.
51. These figures are quoted in A. Greaves, *Crossing the Buffalo – The Zulu War of 1879* (Weidenfeld & Nicolson, 2005), p. 316.

52. David, *Zulu*, p. 366.
53. Greaves, *Crossing the Buffalo*, p. 328.
54. Preston (ed.), *South African Journal of Sir Garnet Wolseley*, p. 50.

Chapter 7
1. David, *Zulu*, pp. 379–80.
2. Ibid., p. 380.
3. Ibid.
4. I. Beckett, *Great Battles – Rorke's Drift and Isandlwana* (Oxford University Press, 2019), p. 103.
5. Clement, *The Glamour and Tragedy of the Zulu War*, p. 328.
6. Beckett, *Great Battles*, p. 76.
7. E. Spiers, *The Late Victorian Army, 1868–1902* (Manchester University Press, 1992), p. 244.

Conclusion
1. TNA, Colonial Office Papers 879/16, 204, No. 151.
2. Clarke, *Zululand at War 1879*, pp. 121–2.
3. Ibid., p. 126.

Bibliography

Place of publication is London unless otherwise stated.

Alister Williams, W., *Commandant of the Transvaal– The Life and Career of General Sir Hugh Rowlands, VC, KCB* (Wrexham, Bridge Books, 2001).

Beckett, I., *Great Battles – Rorke's Drift & Isandlwana* (Oxford University Press, 2019).

Boyden, P., A. Guy and M. Harding (eds), *'Ashes and blood' – The British Army in South Africa 1795–1914* (National Army Museum, 1999).

Castle, I. and I. Knight, *Fearful Hard Times – The Siege and Relief of Eshowe, 1879* (Greenhill Books, 1994).

Clarke, S., *Invasion of Zululand 1879 – Anglo-Zulu War experiences of Arthur Harness: John Jervis, 4th Viscount St Vincent; and Sir Henry Bulwer* (Johannesburg, The Brenthurst Press, 1979).

Clarke, S., *Zululand at War 1879 – The Conduct of the Anglo-Zulu War* (Houghton, The Brenthurst Press, 1984).

Clayton, A., *The British Officer* (Longman, 2006).

Clement, W.H., *The Glamour and Tragedy of the Zulu War* (John Lane, The Bodley Head, 1936).

Colenso, F., *History of the Zulu War and its Origins* (Chapman & Hall, 1880).

Cope, R., *Ploughshare of War: The Origins of the Anglo-Zulu War of 1879* (Pietermaritzburg, University of Natal, 1999).

Corvi, S. and I. Beckett (eds), *Victoria's Generals* (Barnsley, Pen & Sword, 2009).

Coupland, R., *Zulu Battle Piece – Isandlwana* (Tom Donovan, 1991).

Cunynghame, General Sir A.T., *My Command in South Africa 1874–8* (Macmillan, 1879).

David, S., *Military Blunders – The How and Why of Military Failure* (Robinson, 1997).

David, S., *Zulu – The Heroism and Tragedy of the Zulu War of 1879* (Viking, 2004).

Delavoye, A., *Records of the 90th Regiment (Perthshire Light Infantry)* (Richardson & Co., 1880).

Edgerton, R., *Like Lions They Fought – The Last Zulu War* (Bergvlei, The Free Press, 1988).

Emery, F., *The Red Soldier – The Zulu War of 1879* (Bergvlei, Jonathan Ball, 1983).

Farwell, B., *Eminent Victorian Soldiers – Seekers of Glory* (Viking, 1986).

French, G., *Lord Chelmsford and the Zulu War* (Bodley Head, 1939).

Gillings, K., *Discovering the Battlefields of the Anglo-Zulu War* (Pinetown, 30 degrees South Publishers, 2014).

Gon, P., *The Road to Isandlwana* (Johannesburg, A.D. Donker Publisher, 1979).

Greaves, A., *Rorke's Drift* (Cassell, 2002).

Greaves, A., *Crossing the Buffalo – The Zulu War of 1879* (Weidenfeld & Nicolson, 2005).

Greaves, A., *Isandlwana – How the Zulus Humbled the British Empire* (Barnsley, Pen & Sword, 2011).

Greaves, A. and B. Best (eds), *The Curling Letters of the Zulu War – 'There was Awful Slaughter'* (Barnsley, Pen & Sword, 2001).

Greaves, A. and Kkhize Xolani, *The Tribe that Washed its Spears – The Zulus at War* (Barnsley, Pen & Sword, 2013).

Guy, J., *The Destruction of The Zulu Kingdom* (Longman, 1979).

Haythornthwaite, P., *The Colonial Wars Sourcebook* (Arms & Armour Press, 1997).

Hunt, T., *Ten Cities that Made an Empire* (Penguin, 2015).

Knight, I., *Brave Men's Blood – The Epic of the Zulu War, 1879* (Greenhill Books, 1990).

Knight, I., *British Forces in Zululand, 1879* (Oxford, Osprey, 1991).

Knight, I., *'By the Orders of the Great White Queen' – Campaigning in Zululand through the Eyes of the British Soldier, 1879* (Greenhill Books, 1992).

Knight, I., *'Go to your God Like a Soldier' – The British Soldier Fighting for Empire, 1837–1902* (Greenhill Books, 1996).

Knight, I., *With his Face to the Foe – The Life and Death of Louis Napoleon, The Prince Imperial – Zululand 1879* (Staplehurst, Spellmount, 2001).

Knight, I., *The National Army Museum Book of the Zulu War* (Sidgwick & Jackson, 2003).

Knight, I., *British Fortifications in Zululand 1879* (Oxford, Osprey, 2005).

Knight, I., *Zulu Rising – The Epic Story of Isandlwana and Rorke's Drift* (Macmillan, 2010).

Knight, I. and I. Castle, *The Zulu War – Then and Now* (After the Battle Publications, 1993).

Knight, I. and I. Castle, *Zulu War 1879 – Twilight of a Warrior Nation* (Oxford, Osprey, 1994).

Laband, J., *Rope of Sand – The Rise and Fall of the Zulu Kingdom in the Nineteenth Century* (Johannesburg, Jonathan Ball Publishers, 1994).

Laband, J., *Kingdom in Crisis – The Zulu Response to the British Invasion of 1879* (Barnsley, Pen & Sword, 2007).

Laband, J., *The Land Wars: The Dispossession of the Khoisan and AmaXhosa in the Cape Colony* (Cape Town, Penguin Books, 2020).

Laband, J. (ed.), *Lord Chelmsford's Zululand Campaign, 1878–1879* (Stroud, Army Records Society and Alan Sutton Publishing, 1994).

Laband, J. and I. Knight, *The War Correspondents – The Anglo-Zulu War* (Stroud, Sutton Publishing, 1996).

Laband, J. and J. Matthews, *Isandlwana* (Pietermaritzburg, Centaur Publications, 1992).

Laband, J. and P. Thompson, *A Field Guide to the War in Zululand and the Defence of Natal 1879* (Pietermaritzburg, University of Natal Press, 1983).

Lehmann, J., *Sir Garnet: A Life of Field Marshal Lord Wolseley* (Massachusetts, Houghton Mifflin Company, 1964).

Lock, R. and P. Quantrill, *Zulu Victory – The Epic of Isandlwana and the Cover-Up* (Greenhill Books, 2002).

Mackinnon, J.P. and S.H. Shadbolt, *The South African Campaign of 1879* (J.B. Hayward & Son, 1882).

Manning, S., *Evelyn Wood V.C. – Pillar of Empire* (Barnsley, Pen & Sword, 2007).

Manning, S., *Soldiers of the Queen – Victorian Colonial Conflict in the Words of those who Fought* (Stroud, Spellmount, 2009).

Manning, S., *The Martini-Henry Rifle* (Oxford, Osprey, 2013).

Manning, S., *Bayonet to Barrage – Weaponry on the Victorian Battlefield* (Barnsley, Pen & Sword, 2020).

Miller, S. (ed.), *Soldiers and Settlers in Africa, 1850–1918* (Leiden, Brill, 2009).

Miller, S. (ed.), *Queen Victoria's Wars – British Military Campaigns, 1857–1902* (Cambridge University Press, 2021).

Moodie, D. (ed.), *John Dunn Cetywayo and the Three Generals 1861–1879* (repr., Barnsley, Pen & Sword, 2014).

Morris, D., *The Washing of the Spears – The Rise and Fall of the Zulu Nation* (New York, Simon & Schuster, 1965).

Mostert, N., *Frontiers – The Epic of South Africa's Creation and the Tragedy of the Xhosa People* (Pimlico, 1993).

Norris-Newman, C., *In Zululand with the British Throughout the War of 1879* (repr. Greenhill Books, 1988).

Parr, Captain H.H., *A Sketch of the Kafir and Zulu Wars – Guadana to Isandhlwana* (Kegan Paul & Co., 1880).

Peers, C., *Rorke's Drift and Isandlwana, 22nd January 1879: Minute by Minute* (Barnsley, Greenhill Books, 2021).

Percy-Groves, J., *The War of the Axe: Or, Adventures in South Africa* (Blackie & Son Ltd, 1888).

Preston, A. (ed.), *The South African Journal of Sir Garnet Wolseley, 1879–1880* (Cape Town, A.A. Balkema, 1973).

Prior, M., *Campaigns of a War Correspondent* (Edward Arnold, 1912).

Ross, R., *The Borders of Race in Colonial South Africa – The Kat River Settlement, 1829–1856* (Cambridge University Press, 2014).

Smith, K., *Harry Smith's Last Throw – The Eighth Frontier War 1850–1853* (Barnsley, Frontline Books, 2012).

Smith, K., *The Wedding Feast War – The Final Tragedy of the Xhosa People* (Barnsley, Frontline Books, 2012).

Smith, K., *Dead was Everything – Studies in the Anglo-Zulu War* (Barnsley, Frontline, 2014).

Smith, P., *Victoria's Victories – Seven Classic Battles of the British Army 1849–1884* (Tunbridge Wells, Spellmount Ltd, 1987).

Spiers, E., *The Late Victorian Army, 1868–1902* (Manchester University Press, 1992).

Spiers, E., *The Victorian Soldier in Africa* (Manchester University Press, 2004).

Spiers, E., *The Scottish Soldier and Empire, 1854–1902* (Edinburgh University Press, 2006).

Stapleton, T., *Maqoma – The Legend of a Great Xhosa Warrior* (Cape Town, Amavu Heritage Publishing, 2016).

Stossel, K., *A Handful of Heroes – Rorke's Drift – Facts, Myths and Legends* (Barnsley, Pen & Sword, 2015).

Sutherland, J. and D. Canwell, *Zulu Kings and their Armies* (Barnsley, Pen & Sword, 2004).

Thompson, L., *A History of South Africa* (4th edn, Yale University Press, 2014).

Vandervort, B., *Wars of Imperial Conquest in Africa, 1830–1914* (University College London Press, 1998).

Wade, S., *Empire and Espionage – Spies in the Zulu War* (Barnsley, Pen & Sword, 2010).

Walford, N.L., *Mr Archibald Forbes and the Zulu War* (Uckfield, The Naval & Military Press, 2010).

Williams, C., *The Life of Lieut.-General Sir Henry Evelyn Wood* (Sampson Low, Marston & Company, 1892).

Wood, E., *From Midshipman to Field Marshal: 2 Vols* (Methuen, 1906).

Wood, E. (ed.), *British Battles on Land and Sea, Vol. 2* (Cassell, 1915).

Worsfold, B., *Sir Bartle Frere – A Footnote to the History of the British Empire* (Thornton Butterworth Ltd, 1923).

Journal Articles and Theses

Bailes, H., 'Technology and Imperialism: A Case Study of the Victorian Army on Africa', *Victorian Studies*, Vol. 24, No. 1 Autumn 1980, pp. 82–104.

Harries-Jenkins, Gwyn, 'The Development of Professionalism in the Victorian Army', *Armed Forces and Society*, Vol. 1, No. 4, August 1975.

Manning, Stephen, 'Private Snook and Total War', *Journal of the Anglo-Zulu War Historical Society*, 13 (2003), pp. 22–6.

Manning, Stephen, 'British Perception of the Zulu Nation Before and After the War of 1879', *Journal of the Anglo-Zulu Historical Society*, 17 (2005), pp. 17–22.

Manning, Stephen, 'Foreign News Gathering and Reporting in the London and Devon Press: The Anglo-Zulu War, 1879 – A Case Study', PhD, Exeter, 2005.

Manning, Stephen, 'Learning the Trade: Use and Misuse of Intelligence during the British Colonial Campaigns of the 1870s', *Journal of Intelligence and National Security*, Vol. 22, October 2007, No. 5.

Online Articles and Research Sites

Hansard – https://hansard.parliament.uk.

History of the 90th – ripandrevmedia.ca.

Queen Victoria's Journals – https://www.royal.uk/queen-victorias-journals.

Theal, G. (ed.), *Records of the Cape Colony* (1897–1905) – www.egssa.org/1820-settlers/index.php/records-of-the-cape-colony.

Index